The development of
social welfare in Britain

The development of
social welfare in Britain

ERIC MIDWINTER

OPEN UNIVERSITY PRESS
Buckingham • Philadelphia

Open University Press
Celtic Court
22 Ballmoor
Buckingham
MK18 1XW

and

1900 Frost Road, Suite 101
Bristol, PA 19007, USA

First Published 1994

Copyright © Eric C. Midwinter 1994

A catalogue record of this book is available from the British Library

ISBN 0 335 19104 5 (pbk)   0 335 19105 3 (hbk)

Library of Congress Cataloging-in-Publication Data
Midwinter, Eric C.
    The development of social welfare in Britain / by Eric Midwinter.
        p. cm.
    Includes bibliographical references and index.
    ISBN 0–335–19105–3.   ISBN 0–335–19104–5 (pbk.)
    1. Social service—Great Britain—History. 2. Public welfare—
Great Britain—History. 3. Great Britain—Social policy.
I. Title.
HV245.M53 1994
361.941—dc20   93–21335
                                                          CIP

Typeset by Graphicraft Typesetters Limited, Hong Kong
Printed in Great Britain by Biddles Limited, Guildford and Kings Lynn

Contents

Preface: How best to use this book

This book is intended for students of academic and professional courses of high level dealing with or touching upon the world of social welfare and allied issues of social provision in the United Kingdom. In an attempt, as succinctly as possible, to cover the subject comprehensively, its historical range is from medieval times to the 1990s, and its thematic grasp encompasses: poverty, together with income maintenance and welfare; health, with sections on public housing; education; and crime and policing. Moreover, some effort has been made to include at each stage a modicum of comparative material, usually drawn from continental Europe and North America, and, as necessary to complete the tale, specific thoughts and information have been added on gender, race and other special features.

The challenge has been to shape so huge an amount of material between two covers not too far apart, that is, a reasonably sized and a reasonably priced book. The hope is that, for many students, it will serve as a basic textbook, enabling them to examine the essential facts and to consider the essential arguments about these important matters. In this connection, a number of prior decisions were made about the thrust and plan of the book, and it is felt that they will act as a rough guide to using the book as a tool of study.

The continuous narrative

This is a textbook in the traditional sense. In other words, it is a continuous narrative, unbroken by references, footnoting or bibliographical data, aimed at the busy student who needs to acquaint him or herself with the progressive stages in the development of social provision. In that sense, it offers an account which tries to balance a continuing analysis of social ills and their treatments with a sufficiency of factual amplification. It is believed that, for most students on most courses, each section of each chapter provides an optimal coverage of the topic in hand. Of course, no book should or could stand alone, and advice on further reading follows at the end of each chapter.

However, as a first and last resort, there should be found here a measure of basic adequacy at each stage.

The books referred to at the chapter ends have often been basic to the thinking and writing of that chapter, and they should accordingly be useful to students, even if several of the publications may have to be traced through college and other libraries. For fuller detail, there is a comprehensive list of new or recent books, all readily available, at the end of the book, beginning on page 169. These books are necessarily weighed toward the contemporary and near-contemporary scene. They are arranged, for ease of reference, in the same sections into which each of the chapters is divided. Finally, a study of this kind invariably throws up many new terms and concepts, and it was felt that a glossary of such terms would be helpful. Reference is made to this in the summary at the beginning of each chapter, and the glossary itself begins on page 174.

The sectional division

The Introduction apart, the eight chapters adhere fairly rigidly to a set chapter pattern, addressing the themes outlined in the Introduction in standard form. This has been done for two reasons. The first is to discipline what might easily have become untidy and unmanageable material into rational segments for the practical use of students. The second is to guide those students who may be at a point in their studies where they need to follow through a particular topic, such as poverty or education, over a lengthy time period: they will find that the subject turns up at the same place in each chapter for that ease of reference. These sections are as follows.

Summary of chapter contents.
Social and economic background of the period under review.
Common factors of social provision.
Approach to poverty.
Approach to ill-health (this embraces public housing, which evolved out of public health, and is treated specifically from Chapter 5).
Approach to ignorance.
Approach to crime.
Comparative features (i.e. parallel developments etc. in other countries).
Specific features (e.g. comments on the particular status of women, children, disabled people, people from ethnic minorities etc.).
Conclusion.

1 Introduction: Social casualty and political response

Summary

This introduction argues that all human societies are faced with social or 'welfare' problems, and that, at bottom, all societies must respond in some way. There is, eventually, the fear of social breakdown to prompt some sort of saving response. In this context, social provision is broadly defined as meeting the grave problems of sickness, poverty, ignorance and crime. But it is also argued that there are common threads by way of solutions. Four such consistent pointers are stressed:

- some balance of public and private provision is normally to be found;
- there are compromises as to whether the services are organized centrally or at more local levels;
- there are constant debates as to whether treatments should be delivered personally, at home, for instance, or whether recipients should be treated in institutions;
- there are likewise decisions to be made about making provision in cash or kind.

In general, there is an emphasis on the continuous – and the contentious – nature of the 'welfare state' debate across the ages and, indeed, across the globe. The introduction also indicates the format of the book, pointing out the pattern each chapter follows, in the hope that this will be of assistance to its readers.

> The chapter introduces several important concepts, all of which are included in the Glossary at the end of the book. These are: poverty – sickness – crime – ignorance – utilitarianism – intolerability – expediency – centralism and localism – institutionalism.

The common social problems of society

Those familiar with the the Old Testament book of Deuteronomy may recall this injunction to the ancient Hebrew community:

> And thou shalt have a paddle upon thy weapon; and it shall be, when thou wilt ease thyself abroad, thou shalt dig therewith, and turn back and cover that which cometh from thee: For the Lord thy God walketh in the midst of thy camp, to deliver thee, and to give up thine enemies before thee; therefore shall thy camp be holy: that he see no unclean thing in thee, and turn away from thee.

This placing of cleanliness next to godliness is very instructive. In its recommendation of instant sanitation it reminds us that social problems have, since the dawn of socialized humankind, been pressing. The Old Testament reveals the Hebrews as public health pioneers, with a markedly developed social conscience, eager to protect the many against the hazard of the foolhardy or offending individual.

Perhaps the crucial factor in this process was the massive shift in socio-economic life associated with the Agricultural Revolution, the earliest evidence for which dates from about 7000 BC and from the area of Jericho. Humans moved from the food-gathering or Mesolithic to the food-producing or Neolithic stage. By controlling the growth of plants, rather than by just plundering them, and by domesticating animals, rather than by just hunting them, humans, some nine or ten thousand years ago, thus altered the whole perspective of life. The Neolithic Revolution is properly associated with a great expansion in population – world population rose dramatically from about ten million in 10,000 BC to approximately 700 million in about AD 1750, on the eve of the Industrial Revolution. This meant larger groups than the penny numbers of the ancient predatory economy, and it also meant settlement, so that nomadic camp, village and, eventually, town life evolved. Social and cultural elaborations begin to appear: personal ownership; political and military organization; legal and moral codes; literacy; and sophisticated rites and arts. Jericho, for instance, housed three thousand souls, reliant on engineering to irrigate their fields efficiently, and requiring an effective political system for its maintenance.

It is apparent that, at least from this point, social problems emerge. For a human society, once constituted, is subject to social afflictions, whereby there are diversions from what, legally or culturally, is fondly regarded as the norm. When humans hunted and gathered food, possibly just in small family groups, that degree of relativity was unknown or unimportant. There was a singularity of existence, with little room, for example, for one person being poorer than another. And, in the final analysis, the human living in complete isolation must find it difficult, obviously enough, to think in terms of group or social relationships. The recluse, segregated from human contact, cannot really suffer poverty or commit crime, for there is no way of making that comparative distinction upon which *social* issues depend.

Once settled groupings exist, people must perforce toe the party-line of social conformity – but some find it difficult. The Hebrew shepherd, neglectful of his hygienic office, would have caused a public nuisance. He may have been provided with the necessary 'paddle' or he may not; he may have lost it, or he might have been lazy or stubborn. No society is, in effect, Utopian, in so far as that envisages an absence of social problems. The reverse is patently true. It is impossible to think of a human society that has not had its full hand of social problems. Turning, by way of theological balance, to the New Testament, we learn from St John that 'the poor always ye have with you'. Now that is as truthful a generalization as social history might reveal; except to add that, for largely self-evident reasons, the poor are not so much in good as bad company. The sick, the ignorant and the criminally inclined are always with us as well.

A common pattern of social problems

Social problems are notoriously interlinked. The poor man may be more vulnerable to sickness or more likely to be ignorant or more tempted by the blandishments of crime. Moreover, the definitions are constantly changing, according to the nature and mores of the society in question. It is a chaotic world, where there are few, if any, absolutes. Ordinarily, it is about people who are poorer, sicker, less clever or more criminally inclined than other people. For convenient purposes of study, however, some acceptable degree of tidying up must be sought. Several such lists of issues exist, including William Beveridge's famous five giants to be slain: 'disease, ignorance, squalor, idleness and want'. These were the ones he addressed in his eponymous report, published in Britain during the Second World War.

An attempt has been made here to select a division of social ills which, as well as insisting on the nature of that condition, also hints at the parameters of its treatment. In effect, such a selection has already been implied, in the urging that there are, perhaps, a depressing quartet of discernible problems and possible answers. The Four Horsemen of the social Apocalypse are, therefore, deemed to be, for the purposes of this study, poverty, sickness, crime and ignorance. It is an awesome foursome, which is mirrored by the devices of income and allied maintenance, health provision, law and order, and education, as its possible and relevant treatments. Taking a closer look at each of these, one might define them as follows:

1 *Poverty*. Where members of the community are insufficiently resourced to live anything like adequate lives, as determined and assessed by the economic circumstances of that community. The chief cause is a lack of work or scantly paid labour, and, by that token, it embraces poverty among those barred from work by, for instance, old age or disability.
2 *Sickness*. Where members of the community are reduced by forms of illness from anything like reasonable participation in what is regarded as the norm for that community.
3 *Crime*. Where members of the community are driven, for whatever reasons, to deviate from the legal standards imposed by that community.
4 *Ignorance*. Where members of the community find themselves unversed in

the skills and information required for reasonable involvement in the day-by-day life of that community. This applies wholly, but by no means exclusively, to the socialization of younger members of that community.

These may sound uncomfortably close to truisms, but it is important to establish some ground-rules, and, in this general case of social difficulty, the descriptor of some deviation from the agreed or accepted norm is pressed. However vague or unconscious they may seem, some yardsticks exist in every community of what, by and large, constituted 'ordinary' life. To reverse the point, and to deal in the positives rather than the negatives, there are usually common accords about having adequate income, about decent health, about civic behaviour and about reasonable education.

By adopting the touchstone of diversion from normalcy, the relative nature of social ills is stressed. Of course, one could adopt absolute standards of sheer poverty, where people are faced with rank starvation, of only such sickness as is death-threatening, of complete and destabilizing outbreaks of lawlessness and of total illiteracy. But this, historically and geographically, is none too helpful. This is the story of how communities – and especially British society – have tackled these problems. A key feature is that the norms change significantly. Few old age pensioners now, whatever the degree of their impoverishment, face the dire straits of some of their forebears a century ago, while they, in turn, were, on absolute standards, still better off than thousands of elderly people presently living in the Third World. Similarly, the skills of reading and writing were less necessary in British society two hundred years ago than most would believe them to be today, while, alternatively, other skills were required more than is currently the case.

We have noted the interconnection of these categories of social casualty. The Four Horsemen of the social Apocalypse ride in strict formation, rather like a coach of state and four, harnessed tightly together. Nevertheless, because we are concerned not only with problems but with intended solutions, it is rational to proceed in sectional format, for, on the whole, the response of society has been of that order. Put briefly, there have been attempts to treat poverty with financial subventions and sometimes benefits in kind; ill-health through medical and social services; crime through all manner of policing and punitive devices; and ignorance through schooling. These are well-rehearsed and well-understood, and, chapter by chapter, that four-fold categorization will be deployed.

Because the division is, at very best, artificial, some aspects of social welfare will have to be fitted in at the most suitable rather than the ideal point. A major example is housing. In British and, indeed, some European practice, the initiatives to do with accommodation, observed as a social matter, were instigated by public health requirements. Thus the early history of public housing is encompassed in the sections on health. Latterly, the political approach to housing has been couched more in terms of shortage of money, a frequent cause, needless to say, of homelessness or poor shelter. Notwithstanding this, the later history of public housing has been retained, for convenience's sake, in the sections on health.

Similarly, there appear to be clear links between education and employment, with all that entails for poverty or its converse. But, as we may discover, these are perhaps more blurred than first and superficial sightings might suggest – there is, for instance, some testimony to indicate that educational systems are as much to do with assuaging underemployment as preparing for employment itself.

These are no more, to exchange the equine metaphor for a maritime one, than warning shots across the bows of this four-masted barque. They are a reminder that, in choosing a four-fold chart, one is embarking on an approximate voyage of discovery, and not on a well-advertised tour. The ship of social welfare carries a flag of convenience, not an authoritative banner.

A common motive for response

Why do societies respond to these needs when they arise? In one sense, and in that all organized societies face social posers of the kind enumerated here, it follows that they all respond in some fashion, be it no more than a refusal to act at all, rather after the fashion of the 'do-nothing' monarchs of medieval French history. In fact, the political authorities of all societies intervene quite firmly on most if not all these matters, and at all times. There are several reasons why they do so, but one is probably dominant. Time and again, the signal for intervention occurs when the community at large, usually as represented by its ruling establishment, perceives, rightly or wrongly, that the effects of the social ills are threatening the social fabric.

This returns us neatly to the concept of social problems being inherent to civilized settlement and organization. For it is when that socio-economic order is menaced that the problem is recognized and endeavours are made to solve it. Without undue cynicism, it is suggested that, as in the case of the errant Hebrew who refused to remove and bury his waste products with his 'paddle' or shovel, there is the rub. It is the amount of public nuisance, or even danger, that might be caused to the generality of people that leads to political solutions. Poverty and unemployment *en masse* might lead to unruly disorder, tearing at the very stability of communal life. Sickness might reduce the economic tempo of a community, and, especially in the example of epidemic disease, might threaten the healthy majority. Crime is, self-evidently, likely to damage the social realm, its depredations perhaps falling heavily on the wealthier classes. Ignorance – that lack of socially useful skills – places a knife at the heart of the continuing survival of the community.

In a word, social welfare and provision is, on balance, motivated rather more by the need to protect the many than to succour the few. Where social ills are not, within the value-systems appertaining in a given community, creating this kind of nuisance or threat, then there are many illustrations of what Sir Robert Walpole called *'nihil movere'*, of letting sleeping dogs, however sick or malnourished, lie.

Of course, a welter of other reasons may be bidden to support the good old cause of social provision. They may be drawn from religious doctrine, from political science, from philosophic and ethical treatises, from political opportunism, from humane and liberal beliefs, from all manner of ideas and notions. Often, justifications for action will be assembled from several of these corners, like the permutations of football pools, and acts will be rationalized by reference to them. But, at bottom, most major shifts in the history of social provision are attended by this factor: the fear that, unless something is tried, the social commonwealth will be undermined in whole or part.

It is instructive to go directly to Jeremy Bentham (1748–1832), the classic exponent of individualism, to learn of his view of this. In his *Theory of Legislation*, he said that the two chief 'subsidiary ends of legislation', within his general concept of the greatest happiness for the greatest number, were 'security' and 'subsistence'. He claimed that the government which failed to ensure the 'subsistence' of the indigent members of society was, in fact, hazarding the 'security' of its more prosperous members. To let one's fellow-countrymen suffer undue hardship, irrespective of whether they were deserving or undeserving, was not 'utilitarian', not, that is, politically expedient; for it took the risk that the dispossessed might rise in assaults on the very private property Bentham was anxious to protect.

It would be hard to find a more clear-cut justification for the place of expediency as the crucial factor in social provision. Self-preservation, and the fear of social unrest, leading often to somewhat grudging amelioration of social troubles, will be a consistent theme of this history. Sometimes it has been the ghastly or scandalous nature of the problem which has provoked action: this is what, in respect of Victorian England, has been called the 'intolerability' theory. Society found it was simply obliged to respond to the sheer horror of the troubles.

Of course, wherewithal is the critical moderator even of 'intolerability'. Judgements about social unrest or threats to the body politic have had to be made with an eye on resources, for, if they did not exist or were perceived not to be readily available, the balance of 'security' and 'subsistence' might be a harsher one to find. This is why it is important to include a modicum of economic history in a study of social welfare. This has not always been the case in the past, and examinations of welfarism, for example, have occasionally been kept separate from studies of the workings of the economy. Emphasis has rather been placed on the political theory of welfare debate and legislation. This has its place, especially as it frequently occasions the timing and the flavours and the nuances of such activity. But current commentators are much more inclined, and rightly, to acknowledge the strict reliance of the one upon the other. Behind the rhetoric, for instance, of much modern beating of the drum of self-help and privatism lies, across the world, anxieties about the depressed state of the world economy.

The reverse is also true, and this has been even less well-regarded. Excursions into generous social welfare schemes may be as economically motivated as retreats into more niggardly programmes. Several of the major ventures into public welfare schemes, for instance, in the 1960s and 1970s – again, in different parts of the world – were economically driven, with the aim, among other features, of stimulating employment. The economic motif is, then, the other face of the 'expediency' factor: in other words, it normally has to be economically as well as socially expedient before welfare and allied provision is attempted.

Common solutions

Once a community has decided to respond to some cry for social action, and although the colours and traits of social provision are multifarious in the extreme, it is possible, at base, to distinguish certain types of solution or attitude throughout the story of social welfare, at home and abroad. Four such seem to be of most import. Rather like the previous division into sorts of social ill, they are a trifle arbitrary, a matter of convenient listing in the interest of simpler academic scrutiny. In chief, they represent an attempt to offer a short check-list for the examination of any form of social provision, anytime, anywhere.

The public/private compromise

Possibly the most significant of these elements is the proportion of intervention by the public authority, and, conversely, what is left to the responsibility of the individual person and his or her family. This is often viewed as a question of political science, its extremes marked by total state control versus complete liberty for the individual. In practice, both those positions are untenable in the pragmatic world of everyday reality. The very organization of humans into political communities confers some power to the public authority, while an embargo on all personal acts is well-nigh impossible to uphold. Political theory, for this purpose, masks as much as it reveals. Irrespective of the ideological wrappings and finery of any form of public intervention, the true measure lies in its extent and influence on the day-by-day life of the citizen. Throughout the history of social welfare – which, in effect, is identical with the history of civilized endeavour – the quantity and quality of public intercession have varied enormously. At any point, one is able to stop the historical clock and estimate how much by way of education, crime prevention, alleviation of poverty and treatment of sickness is undertaken by the state or other public agencies, and how much is left in private hands.

What is important is the realization that the public/private dilemma is not new: it is not an avant-garde row between social democrats or socialists and conservatives, it is the genuine stuff of pragmatic politics throughout social history.

The central/local compromise

Given that there is almost always a modicum of public provision, even if it is only in the essential field of law-enforcement, the next question touches on the division of this public activity. Certainly from the point where political entities grow in complexity – and the nation-state will obviously be the main frame of reference for this study – discussion mounts as to how much might be administered directly from the centre, and how much should be delegated to regional or local authorities. In Britain, as we shall constantly have cause to note, in old Elizabethan and new Elizabethan times alike and at all times, there has been and is an often uneasy resolution of the dilemma. There always appears to be a rather restless striving for advantage as to how much or how little power and resources are made available by delegation to localized levels of decision-making.

Again, one must recognize that the quarrel of Conservative governments centrally with Labour-controlled local authorities in the 1980s and 1990s is no more than a continuance of that lengthy and epic saga: it is no new phenomenon.

The domestic/institutional compromise

The other two topics are about methodology, not control of delivery. The first of these relates to another age-old question, posed in modern guise by discussions of domiciliary care in the community as opposed to care in residential facilities, as to whether services should be individual or collective. That is, should one 'institutionalize' social casualties together for ease of treatment and of control, or should one endeavour to provide for them piecemeal in their community?

There is no doubt that, over time and in many areas, social reformers of all brands have been fertile in their invention of institutions in which to corral like and sometimes unlike groups of social victims or offenders. The treatment of ill-health offers some spectacular illustrations of the opposites. On the one hand, there might be the exclusion, by quarantine, or some other isolating device, of the sick person – a pertinent reminder, incidentally, that much social provision was about the protection of the majority, not the helping of the oppressed. On the other hand, there might be the collection of sick people into often large infirmaries or hospitals. In the field of law-enforcement, the original Anglo-Saxon relied more on punishments applied in the community context, while the latter-day Anglo-Saxon depends more on the incarceration of groups of offenders in prisons.

The cash/kind compromise

The second of the two pairs of methods is closely associated with the first. It raises the question of whether provision should be in cash or kind, and, once again, students should be on the look-out for this issue at all parts of their studies. Education is, in fact, not a bad example of the genre, for, on the whole, public educational services have been proffered in kind, and in institutional kind at that, by way of schools and colleges. None the less, the use of grants, especially for college maintenance, is also part of the system. The alleviation of poverty is perhaps a more concrete example. Over centuries the battles have raged as to what amount should be given in cash and what in kind, either personally, in bread or coals, or institutionally, in the workhouse or its equivalent.

Many have been the ethical and economic arguments that have ensued over this issue. Today the mix remains, although the emphasis is currently on the direct payment of cash in doles or other subventions to those in need. None the less, the habit of giving in kind has not been ended – the meals on wheels service is but one instance of this.

The common threads

This final résumé of four types of 'compromise' in the business of social welfare completes a *tour d'horizon* in which the theme of continuity has been to the fore. The kinds of social ill, the motivation behind efforts to resolve them, the sameness, at heart, of the solutions broached – these are constants in the tale, however vivid the variety of technical and administrative detail.

It is a lengthy and at times complex story. In relating it, along the lines indicated, it is also hoped to make reference to analogous happenings in other parts of the world, in particular Europe and North America. This is done for comparative purposes, to avoid the danger of thinking that Britain has somehow managed to develop welfare mechanics in a sort of geographic vacuum. There are also issues which necessarily run laterally across the major strata of poverty, ill-health and the rest. These have properly grown in prominence during the past few years, and they relate to such matters as family and gender, or the place of ethnic minorities. Special attention will be given, as appropriate, to those critical questions.

All these amount to common threads, and the texture of every chapter will find those threads represented in very similar patterns. It is a large and it is a complicated subject, but there can be little doubt that, for the student working or preparing to work in these vital fields, an understanding of their historical development is the necessary prerequisite to operating intelligently and critically within them today. As Winston Churchill said, 'the use of recriminations about the past is to enforce effective action in the future'.

Advice on further reading

Two interesting books to read in connection with this introductory statement about the interlock of social welfare and political and economic stability might be:

Marshall, T. H. (1965) *Social Policy*, Hutchinson, London.
Pinker, R. (1979) *The Idea of Welfare*, Heinemann, London.

For the necessary social and economic background, the following single volume comes highly recommended, and will be useful for all succeeding chapters:

Morgan, K. O. (ed.) (1988) *The Oxford History of Britain*, Oxford University Press, Oxford.

Each of the following chapters will end with similar advice on further reading of an introductory kind. Many useful books, however, deal with themes rather than periods, and cut across various chapters. This especially applies to the later chapters, for, obviously, there is considerably more literature on the more modern periods. At the end of the book, beginning on p. 169, will be found a comprehensive list of further reading, provided under the headings of the chapter sections, i.e. Social and economic background, Common factors of social provision, Approach to poverty, Comparative features etc.

2 Medieval life and welfare

Summary

In medieval England may be found both the origins and the antithesis of modern society. An analysis of medieval social issues has, therefore, a dual purpose: it serves to demonstrate how, whatever the clime or time, social ills do occur and do oblige the authorities to make some response along relatively similar lines; and it serves to show how some modernistic practices and attitudes are rooted in ancient beginnings.

Social life in medieval times was necessarily small in scale, dependent, as it was, upon a fairly domesticated range of agriculture. This, in turn, meant that any attempts, for instance, to alleviate poverty or grapple with crime were correspondingly small in ambit. In so far as the state existed in the sense of a 'kingdom', it certainly took an interest in these things, but, in everyday practice, much was left to local action.

Key terms and phrases in this chapter, which are included in the glossary, are: the natural economy – self-help and self-sufficiency – feudalism – atomism – communalism – corporate and contractual practices – subsistence – the Church and charitable activity – almshouses – socialization.

Social and economic background

It is more than passing or antiquarian interest which should prompt an appraisal of medieval England. Apart from the discovery there of the origins of some present-day welfare mechanisms, it serves the other purpose of demonstrating how societies different in style from our own are faced with basically similar problems. At the extremes, the medieval period might be described as beginning with the fall of the Roman Empire, somewhere around the fifth century AD, and enduring until the complete manifestation of the full-run nation-state, which might be marked by the zenith of Tudor kingship in the sixteenth century. It would be foolish, then, to discuss a thousand years blandly, as if there were little change or development of knowledge or of institutions throughout that long era. Its political and religious history was especially varied and colourful. Nevertheless, one might, without undue simplification, point to certain underlying generalities of social and economic existence, provided one bears in mind that these are predominating rather than exclusive characteristics.

For many centuries the economy was largely agrarian. Some of this agricultural activity led inevitably to manufacture, trade and town-life, but this was ever a minority interest. In 1086, at the time of the Domesday Book, over 90 per cent of the population lived on and off the land. In a variety of legal formulations, they were composed of a peasantry very much in the thrall of a small but powerful group of landlords. At this juncture less than two hundred tenants-in-chief and a hundred great ecclesiastical bodies controlled three-quarters of the landed wealth of the country. They often had subtenants who, as knights or lords of the manor, oversaw the immediate activity of the key agricultural settlement.

This estate was typically the manor, convergent, frequently but not always, with the single village. Here relatively small groups of families huddled together and laboured upon crops which, optimally, paid for their rent and their keep. The bulk of the produce was used to preserve livelihood. It was predominantly a natural economy, one predicated upon self-sufficiency. Service on the lord's own holdings was part of the contract, although, later, many of these services in kind were commuted to rentals.

At the time of Domesday there were some 13,000 settlements of this kind in England, and, at the time of Edward I in the thirteenth century, there were about 10,000 English manors. These honeycombed the countryside in amazing abundance, and the conquest of the land was well advanced – 80 per cent of the arable land available when the 1914–18 war began had been under the plough at the time of the Battle of Hastings. They were necessarily farmed on a small scale. The population was some 1.25 million in 1086, and, against the countertide of famine and plague and with several rises and falls, it had only doubled by the onset of the Tudors in 1485.

It took much land to support few people, and many people to farm little land. The farming process was a settled but unprogressive one, scarcely changing or leaving scope for change over this time. Although terrain naturally made for some differences, it was essentially a matter of farming one's own holdings, usually spread over relatively huge tracts of acreage, while other areas were left fallow for recuperation. Techniques were rudimentary, uniform, wasteful and unchanging, with livestock ordinarily grazing on common land, and productivity perhaps four times smaller than might be expected today. Little wonder that the common people might be, in the euphemistic phrase, 'harvest sensitive', subject to malnutrition and death as winter menaced.

The talk in classroom history of 'fields' and 'strips' has misled countless youngsters into an underestimate of the quantities actually involved. A virgate – a rough measure of land area – was customarily regarded as sufficient to maintain a family, and that might have been, according to land usage and local custom, anything from 15 to 80 acres, but typically was around 30 acres. Thus the acreage of a manorial 'field' covered a vast terrain, while a 'strip' might be the size of a football field. One must visualize comparatively self-contained bands of no more than scores or a few hundreds, slowly and laboriously tearing a bleak living from great expanses of countryside.

Communication was very limited, and, although there was probably more personal mobility in medieval England than was once thought, travel was arduous and uncomfortable. Towns were at a discount, particularly in the early part of this period. By the fourteenth and fifteenth century, there was a burgeoning of urban life, as trade prospered more, but, for the bulk of the period, London, with a population of about 50,000, was the only town of prominent note and certainly four times bigger than any other township. All these factors conspired to leave the huge majority of the population co-cooned within their immediate vicinity, and, irrespective of whether they were or to what extent free or unfree in law, they were clearly chained to the economic dictate of the feudal system.

Common factors of social provision

Automatically, this type of life-style created a singularity of approach to the provision of welfare or justice. An atomistic socio-economic structure obviously led to an atomistic ambit for social provision. It was not that barons and kings did not matter. In varying degrees of uneasy alliance and outright conflict, they attempted to rule and defend their baronies and realms, and this is especially true in terms of their influence on policing and judicial process. For the rest – the alleviation of poverty and sickness, let alone ignorance – they had neither the scope nor the will, and, even in the matter of law and order, much was left to local oversight.

An overlooked aspect in the history of social provision tends to be its administrative mechanics, perhaps because accounts of bureaucratic machinery are a little dull, compared with the heady tales of political derring-do or the stimulating stuff of ideological wrangling. But, without such machinery, social reformers may whistle in the wind, and, quite simply, the organizational devices for the enforcement of regular social policies were not available to medieval rulers, even if they had been interested in such concepts.

A corporate system

At the base of the towering feudal pyramid, with its interplay of service and protection agreements, dwelt the huge mass of the people. The formal feudal system was not in being everywhere nor all the time in medieval history, but that feudal tendency, with a landed warrior class in dualism with a tied peasantry, was very general throughout this long period. It followed that, by and large, men and women relied on their immediate grouping, typically the manor and/or the village, for social succour. Although much depended on the good will and efficiency of the lord of the manor and his officers, there was plenty of scope left for communal identity. The work in the great fields could only proceed by common consent and in some concord, and decision-making was often at the behest of the collective will. In turn, this must have determined how some of the social problems were tackled.

One must not, as some historians have done, idealize this tendency into some form of cheerful democracy. The feudal bonds ensured that this was seldom, if ever, the case. None the less, on a workmanlike and everyday basis, there was a solid communalism about manorial life. G. M. Trevelyan, the celebrated liberal historian, has gone so far as to suggest that, in many practical senses, the medieval peasant was 'freer' than the Victorian agricultural labourer.

This primitive corporate approach was very much in line with a central theme of medieval life, in which people were ready to relinquish their individual rights or wishes to a degree alien certainly to today's citizens. It might be argued that the withdrawal of human rights was more compulsory than voluntary, but, at least in part, there was a willingness so to proceed. And historians have been quick to point out that, given its longevity, the system must have had sufficient advantages for it to have held sway.

The role of the Church

In the Introduction, the crucial dichotomy of public and private provision was discussed: in medieval times, the public sector, as represented by kingship or regional, usually shire, governance, was necessarily inconsistent and feeble, at least for daily reference. Men and women could scarcely cope in their entirely private capacities, and thus forms of corporate endeavour grew, not only in the countryside but in the newly born towns and elsewhere. This was to be of much significance in terms of social policy. It was largely founded in the medieval notion of contract, some reciprocal measure of mutual advantage, the salient example being, of course, the use of land at a number of levels in return for some form of protection. The trading guilds of the towns, the orders of chivalry and the monastery are other illustrations of this, with, respectively, merchants, knights and monks grouped together with a mutual purpose and common rules.

The Church played, often in this corporate shape, a vital role in medieval life. In effect, it shadowed the feudalistic pyramid, from the apex of the papacy, via, in English practice, the Archbishopric of Canterbury, the bishoprics, the static monastic orders and the mobile orders of friars, down to the frequently unschooled parish priest, ministering to the village. Medieval life, brutish and fragile, and negotiated in fairly enclosed format, found its perfect counterpoint in the Christian promise of eternal glory, and set much store by the Church. The contract was again to the fore, with the idea of becoming 'God's debtor', by dint of one's good and earthly works being exchanged for salvation.

The Church played a major part in most aspects of social policy, both as stimulant to action and as direct activator, and there is no more vivid instance of the medieval origins of current British practice in these fields than the persistence of this tradition. In summary, then, one finds that medieval social provision was, in consequence of the self-contained nature of the economy, oriented around the home and the local farming group, but with a firm overlay of Church teaching and activity.

Approach to poverty

Of all the four aspects of medieval social casualty, poverty may be most summarily dismissed. The mass of people lived at not more than subsistence levels and their possessions were scanty in the extreme. Clothes and cooking utensils, let alone homes, were made on a do-it-yourself basis, or with the help of village-based craftsmen. The distinction between poverty and non-poverty in such situations is hard to spot. While much of the farming was by common consent and action, produce tended to be family-based, throwing the upkeep of the home squarely on the peasant. None the less, in such tight-knit communities, there must have been a certain amount of neighbourly or kindred assistance, and something would depend on whether the lord of the manor was kind or effective or both in the discharge of his duties.

Given such commonalty of agricultural process, it is obvious that villages sank or swam together – a bitter harvest or sharp drought would affect everyone jointly. The medieval yearning for the merry month of May was no idle conceit: often it would be a grim question of whether the stored grain and the salted meat would, in fact, support life until the advent of the sunnier spring. The quality of life had its ups and downs throughout the year, as well as year by year. In the better times, life could be pleasant enough, with a reasonable diet, and it would be wrong to write off the medieval period as entirely impoverished. What is apparent is that manors and villages were very much thrown on their own resources, and there was little help forthcoming from elsewhere. Naturally, the poorest, the landless, the oldest, would tend to suffer most at times of difficulty.

As well as famine and animal diseases, there were the occasional ravages of localized warfare. The record of manorial or village conflict seems good – there are precious few instances of manor warring against manor – but a little higher up the chain of command was a warrior class which, in varying ways, might be up to more bellicose mischief. So there was also the threat of disruption of that kind. The medieval siege offers a sombre picture of such strife. It was the custom, on a Europe-wide basis, to push the weak and feeble outside the besieged fortification, to save on food and water; they would be driven back by the assailing force, who had no wish to add to their ration-strength. This early example of the poverty trap is one likely derivation of Gregory's coinage in *Romeo and Juliet* about the weakest going to the wall.

The Church and the poor

The one exception to the general rule of home-based support was the Church. In parts a wealthy organization, because of its collection of dues from the laity and because of, on many monastic estates, the richer efficiency of its farming method, it was in a position to offer some help to the beggared and destitute. In more primitive times, the churches had been more charitable societies than buildings, with gifts or endowments for alms for the poor representing the early deployment of Christian philanthropy. In medieval times these customs were largely sustained on a parish basis, although there were unfortunate signs of this charitable function being obscured by feudal practice, resulting in the revenues finding their way into ecclesiastical or even private coffers.

Alms-giving and almshouses

At the high point of medievalism the chief foci for this Christian aid became the monasteries, with alms and food distributed 'at the gate', as the term was, or actually delivered to the poor person's home. Eventually almshouses were built – there were four, for instance, at Canterbury, two of them endowed by Archbishop Lanfranc in 1084. It is important to identify these as probably the first (certainly since the Roman Empire) institutional answers, as opposed to cash and kind answers, to social trouble. They are the beginnings of a long line of institutions, including the workhouse and the residential care home, which offered a non-domestic package to the weary and indigent person. They were few in number, but of great conceptual significance for the future.

Christian teaching about charitable giving has ever been a motive for such philanthropy, even when it has been formalized in tithes and other payments. Without undue cynicism, it must be added that – and this is very true of the medieval period, with its underlining of contract – alms-giving has also been utilized as a kind of afterlife insurance. With a simple view of rewards and punishments prevailing, it is hardly surprising that the givers had in mind their own souls rather than the bodies of the recipients. Either way, it meant that too little thought was given to the social outcome of the activity (a not uncommon trait of social policy throughout the ages). This, coupled with the sporadic incidence of the monastic and allied centres, resulted in a very patchy and, its critics have urged, wasteful and indiscriminate process. One may perhaps spot in these criticisms another first. It has been said that such disorganized alms-giving increased as much as it relieved poverty, a forerunner of that hardy competitor in the welfare race, the scrounger who grabs what's offered rather than works for a living.

These images were to be mirrored in the towns, almost all of which were little more than walled villages, with populations of a couple of thousand people. The Church, in receipt of funds including legacies, often designated for church building, remained the chief source of the relief of the poor. In the later middle ages, the municipal authorities, growing in confidence, began to offer some help. The merchant and craft guilds, again true to their medieval roots of corporate action, started to conduct more secular charitable pursuits, their direct aim being the maintenance of widows and orphans of fellow-members, and other group-based relief, including the occasional almshouse.

Approach to ill-health

It is important to assess health as a comprehensive matter of the social environment, rather than in the more restrictive setting of the interchange of sicknesses and treatments. The middle ages were severely disadvantaged by, as modern eyes would see it, lack of knowledge, and assuredly by lack of nutrition. Families were often debilitated, indeed killed, by poor nourishment. Then there were epidemics, notably the Black Death, a virulent form of bubonic plague, which struck Britain most fatally in 1348–50, carrying off a third of the population. It returned in the 1360s, and outbreaks continued until the late seventeenth century, when larger brown smooth-haired rats began to drive out the smaller but rough-haired variety. Spread by the fleas infesting these black rats, the plague's connection with filthy conditions led to its inflicting the harshest damage on the towns.

In turn, this reminds us that there were advantages. The sparse and thinly spread population of the countryside was, a highly infectious disease like the bubonic plague apart, relatively immune from some illnesses, especially as sewage – a potent source of sickness in the coming centuries – was normally utilized for fertilizer. Fresh running water was not usually a problem, as settlements naturally sought out such a source, which would provide for both human and agricultural use.

The self-help principle was, of course, uppermost. There might have been a medical man – an apothecary – in the town, although his ministrations might not have been of the most efficacious, but localized rural communities had to fend for themselves. Minor ailments – like colds or constipation – were treated with herbal remedies, some of which are still extant today, while physical damage was met by somewhat primitive first-aid. It should be added that the medieval Briton in all degrees of society was, unsurprisingly, a heavy boozer, with the lower orders partaking of ale, mead and cider. Curiously, fruit was often sedulously avoided, and diets also tended to be short on vegetables, so that scurvy was another constant threat.

The Church and sickness

The Church, ever-present in the medieval mind, took up two slightly contradictory stances. One was to regard sickness as the visitation of divine retribution or the work of the devil – much of the response to the Black Death was of this flavour. This led to a certain resignation in the face of major illness. Life was, after all, a brief prelude or testing-ground, prior to the hoped-for joys of eternity. It is also likely that some of this association of critical ill-health with supernatural forces predated the Christian influence, and was well-established in pagan forms.

However, the Church was alternatively interested in the treatment of the sick as a charitable service, often in close relation with its work for the poor. Thus the almshouses were sometimes designated for blind and handicapped people, who, needless to say, were likewise poor people. Almshouses would occasionally be located away from the major accommodation for the succour of lepers, a generic term used to cover all those with disfiguring diseases. Nursing and hospital orders were part of this charitable work, while the travelling Franciscan or 'grey' friars did what they could to tend the sick. Looked at objectively, both these aspects of clerical interest are an illustration of the age-long proclivity for the priesthood in all pre-modern societies to seize responsibility for physical and mental health.

The beginnings of hospitals

The humble almshouse, therefore, assumes an even mightier significance, for it is the progenitor of the hospital as well as the workhouse. Truth to tell, there had been hospitals of sorts in the classical civilizations, with their well-developed city life – the *valetudinaria* of the Roman Empire, for example. However, in the long aftermath of the downfall of that imperial regime, it was the Church which first struggled to construct institutions. The almshouses were usually administered by a priory and funded by tithes, monies obtained from the lay people. The earliest of London's famous hospitals were St Bartholomew's and St Thomas's, founded respectively in 1123 and 1200 in this tradition. They provided asylum for poor, sick, aged and disabled people, and for a number of orphans. They were little more than nursing shelters, and, as testimony to this compassionate, if passive, role, what passed then for a profession of apothecaries, surgeons and blood-letting physicians was wholly uninvolved with these ventures and ordinarily operated from its members' own homes.

It follows, too, that these pioneer agencies were situated in towns, where the trading guilds were also beginning to consider their position apropos health and welfare, and where the richer merchants and citizens were making bequests for just such purposes. In consequence, and as with the amelioration of poverty, huge swathes of the population were left scarcely touched by such developments, and the availability of nursing care had little to do with any estimate of need. Patchiness of incidence is another theme with a long history in the annals of social policy.

The conclusion must be very like the one reached with respect to medieval poverty; that is, over against self-help as the major key was to be found the Church, playing, in minor key, a role as present opinion-former about the nature of illness, and as future trend-setter in respect of institutional organization.

Approach to ignorance

Like health, education has a broad context, and should not be limited to the convention of schooling and literacy. In this wider social sense, ignorance is about the inability to adapt to and survive in one's appropriate community. Inevitably, this chiefly concerns the socialization of children, the insistence that they are properly inducted into the economic practices and social mores of their society. In the last analysis, the child of the medieval peasant who could not snare rabbits was ill-educated.

This relativity of ignorance to need is a significant concept, and will be a recurring one, especially when the mixed motives of institutionalized schooling come to be tackled. For now, the relief of ignorance in medieval times was, like so much else, a family matter, with children fairly quickly having to learn the all-round skills of husbandry, the household and, eventually, manorial custom or its equivalent, with, possibly, some martial arts, such as archery, in addition. The learning was done from parental and sibling models and through habit and practice. There might have been, additionally, some rudimentary instruction from the parish priest, frequently in the porch of the church, on the basics of Christian belief.

The Church and education

In a more sophisticated sense, it was, inevitably, the Church which offered education as normally perceived. By the fourteenth century there were, in fact, over three hundred schools, usually quite minute in scale, and in the control of the monasteries, cathedrals, hospitals or chantries (chapels principally concerned with intercession for the dead, a matter upon which the medieval mind was furiously concentrated). Secular clergy provided the elementary instruction in theological and Latin studies. Here clerks and priests received their early education, and there were some openings for clever boys (but not girls) of lowly origins.

The foundation by William of Wykeham in 1382 of Winchester School (and although its express purpose was prayers in perpetuity for his soul) marks the first genuine attempt to establish an educational base, self-centred and unattached to any monastery or abbey. It included provision for 'the sons of noble and powerful persons' and thus was described by A. F. Leach as the 'germ of the public school system' in his *Schools of Medieval England*, written in 1915. Eton followed suit in 1440, in both fashions – it was intended for much the same type of youth and it was pledged to pray for the salvation of Henry VII's immortal soul.

Beyond and above this layer of schools were the two universities of Oxford and, of lesser authority at this stage, Cambridge, each with slowly growing sets of ecclesiastical colleges, as their titles still recall. Until the collegiate system took root, undergraduate life, which often began at fourteen years of age, was squalid and uproarious, but it provided the only mark of higher education and a footing in the medieval professions. Although the theological and classical curriculum appears arcane to the present eye, it was then immensely utilitarian, for the Church, canon law and many posts in administration and teaching were dependent on such knowledge. There was some training of physicians, but, as we have noted, much medical practice was considered, if not immoral, then unseemly and unfit for the cleric, leaving cupping and leeching (for bleeding purposes) and teeth extraction to the modest barber. As for the nobility, both girls and boys were, according to the best practice of the time, placed at the age of about seven in another household to learn the accomplishments relevant to that class.

In the towns young people learned their trade, their faith and their customs within the family circle or, increasingly, under the rule of the guild. The concept of apprenticeship was evolving. Apart from the urban trades, it was to be seen in the rising Inns of Court, where men prepared themselves for work in the common law. Although these were more secular processes, the authority of the Church was never basically challenged.

The corporate approach to education

The prevailing tenets of medievalism are to be observed in almost all these branches of education. Apart from the obvious example of Church influence, the corporate and the contractual themes of medieval thought were notable. The university, as a congregation of scholars; that peculiarly English agency, the residential college or school, as a commune of students; the Inns of Courts, as a collective of lawyers-in-training; the great household, as a miniature court of young noblemen and women: these are excellent instances of the corporate genre. Next, the mutual relationship of tutor and student; of professional or tradesman and apprentice; of older and younger nobleman, the latter as page, then squire: these are illustrations of an education or training, inclusive of social and pastoral care, given in exchange for assistance in the task in hand. In these several ways, the knock-for-knock nature of the medieval contract is exhibited.

Overall, medieval attitudes to education stayed strictly close to the fundamental beliefs and life-style of the age, with the great majority of people in receipt of only familial socialization. That said, it would be wrong to dismiss medieval education out of hand. In the beginnings of apprenticeship and in the influence of the Church may be seen themes which remain important in the 1990s. Nor was ignorance, in the literal connotation, too desperate, especially remembering that this was a largely oral culture, with books, in those pre-printing days, expensive and scarce. Even in the universities the instruction was mainly oral. But there were readers and writers, and it has been estimated that, taking the middle of the fourteenth century as a rough and ready vantage point, some 3–5 per cent of the population were literate in English, Latin or French.

Approach to crime

Of the four chief social problems crime is the most overt and tangible, an ever-present in all societies. In consequence, the medieval political response was more elaborate *vis-à-vis* lawlessness than poverty, disease or education.

The struggle to maintain due order had to be undertaken at all levels. The landed warrior class was often locked in combat, as Britain suffered feudal warfare, of which the War of the Roses was the prime example. Raiding, especially at the borders with Scotland, was another aspect of this same unease. One must again recollect that this period, at its extremities, covers a thousand years, so that any statements are by way of illustration rather than even broad generalization.

Shire and sheriff

For centuries the English monarchy sought to make good its sway by the shire system. The shire-reeve or sheriff attempted to safeguard the king's interest over an area which, of course, became the base for English local government ever since. Western film buffs will recognize that the office was to have global manifestation – and the *posse comitatus*, the band raised by the sheriff to help keep order, might ring similar bells. The sheriff presided over the shire court, which was made up of the shire's great and good, and which was the repository of county custom. The shires were subdivided into hundreds or wapentakes, with a similar court, and when parliament evolved, it was based on shire representatives meeting to form a countrywide royal court.

By the fourteenth century itinerant, that is travelling, judges, who might keep some check on the often venal sheriffs, were well-established but the genuine counterweight was the utilization of knights, burgesses (leading townsmen) and gentry as unpaid agents of local government. At its most formal, this was best secured, by the fourteenth century, through the office of justice of the peace. From the viewpoint of social welfare at large, what is now important to note is that these various officers – sheriffs, justices of the peace – found their duties much widened as time went on. Very soon they had responsibilities for administrative as well as judicial functions, and in them may be seen the origins of local governmental officialdom today.

As towns developed, they began to organize legal and, alongside this, administrative machinery, and this was to be another source of future local government. The Church, as ever, played a significant part. Canon, that is Church, law was prescribed for those in clerical orders, and it must not be forgotten that prelates and abbeys were often huge land-holders, with all that entailed by way of jurisdiction. The teaching of the Church, with its strict adherence to the providential ordination of men's status and estate, acted like an ideological cement throughout society. Medieval religion was tailor-made for peasant communities, emphasizing, as it did, the static nature of human life and, of course, the association of sin and crime.

Village law – the origins of the jury

Much of this probably washed over the ordinary serf or villein, toiling ceaselessly over his paltry harvests in his remote village. The manorial court acted as the lower-level equivalent of the shire and hundred courts, with many of the suits and disputes, as in those higher tribunals, concerned with matters of land usage and possession. Law in rural communities tends to depend more on custom than on writ, and medieval England was no exception. Generally speaking, however, England was badly policed. Although in some reigns – those of Henry II and Edward I, for instance – a more serene atmosphere prevailed, the chaotic atomism of society did not make for peace. The rigid character of medieval life inevitably led to a crumbling at the edges, with, at all levels of society, a minority of men and women finding themselves, for all manner of reasons, rootless. The outlaw figure of Robin Hood serves as a medieval figure just as potent as a scheming Sheriff of Nottingham.

The most spectacular outbreak of lawless behaviour was the Peasant's Revolt of 1381. An analogue, so to say, of the Black Death in health terms, and, incidentally, in part caused by the labour shortage subsequent to that disaster, it created much fear and confusion, and Richard II needed luck, courage and troops to ensure it was suppressed. One of the peasants' grievances – the poll tax – was to create much the same difficulties for the government six hundred years later. Ordinarily, however, it was the sporadic round of murder, violent robbery, rape and assault which might affect everyone, high and low.

For much of the time, people were thrown back on their own devices, as we have observed they were in all other social fields. By and large, what is sometimes called the 'know-everyone' system was deployed. This relied on the inhabitants of small-scale communities living in one another's pockets, far removed from the anonymity of urban existence, so that all could keep an eye on one another, and everyone knew the likely culprits. From Anglo-Saxon times onwards, and with a major tightening under the Normans, this method of self-regulation was sophisticated into groupings of ten or twelve men who had to take responsibility one for the other. These were known as tithings or frankpledges, and they were customarily inspected by the sheriff or his officers to ensure that all lower-class men were so engaged. This joint surety, for policing, for handling reports of suspicious and for good behaviour, is another instance of the corporate nature of medieval life. It is also an excellent illustration of the fashion in which men, and thus their families, were tied to the land and their home village.

Although affairs moved slowly and obscurely in medieval times, some of the roots of the jury system are evident enough in this process. Especially by the reign of Henry II, the use of inquisition and judgement of peer-groups of neighbours, at the appropriate social ranking, was finally replacing the ancient trials by compurgation (the swearing to one's honour by friends), by ordeal and by battle. Shackled remorselessly to the land as it undoubtedly was, the tithing does have some of the hints of more democratic citizenship.

The rise of the constable

As community life became more integrated, the manorial courts and courts leet (meeting twice yearly in some areas to sort out petty crime) became rather more important, and, in succession to the tithing or frankpledge mode, the office of parish constable arose. It was beatified in a Statute of

1252, and defined as an agency for collective responsibility. The Statute of Winchester of 1285 again addressed the issue. It set out the need for a chief or high constable for the hundred, with a petty constable for the village or the tithing. This legislation embraced the needs of the townships. The system of Watch and Ward – the one for day and the other for night – was endorsed.

The pivot of law and order now became the constable, for he was responsible for the 'presentment' of offenders at court and for the raising of the hue and cry, that famous and noisy example of collective action. He became the appointed subsidiary of the local justice of the peace – whose duties were more clearly outlined in an Act of 1361 – and this was originally a voluntary post, undertaken on rotation. It later became subject to substitution by payment, as men found themselves too busy or unwilling to serve, and, gradually, the paid office of parish constable was to emerge. It is very important to grasp the origins of British policing in the civic ordinariness of village life. Unlike some of the more military continental models, British policemen and policewomen stand foursquare on the notion that they are normal citizens undertaking duties which any fellow-citizen might or should.

So much for the more formal measures. As with all their other social troubles, medieval peasants and villagers had eventually to copy what often their betters were guilty of, and take the law into their own hands. With fist, club and bow, the English peasantry had sturdily to protect itself as best it could against the incursions of robbers, raiders or other marauders. Although the arrangements for law and order were more elaborate than in other social fields, self-help remained of the essence during large tracts of this lengthy period. The stuttering attempts to formulate offices, like that of the justice of the peace or the constable, or to think haltingly about the needs of local governance, are, for practical purposes, of future rather than present interest.

Comparative features

Granted the relatively small size of most medieval communities across Europe and the main reliance of most people on subsistence agriculture, there was a curious sameness about medieval European life. In some regards, it was a most unified civilization, to the point where today's Euro-federalists might turn green with envy. Occasionally, great stretches of land were in the political thrall of this or that Emperor, or one or another of the mighty kings could hold massive sway. But it was not really political union which gave Europe such uniformity in the middle ages.

This sameness lay more in what might be termed the horizontal structure of European life, whereby strands of belief and practice were held in common across the continent. The obvious and main example is the Roman Catholic Church, with its ministry in dominion over the whole of Western Europe, from the apex of the papacy to the base of the parish priest. We have noted something of the Church's involvement in education, the law and other matters, and this held true across Europe. It underpinned the latinity of the culture. Latin was the Esperanto of the age, enabling educated men to hold converse anywhere in Europe. University life, for instance, was very similar wherever the scholar might find himself. Feudal law and custom, including the rules of warfare, was another cross-regional binding, one very much influenced by clerical teaching.

It is difficult to overestimate this commonness of cultural and intellectual comprehension. Franciscan friars were mobile in many lands, tending the distressed, just as Benedictine monasteries were offering charity at their gates across Europe. The 'hospitaller' orders, such as the Knights of St John of Jerusalem, were busy founding shelters for the sick from the twelfth century, while the towns of Italy and the Low Countries were establishing models of welfare which English towns would later follow. The *tables des pauvres* in Ypres in Flanders – feeding stations for the impoverished, current from the thirteenth century – are one example. Because, on the other hand, signs of national loyalty were as yet underdeveloped, it might almost be said that the priest (or the scholar, or the knight, or the peasant . . .) had more in common with his counterpart in another place in Europe than those of another grouping in his own land.

The exigencies of transport brought England closer to the continent. Because sea travel was faster and more reliable than the tribulations of road travel, Calais was 'nearer' to London than was York. The cross-Channel exploits of English monarchs (Henry V is a celebrated example), with English and French regions sometimes held in common, meant that there were closer ties between England and the continent than at any time until the present. All in all, the similarities of English and continental European social life were more telling than the differences. As we shall see, this was to change radically with the onset of modern times.

Specific features

The collapse of the Roman Empire was partially caused by and set in train vast migrations of peoples. The arrival of Angles, Saxons and Danes in Britain was but one facet of this huge movement of ethnic groups. Not all students are aware, for instance, that as the Normans colonized England, they were also colonizing Sicily. These so-called 'barbarian invasions' created a ferment of population change, with the clash of cultures and of arms the motif of early European history. In a sense, the insulated character of medieval life – the sheltered manor, perhaps with its defensive fortification, such as the peel-tower on the Anglo-Sottish borders; the monastery; the walled town – was the essential response to this ceaseless chaos. In terms of European nationhood, few may reasonably claim racial purity, even if they wished to do so. It is worth remembering that ethnic migration has long been a theme of European, including English, history.

Turning to topics such as the place of woman in medieval society, one is faced with male domination, not least given the masculine hegemony of the Roman Catholic Church. The secluded cluster of family life was the main key to existence, and, therefore, women had an important role in farming and household chores, let alone their even more significant role as child-bearer, child-rearer and health counsellor. They worked extremely hard, but they were not brushed to one side: theirs was an integral, if burdensome, part. Some attention was paid to the education of girls in the higher echelons of society. The song schools, attached to clerical foundations, offered some very elementary education, but girls, as was remarked above, received no later schooling. It was thought they would corrupt or distract the boys – an argument still heard in present times when coeducational schooling is heatedly discussed. It was also accepted that marriage or the nunnery was woman's lot and, until many centuries later, the arranged marriage, with land, property or money riding upon it, was the norm. This, needless to say, could bear very heavily on women, although it might be added that men sometimes took it amiss as well. Overall, one must always try to empathize with those from other cultures in terms of their values and expectations, but, even so, the destiny of medieval women was not pleasant and must, as often as not, have been unhappy.

Conclusion

Enough has been said to foster the notion that present-day practices and theories of social welfare owe something to medieval origins. The residential institution, the social welfare 'scrounger', the influence of the church in social matters, the education of girls, the office of constable, the beginnings of local government – these are a few of the examples. Of course, medieval life was at once more intensely localized in scale and more heavily dependent on corporate action and contract than modern life, yet, conversely, through that very corporate strand, as well as the convenience of the English Channel, ties and comparisons with Europe were probably firmer than they are today, in spite of the blandishments of the European Community. The next chapter will describe the parallel growth of the nation-state and the money-economy, and the way in which social problems and their proposed solutions changed accordingly.

Advice on further reading

Some students may find it necessary to delve further into social life in Medieval Britain. Four books suggest themselves for that purpose:

Barlow, F. J. (1955) *The Feudal Kingdom of England 1042–1216*, Longman, London (5th edn 1992).
Bolton, J. L. (1980) *The Medieval English Economy 1150–1500*, Dent, London.
Hilton, R. H. (1975) *The English Peasantry in the Later Middle Ages*, Oxford University Press, Oxford.
Postan, M. M. (1972) *The Medieval Economy and Society*, Penguin, Harmondsworth (3rd edn 1993).

For more specialist enquiries, the student might consult:

Barlow, F. J. (1979) *The English Church 1066–1154*, Longman, London.
DuBoulay, F. R. H. (1970) *An Age of Ambition*, Nelson, London (for its discussion of class, marriage and gender themes).
Bellamy, J. (1973) *Crime and Public Order in the Later Middle Ages*, Routledge, London.
Clanchy, M. T. (1979) *From Memory to Written Record: England 1066–1307*, Blackwell, Oxford (for its account of the development of literacy).
Gies, F. and Gies, G. (1989) *Life in a Medieval Village*, Harper and Row, London.

3

The nation-state and the money-economy

Summary

This chapter covers the 300 years of early modern history; that is, to the dawn of industrialism. It observes the gradual rise of the British nation-state, centralized and omnicompetent, chiefly founded on the growth of a predominantly commercial economy. In turn, this gives rise to nascent attempts at national solutions to welfare questions, and, as the role of the Church changes somewhat, these are sometimes more secular solutions. The Elizabethan poor law is the most famous illustration of this trend, but there are also moves to organize criminal justice on a sounder national footing, to exert national controls over schooling and apprenticeship, and even to undertake some primitive public health activity.

From a broader standpoint, it is of importance to note that, across Europe, similar stirrings were afoot, resulting in that mesh of nation-states, each with a largely money-economy, which remains the basic pattern today. Each of these, like Britain, was faced with social problems of a corresponding type, and each of them felt obliged, on the whole, to meet them in much the same fashion. Thus it might be asserted that, at least by way of origin, the nation-state and the welfare state are as one.

Some of the terms and concepts used in this chapter and included in the glossary at the end of the book are: the money-economy (*Geldwirtschaft*) – the nation-state – sovereignty – omnicompetence – particularism – centralization and decentralization – bipartism – Europeanization – professionalism – the parish – workhouses – justices of the peace – the poor law.

Social and economic background

The evolution of modern out of medieval society was immeasurably slow. Many of the ingredients of early modern life – the towns, kingship, even parliament – were already present in some connotation, while other elements were late in arriving. It is only in retrospect that one could make the decision that a watershed had occurred.

The construction of the nation-state

Gradually, the nation-state was constructed. It was centralized and omnicompetent, where much of medieval authority was diffused through a hierarchy of landed nobility. The War of the Roses in the fifteenth century was the last, colourful, internecine squabble among the grand families for control over the lands of England. Thereafter – and not least because the feudal families were grievously enfeebled by such warring – the monarch was able to assume unimpeachable authority over the nation. His role would, of course, be challenged, and there would be arguments over the succession, but, from here on in, the concept of central power was not to be menaced.

This development happened in tandem with the increasing commercialism of the economy. To deploy the Germanic jargon, there was a switch from the predominantly *Naturalwirtschaft* or feudal economy to the predominantly *Geldwirtschaft*, the money-economy of present times. Neither was ever exclusive, but, gradually, money became as important as, or more so than, land as the key to wealth. Trade depended on secure transit and rational structure. A more peaceful kingdom, allowing greater safety of travel, was one prerequisite of satisfactory commerce; a more systematic organization of coinage, banking and other monetary matters was another. Both relied on a strong central government. In these business affairs, national law was town law 'writ large' – where subsistence farming rested on custom, commercial traffic required a much more methodical regimen.

If not the dawn, then it was the morn of capitalism. The medieval wool trade became the staple component of the new dispensation, a clear instance of the historical amalgam of continuities and changes. The discoveries, with English sailors to the fore alongside those of Portugal and Spain, created novel opportunities for trade. We have noted the restless quality of medievalism, and those internal evidences of strenuous migratory activity. Increasingly, this found expression in the so-called Expansion of Europe. North-west Europe became the focus for an enlarged world, and England sprang from being on the rim of a smaller to being the centre of a larger planet. In the three centuries following the discovery of the Americas, $2\frac{1}{2}$ million kilograms of gold were imported into Europe from this new world, and the money-economy was further enhanced. Columbus himself straddled the two cultures, part medieval mystic, part modern pioneer.

Although the lords and the peasants survived in some fashion, another group, more identifiable with the money-economy, rose in influence. It was a loose combine of squires, land-owners, merchants and senior tradespeople, and the professional men who attended them. Although this has been subject

to countless analyses since by academics and thereby to a dozen interpretations, one must nevertheless acknowledge, in however general the terms, the
growth of a third or middle class, with a major stake in this money-economy
and the nation-state that provided its ambit of concern. And the financial
sufficiency of the new-style monarchy was heavily dependent upon this
group, most insistently for the standing army – as opposed to the old feudal
levy – upon which the external defence and the internal peace of the realm
relied. King and middle classes thus found common cause: no state, opined
the shrewd Francis Bacon, adviser to the Tudors, 'would prospere or be
worshipful undere a poore kynge'.

Science, religion and culture

The other great movements of the hour were at hand to contribute to these
vast changes. The Scientific Revolution, represented in England by such as
Francis Bacon, challenged the traditional orthodoxies, theologically based,
with the harder tack of scientific method. Technically, compasses, telescopes,
firearms and a plethora of improved instrumentality and mechanics made
their telling mark. In turn, it influenced the Administrative Revolution, for
printing, as but one example, very much eased the transfer of power to the
centre and lubricated the cogs of widespread communication. One could
only implement a national bureaucracy when the tools were available.

The Renaissance and the Reformation, whatever their intrinsic virtues,
had a socio-economic role. In England, literature and drama, with
Shakespeare the undoubted fount and genius, were more vivid manifesta-
tions of the Renaissance than the visual arts. The political effect of the
Reformation was a complete abrogation of the international chains of
Roman Catholicism, with the establishment of the Church of England under
the Tudor monarchy. Both emphasized, in practice, the vitality of nationalism
and of the nation-state, within which the individual was significant.
In caricature, where *Everyman*, the mystery play, anonymous of author and
in title, is the characteristic medieval drama, *Hamlet*, a specified individual,
his soul scrutinized by a unique poet, is the characteristic modern play.
Moreover, the connection of Protestantism with the capitalist ethic has
invited much debate, with, for example, the great German sociologist Max
Weber arguing that the one was 'the crucial agent' in the endorsement of the
other.

Medievalism was somewhat polarized in social nature. A human's context
was, for instance, the huge canvas of a universal church and culture, and
the minute shelter of a tiny localized association, such as the manor. The
onset of nation-statehood witnessed a weakening of both those ties. On
the one hand, the feudalized fragments were drawn into a unitary state, and
the bond of medieval association (the manor, the guild, the monastery) gave
way to a clearer, firmer obedience and loyalty to the nation, strengthened,
undoubtedly, by the growth of national consciousness, literature and re-
ligiosity. On the other hand, the shackles were cut with the wider concord,
especially as represented by the Church, the latinity of culture, and the
medieval codes of conduct, for knighthood, for instance. It was as if, to put

it at its crudest, a chunk of Christendom was carved out to form the English, then the British, nation-state.

It is obvious enough, but very important to remark, that each of these ingredients of modernity was at once the cause and the result of its fellow-components. The swirling, cyclic accumulation of this interaction was, in political and economic terms, the commercially based nation-state. Despite the inevitable controversy about such arcane deliberations, many would agree that the 1530s marked the apogee of the English nation-state. Henry VIII was the buoyant and ambitious absolute monarch, as the Church of England was at the point of its creation. And, as its elegant recorder G. R. Elton has described (in particular in his *Reform and Renewal: Thomas Cromwell and the Common Weal*, published in 1973), a central bureaucracy was plainly established. It was then that one might witness the emergence of just such a dynamic entity.

A most meaningful feature of this displacement of the more static medieval format was the passage back of social policy from private hands to the public realm. In contradictory fashion, this also meant that the communal banding of men and women and families gave way to a more individualistic formula. Freed from the cabinned social confines of medievalism, encouraged by new forms of thinking, economics, religion and culture, they could soar more confidently as individuals. But the nation-state, which was the progenitor of this exciting environment, also built in its limitations. One was an individual but with a loyalty now pledged initially not, say, to a manor or a monastery, but to a nation. Public policy, initiated at a national level, certainly replaced the more private endeavours of localized and domestic groupings. Dimly, one can foresee the coming of the citizen: the individual, dependent upon but responsible to the dictate of the state.

Common factors of social provision

For all the migrant waves in the earlier and the feudal quarrels and hostilities in the later part of the medieval period in England, the lot of common humanity was relatively static. In practice and by teaching, there was a certain stability about that way of life, with its immediate allegiance to a lord or a group. Of its very nature, a more dominantly monied economy was rather more dynamic in character, with older conventions much more at a discount.

The money-economy and social dislocation

Nothing changes the core of social problems more radically than the sort of structural revision which the country underwent as the nation-state reached maturity. Predictably, there was fall-out, presenting an overt social difficulty. Newer economic methods, especially relating to more commercialized farming, caused dislocation. People found themselves turned away from the land and from the land-based groupings which had previously sheltered them. At the root of any social questions facing the Tudor monarchs and their successors, right up to the coming of industrialism, was what might generally be termed the 'vagrant' issue.

It needs little underlining that it was the fear of dislocation, rather than concern for its victims, which prompted governmental anxieties. The Tudors, having engineered something akin to a national settlement, were not pleased to note these underminings of social stability. There was a tendency to blame the enclosure of lands, particularly for the extension of large sheep farms, although, in truth, the government, then as now, was apt to mistake symptom for cause. The agrarian and commercial changes of these times brought a general crumbling of the old fabric. 'Horn and thorn shall make England forlorn', ran the doggerel: it was believed that, as sheep-farming grew, the supply of corn would drop, taxation would decrease and the shire levies for military purposes would disintegrate to the detriment of the nation's defences. Apart from the worrying fact that sheep required less labour than arable farming, there were queries about the martial virility of that calling: 'we do reken that shepherds', wrote one gloomy critic, 'be but yll archers'. Even today we still hear that young people are too 'soft' or ill-disciplined for the nation's good, and the call to 'bring back national service' rings out.

Government was in something of a quandary. It noted with pleasure the affluence of a rising class of merchants and traders and the growth of urban life. This was a counter weight to the old aristocracy, a source of reasonable funding via taxation, and a steady ally in most of the internal administration of the kingdom. But, with some justification, they observed, with much less pleasure, that the resultant destitution was a threat to peace, and of a type and on a scale not really experienced previously.

Centralization

Over the two or three hundred years of the early modern state, the governmental response was often vain and ineffective, sometimes attempting to control the economic forces themselves, sometimes trying to deal head on with the social casualties they created. What is apparent, however, and what is of true import for any study of social welfare, is the consolidation of a national system for handling these problems. It was founded in the central authority of the Privy Council, which, in effect, had transformed itself from an advisory forum for medieval kings to an executive agency for the state. Henry VIII's Chancellor, Thomas Cromwell, might be credited for much of this change in the 1530s, and it was reinforced by later leading statesmen, such as Lord Burghley during the reign of Elizabeth I.

Of course, the central authorities could not manage the nation alone, especially as transport and other forms of communication remained unsatisfactory. Heavy reliance was thus placed on the cadres of local gentry, normally operating as justices of the peace, and active on a shire and parish basis. So the story of local government unfolded a little further. Like so much in such stories, it was in part a genuine change, and in part as true a continuity. Medieval monarchs had sought, with the help both of chief officers nationally and of subordinates locally, to weld something of an autonomous kingdom. Now those national agents, central and local, had come into their own, as the administrative skeleton for the new body politic. In nutshell summary, one might risk the twin metaphor that the political entity had changed from a a pyramid, with the king at the apex of a layered hierarchy, to a wheel, with the monarch at its hub.

Another important aspect of this same tale is the evolution of parliament over this same longish period. In brief, parliament, postulated as a medieval legal court, gradually became a political body, something between the monarch's advisory and endorsing assembly and a forum roughly representative of upper and middle class opinion. Slowly, and critically over this three hundred year period, the balance of power between absolute monarchy and parliament altered. The landmarks are well-known. The reduction in regal power during the events in the seventeenth century surrounding the English Civil War and the Glorious Revolution, the growth during the eighteenth century of the office of premiership, crucially in the hands of Sir Robert Walpole, and the corresponding and rudimentary beginnings of party politics – these are illustrations of this. It is interesting to observe, however, that parliament, in another of those tricks of historical continuity, retains to this day the adversarial nature, prosecution and defence, of the standard English court.

Suffice it here to say that sovereignty shifted firmly towards parliament, leaving the position of the monarchy less powerful. The major factor in this significant switch was that, from a situation of fair harmony in Tudor times, the parliament, and the classes it represented, began to need the monarchy less – national security was increasingly certain and the passage of goods and funds, for instance, not as troubled – at a time when the monarchy began to need the parliament more: demands for money via taxation were at the root, along with religious and other aspects, of many of the breakdowns in harmony. Obviously, this is the grossest of simplifications: each turn of the historical wheel was complicated and diverse in character. But the essence of the shift – with parliament left in supreme control – is what seriously matters from the standpoint of social welfare.

Moreover, this radical move in the discharge of sovereign authority is strictly secondary to the more primary business of the ambit for that sovereignty. This remained the nation-state. The shift of authority within the unitary state changed little in terms of the individual's place in society and how he or she might be treated.

Local government

Perhaps of more immediate impact in this respect was the relation of local and central government. Over the years, the organization of social provision has veered, this way and that, along an administrative gamut ranging from the highly centralized to the highly decentralized. Sometimes there was hefty delegation. The Tudors insisted on a central diktat for many matters, but perforce had to leave much detail to local decision-making. In the time of the early Stuarts, Privy Council authoritarianism fell into decay, partly as parliament – in one regard the conglomerate of all those local interests – was in frustrated contest with absolute monarchy. When Oliver Cromwell's Major Generals instituted strong regional rule, based on a division of the counties, in the 1650s, central power, not least apropos social ills, was refurbished. During the eighteenth century there was considerable decay in this respect. The parishes were left largely to their own devices. There were now, incidentally, 15,000 of them, all offering their own brand of widely varying solutions in an exhibition of what has been termed 'parochial *laissez-faire*'. Again, this incessant localism reflected the fact that parliament was an assembly of locally based, property-owning gentry, not over-keen to have their domestic waters muddied.

British political operations, from this time on, became enmeshed in a bipartite or complementary mode. But it was rarely settled for long. Central and local government have since existed in uneasy compromise, with first one and then the other seeming to be most prominent. It is important to latch on to this truth, chiefly because it is extant today and has ever had a marked effect on the organization of social provision. The battles of the 1980s over local government were not by any means novel.

This bipartism raises the question of the place of the individual, for, as we have seen, one of the side-effects of modernism was the release of the individual from the safe, if claustrophobic, membership of medieval congregates. In Aristotle's equation of state and individual – the *polis*, or Greek city-state, and the citizen – there was no place for local government, largely because the city-state was envisaged on so small a scale. How, then, did the parish stand? Was it the partner with the state in interfering in the individual's life? Was it the protector of the individual from state intervention? In a technical sense, there is no argument: the former brooks no denial. The omnicompetent state has, since early modern times, exerted its sovereign will if only to delegate tasks to local agencies or, perhaps, to let things slide and do nothing. The constitutional position is very clear: the state disposes. At bottom, the local authority exists as an expression of national sovereignty, once vested in the king-in-parliament, now, in real terms, in parliament.

Decentralization and individualism have always been confused, and so, as local authorities continue to quarrel with national government, the confusion is sustained. In practice, of course, the technical position has not stopped local government, over the ages, from acting as the protagonist for the individual, using this as its rationale for challenging the over-mighty state. The Introduction promised that this constant see-sawing of local and central government would form one of the common denominators of the narrative of social provision. It was in the creation of the modern state that this dichotomy originated, and it is right to acknowledge that it is not an ultra-modern phenomenon.

It is now time to see what this new panoply of administrative mechanics did for the provision of social welfare between about 1530 and 1830.

Approach to poverty

There is no doubt that poverty was the chief concern of the early modern authorities, especially in its mobile guise, when jobless, landless vagrants were tramping through the countryside. Centralized policy dates from the Statute of 1601, the famous '43rd of Elizabeth I'. It drew together some previous enactments, and rooted the system of relief in the parishes, really the only available unit for such an operation. Each parish was obliged to administer relief through the office of overseer, a term first used in 1572, who was appointed by the magistrates. Overseers, under the guidance of the justices of the peace, could levy rates on poverty to provide for the destitute. In fact, it is believed that 1547 marked England's first direct taxation for welfare purposes, when the City of London, faced with a substantial problem of poverty and sickness, levied such a rate, which, like most taxes, was 'a little grutched and repined'.

The old poor law

Slowly, the poor law came to influence the lives of everybody. It was the only social service, covering many facets of everyday life, from unemployment and migration of labour to infirmity and orphans. It was tantamount to being the local government of the time. A key element was the laws of settlement, which demanded that, on a person becoming chargeable as a pauper, he should be deported to the parish of his origin and catered for there. Immediately one may spot the political aspect of that legislation. It envisaged a stable society, wherein each person had a settled place, and there was a determination to deter that kind of wandering which might constitute a social menace. It involved an approximate fairness, along the lines of present-day arrangements whereby local authorities pay for their inhabitants to accept services in another area, but that anxious concern to keep the realm peaceful was paramount. The 1662 Act of Settlement and Removal eventually became the fulcrum of this policy.

Over these early modern centuries there was considerable mobility of labour, as work altered in type and incidence, driven by the growing commercial forces. Problems arose when the economy was flat and changed in such a way as to throw labourers and tradesmen out of work, and then the inexhaustible arguments broke out over their place of 'settlement'. Something of medievalism remained in this insistence that everyone should be tied eventually to a static group, but, in the post-medieval context, each labourer was an 'individual', with, apart from possible family props, no collectivity – manor, for instance – to come to his aid. Because the parish, with its ecclesiastical dimension, was the unit of control, the Church often retained some interest and, of course, there was still some charitable giving. But the part of charity in religious life weakened with the advent of the Protestant creeds, with their emphasis on 'individual' self-help and salvation; and the whole business was rather more secularized. Local clergymen often played the role of justice of the peace, themselves being part of the local gentry.

Administration and facilities varied wildly, and, if anything, the inconsistencies increased as time wore on. It is worth noting in this connection that, of the 15,000 parishes, 13,000 had populations of less than 800 people in the eighteenth century. By this time there were parish vestries which were elected, and there were others which were closed oligarchies of vicar and church wardens or of farmers and publicans. Some had paid overseers and assistant overseers; some relied on voluntary help. Some had reasonable accounting procedures; some had disgraceful records in this respect, with only the self-interest of the rate-payers as a monitor. Later on in the period, some Select Vestries, as they were called, offered a viable service in some of the larger towns, where the authorities were grappling with very onerous problems. Liverpool and Manchester are examples of this.

Pleasingly enough, the Tudor nursery rhyme, 'Hark, hark, the dogs do bark', recalls how, when 'the beggars have come to town', they are subject to a mixed reception of whippings, brown bread and so on. This degree of inconsistency, with its compound of savagery and humanity, remained the hallmark of the system, incorporating, like so many welfare schemes, a basic suspicion that the victim is either a fool, who should do better, or a knave, who should know better. On the theoretical side, however, it does raise an issue that was to be of much importance in relation to the local implementation of central laws. One of the classic defences of sturdy local government has been its capacity for home-grown solutions suitable to locally understood needs. There were parish vestries which claimed that their particular style of management was relevant to the unique circumstances of their area.

Systems of relief

There were, among this profusion of parishes, some which tried to meet the issue of underemployment, the major factor in poverty, directly. During the eighteenth century, some parishes put the paupers to work on the roads or in the local quarries; some tried the Labour Rate, whereby rate-payers agreed to employ a number of labourers; some used the Roundsman System, with the parish funding local farmers and businessmen to employ paupers at fixed rates. They were probably the exception, however. This attempt to battle positively with the cause of poverty by creating jobs was not widely practised. What was more often to be found was some mix of the two basic modes of treatment, mentioned in the Introduction as the domestic/institutional compromise.

There had been 'tenantries' for the aged poor as early as Tudor times, alongside 'houses of industry' and 'workshops', and even the occasional 'poorhouse'. These gave shelter and sometimes work to paupers and other distressed persons, although they were not available on a vast scale. It is, however, wrong to think of workhouses as a peculiarly Victorian phenomenon. By the latter half of the eighteenth century, there were eight workhouses in East Anglia, while London boasted no fewer than a hundred poorhouses, hospitals and other agencies, some of them run by charitable means. The Liverpool workhouse was especially large for that age, offering shelter to over a thousand paupers. Some workhouses organized schools, while some – at Bolton and Wigan, for example – actually ran at a profit. With forbidding gauntness, there were also 'prentice houses, where pauperized and destitute youngsters were recruited as cheap labour. In 1782 Gilbert's Act foreshadowed the great nineteenth-century reform of the poor law with its encouragement to parishes to gather together and form 'unions' for the upkeep of a workhouse: there were just 67 of these union workhouses by the end of the century.

Crucially, and whatever else they mustered, the parishes gave outdoor relief, that is grants of money or goods to paupers who continued living in their own homes. This has, of course, remained the main method for the relief of poverty across the developed world. Then, since and now, there were politicians, administrators and economists eagerly prepared to demonstrate that these payments were too high and that they constituted a threat to the even tenor of the economy. The story of welfare is consistently visited by this public dilemma: the impoverished menacing the stability of the polity versus remuneration for the impoverished menacing the stability of the economy.

The most celebrated, but by no means the sole, form of outdoor relief was organized by the Berkshire magistrates in 1795, and became known as the Speenhamland system. Wages were subvened from the poor rates in accordance with the size of a man's family and the price of bread. Apart from its general application, there are two minor points of interest. One is that, in the use of family size as a reference point, one glimpses the dim origins of family allowances or child benefits; the other is an equally opaque hint of price indexing in the use of the cost of bread as a measure.

Given the early effects of industrialism, which, by this time, were causing much disruption, some commentators, such as the historian Mark Blaug, have seen in the Speenhamland system a life-saver, without which 'human society would have been annihilated'. With the cost of living rising rapidly, with the small-time craftsman and the rural labourer alike caught up in the pincers of industrial and agricultural change, there was certainly a pressing need for social welfare schemes. Men were finding that their trade was redundant, and that their small-holding had been encompassed by larger agricultural units. On the other hand, the Speenhamland system came in for considerable criticism. It was synthetic and, as such, it impeded the free play of the labour market. Unscrupulous farmers would pay less than subsistence wages and unscrupulous farmhands would avoid work, both knowing that the parish would make up the difference with an allowance from the poor rate. Once again that dilemma is epitomized: that difficulty of finding the correct balance between genuine work and genuine hardship. And, once again, one catches echoes of such debates in today's talk of the poverty trap and work-shy idlers.

Approach to ill-health

The other three aspects of social provision may be dealt with more summarily, in that, where public authority intervened, it was normally through the justices and the parish, the functions of which have already been analysed. As well as overseers of the poor, for instance, there might be found (sometimes in the guise of the same person) surveyors of highways at parochial level. During the eighteenth century some 300 townships and parishes set up, through Improvement Acts, Improvement Commissions which, among other things, might be involved with cleaning and policing. This was about as far as public health went, and, like much public health, the reasoning behind it was often economic, fortified by the need to keep the streets clear as well as peaceful. By the same token, there was frequently great concern expressed about infections among military personnel, for it was obviously risky to have an enfeebled army.

English writers as diverse as Sir Thomas More and Daniel Defoe dilated on the necessity of hygiene and a concern with the social environs, and there were attempts – through the Bills of Mortality in London, for instance, by which weekly house-to-house logs of the dead were maintained, or through ordinary parish registration – to keep abreast of the facts and figures of death and disease. It is suggested by some commentators that the commercialization of the economy, and the growth of town life, stifled the homoeopathic remedies of medieval times, and, in any event, the close-packed confines of the towns made them worse breeding-grounds for disease than the less crowded agricultural communities.

The medical profession

By and large, people relied on their families and neighbours for assistance in ill-health, although, because sickness was a major cause of unemployment, some of the burden fell automatically on the poor law authorities. Sickness, like hunger, was still regarded as a common attribute of ordinary life, and one to be borne with fortitude. On the other hand, the Renaissance and the Reformation combined to release intellectual energies to consider such matters as medicine. Andrew Vesalius of Padua, the great anatomist, led the way in an observational, as opposed to theoretical, approach, and this revolutionized medical knowledge. The most famous English exponent of the new method was William Harvey, who in the seventeenth century demonstrated, by experiment, the circulation of the blood. Many other British scholars and practitioners were to contribute to a Europe-wide quest for a more scientific base for medicine.

The impact of this upon people's health was slow, but the wider acceptance of the doctor as an adviser in health matters certainly grew. This was part and parcel of a general pattern of increased specialism, as town life, commerce and the rise of a middle class supported the development of certain professions. In 1540 Henry VIII had granted a charter to Thomas Vicary, first master of the Barber-Surgeons company, the forerunner of the Royal College of Surgeons; in 1518, under its first president, Thomas Linacre, the College of Physicians had been formed. These attempted to control the practice of medicine, but it was not until the eighteenth century that medical teaching itself was at all organized. From 1726 in Edinburgh, chiefly under the aegis of the anatomist Alexander Monro, and from 1747 in Glasgow, where William Cullen was the main protagonist, medical schools began to develop. These were similar to the existing continental models, and they started to replace the traditional apprenticeship method which had long existed.

Space precludes a detailed listing of the many discoveries and the many doctors who contributed over this time to the extension of medical knowledge.

What, from the viewpoint of social provision, is important must be the growing habit of purchasing medical advice and treatment. Needless to say, it was by no means new; but any large-scale professionalism certainly was. Thus what one begins to observe is the coming of a third option, neither the domestic and neighbourly treatment of disease, nor intercession by the public authority. The prevalence of the commercially oriented doctor is a prime example of what might be termed 'privatized' services.

They assuredly had much to contend with, often by way of epidemics. The sweating sickness in the Tudor era, the recurrence of bubonic plague in a major fashion in the seventeenth century, the disfiguring smallpox of the eighteenth century, the problems in the army and navy of gunshot wounds and of scurvy: there was more than enough for a paid profession to handle. With prejudice and dogma rife, it cannot be said that remedies were always more comforting than the diseases, and, whatever the case, the mass of the people still had to fend for themselves.

The risk of fire

Nor, as a final comment, was disease the only hazard to the social environment. Another dread cause of alarm and injury was fire. Although schoolbook lore homes in on the Great Fire of London in 1666 (just as it emphasizes the Plague in London the previous year, as if forgetful of the many other epidemics that rampaged), the fact is that buildings and whole towns were susceptible to fire, given the proximity of very inflammable buildings. St Paul's Cathedral was burned five times before 1666. Usually it was down to the parish or municipal authorities to rally the citizenry to extinguish these raging infernos – the 1666 Fire was marked by a numbed apathy on the part of Londoners. However, the point is worth pursuing that, with increased commercialism, privatized fire services developed, founded on the insurance companies of London and one or two other large towns. The Phoenix company is often quoted as the most colourful illustration of this tendency.

Approach to ignorance

In a formal sense, the Church continued to play a large part in education, although some widening of syllabus occurred, in consequence of the intellectual awakening associated with the Renaissance, the Reformation and the Scientific Revolution. As we have already seen with medicine, there were moves to establish more institutional training for the professions. Furthermore, and in that highly important borderland of public and private provision, there was an advance in what might again be called 'privatized' services, as more well-to-do people were more likely to pay fees for their children's education.

Shakespeare and his talented confrères apart, the proudest triumph of the northern Renaissance was possibly the flowering of the grammar school, which provided a seat of learning – for boys – throughout England in the sixteenth century. It has been claimed, perhaps a little extravagantly, that no boy lived more than twelve miles from such a splendid agency, but, truth to tell, there was such a school for every 6,000 of the population. Their role was to provide for the commercial and administrative demands of the Tudor state, and it is no accident that the seminal educational treatise of the day, written by Thomas Elyot in 1531, was succinctly entitled *The Governor*. The schools were dedicated to that social discipline which rested on religious and political conformity, with obligatory elements to this end included in a veritable national curriculum, and with teachers having to swear the School-master's Oath, vowing allegiance to Queen Elizabeth and acknowledging her supremacy in religious affairs. Education was regarded as a weapon in 'winning the west for Protestantism'.

Some schools prospered and became patronized by the rich and lordly. They adopted a boarding dimension and several became 'public' (that is, 'endowed' rather than 'private') schools. Wryly, some of these had been intended for the lower orders – Charterhouse, Christ's Hospital – or local boys – Rugby, Harrow. They became the 'great schools' of England, whereas most of the vibrant grammar schools fell into decay during the next two centuries. They were outmoded by changing urban conditions, so that, by the early nineteenth century, there were barely a hundred left, with but 3,000 pupils. The once powerful Leicester Grammar School had sunk, for instance, from 300 scholars to one boarder and three day boys. This was in line with the general decline of eighteenth-century administration.

For the generality of English boyhood over this period, the most favourable educational outcome would have been an apprenticeship, that mix of vocational and pastoral care which was widely practised during this period – 'the Englishman's school', as the celebrated historian G. M. Trevelyan rather finely called it. The system was controlled by central edict, operated by the local magistrates, the salient act being the 1563 Statute of Artificers. As with other legislation, it is unlikely that it was adhered to at all times, but, historically, what is significant is the state's belief that it should behave 'functionally' to rule over so many facets of everyday life. And educationally, the aim, if not always the result, was the production of young people who would conform to the religious and political mores of the day and be able to offer some decent skill to the economy.

Approach to crime

Although any semblance of the medieval motif of group responsibility had vanished by early modern times, the 'know everyone' system continued to operate pragmatically in a country where communities were still small in numbers. As late as 1750 only two British cities had as many as 50,000 inhabitants. The justices of the peace were the hub of the legal system, as they were of almost everything else, and thus, in a real sense, local government and the local judiciary were one and the same. The deputization for the office of constable, as more and more tradesmen and others had no wish to perform the task, had been so rife that, soon, the paid office of constable was the reality. As we have noted, some townships had Improvement Commissions, whose duties included policing, and many places established a day police and a night watch, of varying reliability. The tug between expenditure and efficiency was already apparent in local affairs. There were some voluntary protection societies of a 'vigilante' type, while the landed gentry usually employed gamekeepers and other agents to protect their property. Troops and local yeomanry might be called out on occasions of mob violence.

The 'barbarous licentiousness' of London made mockery of such an antediluvian system and there were men – Henry Fielding, the novelist, or Patrick Colquhoun, who envisaged a centralized police service – who strove to improve matters. But there was much suspicion of state policing, on libertarian grounds, in the eighteenth century, and little was done. None the less, there were, by the 1820s, some 450 day police, under Home Office command, as well as 4,500 night watchmen in the capital. The legendary Bow Street Runners, no strangers, incidentally, to shady trafficking, were part of this set-up. They tended to operate almost as bounty hunters and, after the establishment of the Metropolitan Police, they continued to work for rich clients. They serve as a further example of the 'privatization' of services, a forerunner, in fact, of the private security and detective firms of the modern era.

As for the treatment of crime, capital and corporal punishment, disfigurement, usually in an attempt to identify the culprit (and branding for army deserters was not abolished in Britain until 1879), and forms of exclusion were common. Elizabethan beggars, for instance, might be mutilated, while penal colonies were much used in the Americas and, after the American Revolution, Australia. The notorious 'hulks', with convicts held on ships anchored just off shore *à la Great Expectations*, were an element in that process. Actual imprisonment was much rarer. Jails were originally where prisoners awaiting trial were held, and Henry II had insisted that every county should have one. Gradually, imprisonment replaced many of the other modes as the leading punishment. Convicted criminals were jailed in houses of correction, the forerunners of today's prisons. London's Bridewell was built in 1553. These places became sinks of filth and depravity, and prison reformers, such as John Howard and Elizabeth Fry, were painstaking in their detailed and compassionate criticism of them. Nevertheless, they mark a substantive shift in the annals of crime control, for, as with poorhouses, hospitals and schools, one detects a growing belief in favour of using some institution or other as the centrepiece of policy.

Comparative features

The economic and cultural movements which transformed life and thinking were Europe-wide. The Italian city-state, for instance, had been something of a model for the administration of the new nation-states, while Machiavelli's *The Prince* was hailed as the superb primer of how the clever and successful rulers should conduct themselves. The discoveries, self-evidently, concerned much of Western Europe, and in the field of knowledge Britain had often to learn from elsewhere on the continent – medicine is an example of where Britain lagged behind its fellow-nations.

Nation-statehood

These incidental matters fade into insignificance compared with the overarching creation of a network of nation-states. Arnold Toynbee, the historian of civilization, wrote prophetically of 'a divine right, which is still wreaking havoc in the western world, in the grim shape of a pagan worship of sovereign national states'. The factors we have noted in Britain (that term is deployed with deliberate looseness) were busily at work elsewhere. These included: a money economy; absolute monarchy, accompanied by forceful central administration, including a standing army; an alliance with a rising mercantile class, sometimes represented through a parliamentary forum; usually, a more 'national' stance on a religious settlement; and a cultural and literary upsurge of national consciousness.

This occurred over a long period. England, France and Spain, for instance, might be defined as nation-states from the sixteenth or seventeenth centuries, whereas Germany and Italy were not formally unified until the 1870s. That unification process recalls a very important element. The creation of a nation-state was a two-way development: on the one side, there was a carving out of a political entity from the comprehensive sweep of medieval Europe, with its uniformity of religion and culture; on the other side, there was the gathering together of the 'particularist' segments and regions in and around that entity. This dual process may be illustrated by language. England, for instance, ceased to use Latin quite so much as in medieval times, while, conversely, the south midlands dialect gradually triumphed over the other argots to become the standard English of Chaucer and Shakespeare.

Particularism

Whatever the part played by patriotic sentiment, the *Realpolitik* of nation-statehood lay firmly in the expansion of one component in the amity, one strong region which dominated the rest: Prussia in Germany, Piedmont-Sardinia in Italy, Castille-Aragon in Spain, and so forth. Unification was, in effect, more like internal imperialism. This has had tremendous ramifications. It means that the mesh of European nation-states is constantly and uneasily vulnerable to shifting frontiers and rearrangements, especially at the fringes. The events in Eastern Europe, particularly in what was Yugoslavia, following the end of USSR hegemony, have been but the latest in a centuries-old political game of desperate character. The United Kingdom, the consequence of the over-lordship of England, in real terms the south-east of England, has its similar difficulties. Its 'particularist' regions, notably Scotland, Wales and Ireland, were drawn into English control during the period in question, and from that point they have perceived themselves as 'minorities', seeking, with differing results, degrees of independence. Social provision, as well as other political and social features, was to be an aspect of this.

However, it is what Toynbee called 'the pagan deification of territorial blocs' which constitutes the main lesson. Social provision, in the United Kingdom and elsewhere, was henceforth to be at the behest of the nation-state. Even the most fervent free marketeer would, over the next three or four hundred years, envision the nation-state as the base and resource for the liberal interplay of economics. Few argued against the overt presence of defence or the judiciary as the prerequisites of nationhood, and most saw in the nation the foundation for rivalship, in trade, and, oftentimes, in war, with other such nations. That was to be the common ground, and when and if across Europe, and by extension the European colonies, there were decisions to be made about poverty, crime, education or health, they would automatically be the decrees of the nation-state.

Special features

The place of women was not too much changed by the otherwise tumultuous switch from medieval feudalism to modern nationhood and the cash nexus. The paternalism of political and professional life, its masculine dominance reinforced alike by the new Protestant as well as the traditional Catholic faiths, was not sympathetic to any change in favour of feminist potential. This was to be the major phase, for example, of the witch-hunt, a fiendish campaign directed, in the main, against women. Of course, where economic uplift brought rising living standards, women flourished alongside men, and in the pre-industrial period there some examples of women who distinguished themselves in the rigorous world of business. Even this tendency tended to be extinguished as industrial production did come on stream. The restrictive practice of the defensive-minded professions, which were slowly grabbing control of large tracts of vocational life, was anti-woman. In the world of medicine, for example, the village woman with the old-style remedies was less prominent – and might even be branded a witch – while medical practitioners were inevitably men. The male doctor/female nurse split dates from this era, if not hitherto. The woman who was successful in this early modern world had to be strong-minded, well-to-do, well-connected and lucky.

Conclusion

The ambit of the nation-state cum money-economy remains critical. In Britain, and almost throughout the world, this dualism of politico-economic organization has taken complete hold. It is extremely important to grasp the essentials of its origins and early history, within which one may observe the first burgeonings of today's social welfare thinking and administration. From the role of a sovereign parliament to family allowances, from taxation for welfare to the stirrings of institutional solutions, the three hundred years of Britain's modern, but pre-industrial, history construct the platform upon which was built urban and industrial life, and, ultimately, the conventional welfare state. The next chapter traces the coming of industry, in association with expanding town life and the new, often bewildering, form which social ills in consequence adopted.

Advice on further reading

Four books are recommended as dealing fully and directly with this period:

Clay, C. G. A. (1984) *Economic Expansion and Social Change 1500–1700*, Cambridge University Press, Cambridge.
Coleman, D. C. (1977) *The Economy of England 1450–1750*, Oxford University Press, Oxford.
Hill, C. (1967) *Reformation to Industrial Revolution*, Penguin, Harmondsworth (3rd edn 1992).
Porter, R. (1982) *English Society in the Eighteenth Century*, Penguin, Harmondsworth.

For the theories and methods of social welfare, two books should be used for both this chapter and the remaining chapters:

Brown, M. and Payne, S. (1969/1990) *Introduction to Social Administration in Britain*, Unwin Hyman, London.
Byrne, T. and Padfield, C. F. (1992) *Social Services*, Heinemann, London.

4

Industrialism's impact and the initial response

Summary

The Industrial Revolution created the social frame of reference for modern society. This was characterised by the interplay of three main factors: a massive population explosion; the huge development of factory-oriented manufacturing systems; and the rapid growth of urban settlement. In terms of social casualty, the upshot was more of a 'mass' and less of an individualized problem. Major unemployment, urban epidemic, large-scale illiteracy, heavy crime rates – these became the standard features.

Faced with this new slant on old problems, the so-called 'tutelary state' developed (about 1830–70) with 'preventative' solutions, designed to drive men and women towards improved life-styles. The new poor law, public health reforms, educational subsidies and inspection, the new police forces – these became the standard answers. And the whole apparatus continued to demonstrate a sometimes uneasy partnership of central oversight and local action. Common administrative traits were much in evidence, among them the widespread use of large institutions, such as prisons or schools, of locally elected boards, of qualified professionals, and of centrally organized oversight and inspection.

This chapter introduces several novel and specialized terms and ideas. These include: congregation – mercantilism (bullionism) – *laissez-faire* – individualism – utilitarianism (Benthamism) – the tutelary state – administrative momentum – felicific calculus – less eligibility – workhouses – the sanitary idea – the preventive principle – the miasmatic (pythogenic) theory – the germ theory – the monitorial system.

Social and economic background

If, as the hymn has it, 'a thousand ages in thy sight are like an evening gone', then something of the same is true of this chapter and the remaining ones apropos the previous two. A broad-scale sweep across medieval and early modern Britain, covering well over a thousand years, was but the prelude to a much more intense engagement with the past two hundred years. But the scene has been well and truly set: the nation-state in a cash-nexus.

There have been just two main adaptations within that referential frame. The first has already been touched upon, and that is the growth of constitutional democracy and the decline of absolute kingship, leaving parliament as the sole fount of legal sovereignty. Although, as is well-known, the electorate for this forum has been extended, from a small base of middle and upper class voters, to embrace virtually all members of the population above the age of 18, the fundamental effect has not been to alter that original postulate. Thus it is important always to remember that the United Kingdom is a *parliamentary* democracy, and not, for instance, a popular or an industrial or a decentralized democracy. Rousseau long ago pointed out that the British only enjoyed democracy one day in every five years, that is, at the juncture of a general election, and that between times they forfeited their political will. Certainly, the legislature remains very eighteenth-century-like in its *modus operandi*, so much so that, during the troubles of the 1980s, there were those wont to recall the old Hanoverian jibe that England was 'an oligarchy moderated by riot'. None the less, that switch of omnipotence from monarchy to parliament is of great consequence.

The second of these two major adaptations was the coming of the Industrial Revolution, normally cast as occurring between 1760 and 1830, albeit with many precursors and even more subsequent revisitations. It affected neither the role and ambit of the nation-state nor the commercial basis of that state; rather it effected an enormous change in the substance of national society through its bewilderingly vivid range of technological innovation. This, of course, has been cumulative, even exponential, in its process, so that the lives of men and women have been inexorably altered.

Obviously enough, the most startling effect of industrialism was a huge leap in productivity. Power-driven mechanisms were the key. James Watt's steam-engines were widely adopted after 1785, and by 1800 there were already some 500 in use. With coke-fired furnaces, the United Kingdom's iron production rose from 18,000 tons in 1740 to $2\frac{1}{2}$ million tons in 1850, and that amounted to half the world's production. Coal production increased from $2\frac{1}{2}$ million tons in 1700 to 16 million tons in 1830. New sources of power came on stream. In 1802 William Murdoch introduced industrial gas, and in 1850 the Scots chemist James Young established the basis for the production of petrol. Both were to have far-reaching consequences. Inventions in all fields were on the march: in the 1760s there was an average of twelve patents taken out annually; in the 1820s it was close to 250 a year. In 1741, $1\frac{1}{4}$ million pounds of cotton were spun; by as early as 1787 that figure had jumped to 22 million pounds, and soon the power looms were to accelerate even more. By 1833 no less than 100,000 power looms were in noisy action.

Many are the examples that might be quoted to demonstrate this relatively swift change in the economic landscape of Britain. The social changes were no less dramatic. There is considerable argument over the primacy of all these factors: for instance, did a rise in population lead to a demand for higher productivity, or did higher productivity enable a larger population to prosper? From the more immediate viewpoint of social welfare, one perhaps should major on the outcome, on the scene which came to present itself for those faced with social ills. Socially, there were three significant elements that created the milieux in which industrialism succeeded: the rise in population; the rise in urbanization; and the rise in large units of production. They interacted together, each nudging the others onward into a cumulative spiral, but, with that warning about their interdependence made, it is simplest and quickest to assess them separately.

Population

At the time of the Battle of Hastings in, memorably, 1066, the population of England and Wales was $1\frac{1}{2}$ million. By 1700 it had laboriously grown to $5\frac{1}{2}$ million. By 1831 it had more than doubled to 13 million. As early as 1798 the melancholy Thomas Malthus, in his *Essay on Population*, was predicting catastrophe as the population outstripped the means to feed it. In the event, it appears that the birth rate stayed fairly steady – at about 37 births to every 1,000 of the population – over this time, but that the death rate declined – it was about 30 per 1,000 population in the 1830s – and thus more people survived, especially through the hazards of infant mortality. Thus, despite its bleak toll on human life, industrialism may, on balance, have had an advantageous effect on population. For example, more brick, less wood, in housing; more cotton, less wool, in clothing; or the advent of cheap soap – 300 million pounds consumed in 1790, 650 millions in 1820 – such features may have played a part.

One should never wax too sentimentally about the idylls of a rural existence, shattered by the abrasive awfulness of factory life. There were, in both agriculture and the domestic system of manufacture, the cruelties of child-labour and the risks of starvation and sickness. Certainly, and whatever the causes, the population raced on, and in so doing provided not only a great labour-force for the Industrial Revolution, but an equally great market. The national consumption of tea, for instance, rose from two million pounds in 1750 to ten times that figure a century later.

Urbanization

The impact of this demographic change was most emphatically felt in the towns and cities. Where the nation doubled in population, its towns trebled and quadrupled. In the first half of the nineteenth century, Blackburn's population sprang 500 per cent to 65,000, and Bradford's eight-fold from 13,000 to 104,000. The main cities – London to two million; Manchester from 90,000 to 400,000; Leeds from 53,000 to 172,000 – doubled their populations, and more, in the first half of the nineteenth century. There was a migration of labour into the towns from the country, accentuated by the phenomenon of a growing population anyway. It was the start of a process by which the huge majority of British people would shortly come to be town-dwellers.

The effects on such amenities as water supply and sanitation were soon to be horrific, and, in a variety of other ways, the large town, as the locus of much English life, altered the whole stage for social welfare. Until this time it had primarily been the village and the parish within which men and women had faced social evils alone or in small groups. Henceforth, an anonymity was to characterize much of British social policy, as officials and others struggled to deal with packets of large numbers.

Factory production

Even where manufacture had existed in early modern England, the units of production had, for the most part, been tiny. In the textile trades, for example, the system of 'putting out' had been common, with merchants investing in a mesh of home-based craftsmen. The factory was not unknown, but it was rare. Power-driven production required the assemblage of men and machinery in single places, and thus the factory system grew. In mines, mills, foundries and allied agencies, men, women and children toiled as members of the newly dominant wage-earning labour force, set against the might of industrial and banking capital. It was a remarkable switch. The factory owner and the factory worker became the commonplace economic divisions.

Manchester illustrates the point well enough. In 1782 there were only two mills in that town; by the end of the century there were 52, closely to be followed by 24 iron-foundries and 37 machine workshops. By the middle of the nineteenth century the average number of workers per economic unit was 200, a par which, of course, masked the existence of some very large factories and mines. Where, in medieval and for much of early modern times, nine out of ten workers had been agriculturally based, by this same time the ratio was down to one in five – and, of course, agriculture itself was becoming 'industrialized'. Already a half of the workforce were in the industrial trades, not forgetting those involved in transport, for, first with canals and improved roads, and then with the grandiose peak of the Industrial Revolution, the railways, transportation was a key factor in this process. Incidentally, it is worth mentioning that another fifth – the same number as in agriculture – were in domestic service.

In summary, one might adopt the laconic coinage of the political scientist, Herman Finer, who succinctly utilized the word 'congregation' to describe this joint interaction of social features. More and more people crowded within the ambit of the nation-state; more and more of them crowded into the cramped confines of the towns; more and more of them were packed remorselessly into the tight and intense activity of the factory or its equivalent. 'Congregation' was, and remains, the chief feature of the industrial and

post-industrial periods apropos social policy. Where mechanization and democracy have been the main economic and political adaptations within the
bounds of the commercial nation-state, this density of social existence has
served as the determinant of welfare and allied reforms since the 1830s. In
some fashions, the social changes that accrued from industrialism and its
concomitants have been more challenging than the technological and commercial elements themselves. Certainly, much of the thinking about and
much of the practice of social welfare adopted a radically different line since
these events.

Common factors of social provision

Faced with the horrors of 'mass' social problems, there was no shortage of
proposed solutions. In view of the acceptance of only one general theme by
way of solution, it is worth recognizing how many there were to choose
from, as theorists and commentators queued to offer counsel to successive
governments. Among this multiplicity of advice were included plans to abolish the poor rate altogether, to abandon criminal investigation to bounty-
hunters, to leave sanitary services to private companies to arrange, to allow
the Church a monopoly of popular education, and so forth. As always, there
was strenuous opposition to reforms, from vested interests in such professions
as medicine and civil engineering, from hidebound or suspicious local authorities, from working-class reaction to what was experienced as cruel
treatment, and from a general feeling of conservatism about new and
meddlesome interference in people's lives.

Despite the proliferation of advice and the strength of opposition to the
successful solutions, there emerged a common set of beliefs and practices
about how social evils should be combatted, in particular during the period
from 1830 to 1870. There remains some controversy about the provenance
of the reforms of this period, but there is now no general acceptance of
the older view that this was a period of governmental *laissez-faire*, of leaving
things to find their own level without state interference. By the 1850s Britain had become, apropos government intervention, the strongest state in
Europe.

The debate has more lately swirled around the unconscious or conscious
nature of the reforms. Some suggest that the prime dogmas of *laissez-faire*,
of government keeping strictly to the sidelines of social matters, were
overrun by the enormity of the problems, and that piecemeal and fairly
anonymous devices were empirically wrought to deal hastily with problems.
These snowballed rather, creating a process labelled 'administrative momentum', which resulted, almost inadvertently, in a strong state. Others have
claimed that 'intolerability' – the sheer ghastliness of the problems – so
affected men like the social reformer Lord Shaftesbury that they moved
to act swiftly and overtly. It might be pressed that, eventually, 'blind forces'
and 'intolerability' join in the same consequence, that is, a build up of
governmental intercession; and it is the character of that intervention which
is of prior import.

Jeremy Bentham

What is surprising is the common principles which typified this reforming programme, for, although civil servants may have gone about their business silently behind closed doors, or reformers may have chased their own immediate end, the spirit of utilitarianism was abroad. This set of beliefs is mainly associated with the name of Jeremy Bentham. He began with the premise that man is wholly motivated by his pursuit of pleasure and his avoidance of pain, and that, if all men (and women, although old-time philosophers concentrated entirely on the male of the species) were left free so to pursue, the sum total of all these successful forays in the hunt for pleasure would be the greatest happiness for the greatest number.

This made a great deal of sense to the merchants, bankers and industrialists who were enjoying the profits of the Industrial Revolution. Tudor and Stuart economic theory had instituted many embargoes and tariffs as part of the prevailing mercantilist theory, which viewed economic activity as a sort of cold war with other nations, with the need to show a healthy margin of gold and silver reserves – hence the synonym of 'bullionist' theory – as a sign of victory. Once a strictly controlled trading framework might have benefited merchants, but the corruption, patronage and obscurantism of eighteenth-century politics and law had done little to help and much to hinder the active businessman. Now an individualist creed was very welcome to the bustling entrepreneur. Bentham simply asked of every institution, 'what is the use of it?', that is, does it restrict or liberate man in his search for happiness.

Without venturing too far into the philosophic niceties of Benthamism (such as its apparently incompatible combine, like Marxism, of a mechanistic explanation with a moral purpose) the hardheaded Victorian businessman found it clearly appealing. With Adam Smith and his *The Wealth of Nations*, published in 1776, very much the key text for the commercial side of utilitarianism, the notion of free trade became compelling. It reached its apotheosis with the Repeal of the Corn Laws in 1847, when state protection against corn imports, which artificially kept up the price of bread, was abandoned. There is, of course, a very simple reason why the early Victorians embraced the doctrine of free trade. It worked. At a time when Britain had scarcely a competitor on the world scene, together with a strong navy, an expanding empire, relatively stable political conditions, and sound banking and other financial agencies, businessmen were eager and willing to operate in an entirely untrammelled market.

How could such an individualist doctrine deal with the overwhelming nastiness of social evils? The French historian Halévy has succinctly analysed the bisection of Benthamism into two branches. On the one hand, there was unadulterated self-help, which he called a 'natural harmony of interests', and which is best exemplified in commercial free trade. On the other hand, there was an 'artificial harmony of interests'. This argued that there were too many obstacles in the way of people enjoying the free pursuit of pleasure, many of them vestiges of malfunctioning government practice. Thus the state had a duty to perform a positive role in keeping the ring clear of such barriers, ensuring that there were no impediments to the free play of people's activity. S. E. Finer has been especially helpful in sustaining this analysis, postulating the notion of 'the tutelary state', its task being the guidance of citizens towards the delights of self-help, and the clearance of the social and economic arena so that they might conduct themselves in that libertarian manner.

Edwin Chadwick

There is no doubt that this idea of a *tutelle* of administrative devices, aimed at producing the milieu most propitious for individual action, was most pronounced in the world of social reform. It is most closely associated with the theory's most devoted advocate, Edwin Chadwick, one-time secretary and aide to his mentor, Jeremy Bentham. Sir Edwin Chadwick has never found a notable plinth in the gallery of social reformers: like many another incorruptible zealot, he was grimly unattractive in manner and did not have to seek far for enemies. None the less, he has some claim to be observed as the chief figure in the formation of the modern state as it touches on social provision. He was involved in all the four aspects of social provision under consideration here, although his personal influence on education was not pronounced.

His analysis of all social problems was the same; his solution to each such problem was the same; and his interpretation of what amounted to a vaguely held belief across a decisive body of opinion became the classic theme of social reform at this time. He identified the greatest happiness, rather dourly, as the greatest national product. Unimpeded, people would contribute to this as abundantly as possible, driven thither by their own self-interest. But they were impeded, and especially by poverty, sickness, crime and ignorance.

The synthetic allowance system of the old poor law, by adding money to wages, dislocated the free trade of the labour market, and employer and employees could not negotiate naturally. Premature death and unnecessary illness were other impediments to natural productivity, for unsanitary conditions and feeble water supplies were unnatural causes of sickness, and the result was a savage reduction in the amount of work done. Additionally, the wheels of commerce were literally clogged up by the disgraceful state of the streets, another consequence of scandalously filthy conditions. 'Depredations', such as theft, now constituted a major loss to the gross national product, and, when the fruits of a man's labour were stolen, that again amounted to the nation being unnaturally deprived. Ignorance was a fourth obstacle, for, if children and adults did not understand where their best interests lay, if they were unable, through illiteracy, to staff the novel machinery and offices of the burgeoning economy, if they were, in short, a social menace, then they would have to be educated.

Chadwick's approach to all these joint problems might be summarized under the following headings.

The felicific calculus

Jeremy Bentham had measured the credit of pleasure against the debit of pain in an arithmetic fashion he called the felicific calculus. Chadwick adapted this to finance, to further his desire to identify happiness with productivity. In the most intense manner, he was prepared to cost and itemize the tiniest detail of social life in order to demonstrate, for example, that the poor law, as it existed, was not only inefficient but also cost £7 million annually, and that ill-health and crime cost the nation another £7 million. By hammering away at these many illustrations of cost-effectiveness, Chadwick made a strong appeal to his money-minded fellow-countrymen. He attacked 'mistaken parsimony' in these affairs, arguing that investment at the present would reap future profit. Tax- and rate-payers were sometimes disinclined to accept that the future was all that pressing, but any promptings to reduce levies or increase effectiveness were readily understood.

The preventive principle

Chadwick was, in every instance of social casualty, anxious to 'prevent' its encumbrance, so that people might be freed or, rather, forced to be free. As will be seen, there is a world of difference between prevention and treatment. Stopping people from becoming paupers, patients, criminals or illiterates was the name of Chadwick's game, not reacting once it had happened. He placed a great emphasis on the precept of 'less eligibility', especially in respect of poverty and crime. Harsh rules about poor relief, critically the basic unpleasantness of the workhouse, and intense policing, coupled with swift and certain punishment, would, he believed, make being either a pauper or a felon 'less eligible' than being employed or well-behaved. It is obvious that Chadwick disagreed with reformers like John Howard who wished to make prisons more agreeable. Similarly, water supply, flushing the filthy sewage from the gruesome slums of the towns, and subsidized schooling would 'prevent' much ill-health and ignorance. In concept, Chadwick's preventative doctrines had much to commend them, whatever the difficulties they encountered in practice. They did not hold main sway for long. They were soon overtaken by an accent on reactive as opposed to proactive policies, and there, by and large, the balance has remained.

The tutelle

There remained the mechanisms which would implement the hypothesis of the tutelary state. In typically Benthamic manner, there was an impatience with any reverence for the outdated and outmoded institutions of yore. Not the least of Chadwick's influence has lain in his organizational inventiveness, as he strove to find new ways of dealing with new questions. These, at Chadwick's behest, were three in number.

First, he insisted on locally elected committees, usually supervising a specific subject in its natural ambit of control. A good example of that might be his wish to see a board of health administering an area of natural drainage.

Benthamites believed that it was advantageous to identify the interests of governed and governors as closely as possible for the maximum good.

Second, Chadwick was a forceful adherent to the value of professionalism. At all times, he fought to replace what he saw as bungling amateurism with vigorous and dedicated officials, preferably holders of a 'prescribed qualification'.

Third, he invariably constructed a central body to overlook each national service, to advise, to hold residual powers of control and, crucially, to employ an itinerant group of inspectors. That was a device borrowed from that other part-Benthamic success, factory legislation, for which, from the 1830s, the role of factory inspectors had become critical. That constant theme – the relative powers of central and of local authorities – was to be redefined and re-evaluated in this process.

That is not to say that all these mechanisms were wholly successful: several broke down under the burden of the problem and the oversimplicity of the solution. However, they were to be found, in some shape or form, in all early attempts to resolve troubles in the four areas under review. In these fashions Chadwick and his colleagues sought to revolutionize the approach to and the organization of Britain's social agencies. Right down to the lowest levels of municipal and parochial authority, ears were cocked to the siren call of cheaper and more effective services.

He was assisted by one major factor. The pressure – the 'intolerability' – of the situation adversely affected the middle classes, the very people who held the reins of power, to a large degree nationally and almost entirely locally. As well as grudgingly bearing the onus of both central and local taxation, it was their businesses which were threatened by robbery and mob violence, by absenteeism because of sickness, by poorly instructed workers and by the synthetic cosseting of the labour mart. Their families also ran the gauntlet. Apart from burglary and other such evils, there was the hazard of disease: once it had taken a hold, cholera failed to discriminate between servant and master.

There was thus a predisposition to listen and attend to what sounded like a commonsensical analysis, vigorously pressed, and one which was in kilter with the prevailing economic thought of the hour. As with factory legislation, aimed at protecting women and children from unduly long hours and insufferable conditions, there were others in the campaigns. Humanitarianism and philanthropy, fostered by the established and the non-conformist Churches, was a main influence. Nevertheless, it was the utilitarian methodology, usually as prescribed by Chadwick, which had the most potent contribution to make, especially administratively. How these principles were screened through into reforms in each of the four defined fields of social welfare will be the topic of the next sections.

Approach to poverty

In 1832 there were 1.5 million paupers in England and Wales, a tenth of the population. The 15,000 parishes ran a wasteful and confused system at a cost of ten shillings (50p) a head of population, much of it given in doles to the unemployed. It must be added that, on the one hand, prices had of late been rising faster than wages, and that factory work left many fewer people able to grow their own supplementary produce. On the other hand, the often flourishing economy meant that the gross national income was around £400 million annually, out of which £7 million – a mere 2 per cent – for the one and only social service seems a fleabite. None the less, the perception was of workers artificially tempted not to seek employment.

The new poor law

It was strongly argued by the likes of Edwin Chadwick that this constituted a double-bind: there were losses of production because of the paupers' indolence; there were losses in poor rates to sustain them in that idleness. This was an encroachment on the free play of the market, and the Workhouse Test was constructed to 'prevent' this anathema. It was determined that life in the workhouse would be less comfortable – 'less eligible' – than life on the lowest wage rung, with the purpose of driving paupers into useful employ. Alongside this, it was decided to cut wasteful outdoor relief – whereby paupers were given money and occasionally bread or coals for their own use at home – as much as possible. In this we see a definite theoretical shift from the domestic to the institutional, and from the cash to the kind, solution. Including a number of workhouses of varying quality already in existence, there were, by 1847, 707 workhouses, with 200,000 places in all. The number of such baleful institutions continued to grow: the first models for the new workhouses were designed by Sampson Kempthorne, while the architect G. G. Scott is said to have been responsible for over 750 such plans.

It was the Poor Law Amendment Act of 1834 which set this massive reform in train, and it has been variously branded as 'genuine radical legislation' and 'social fascism'. It represented all three branches of the *tutelle*. There was a central board – the Poor Law Commission until 1847, then the Poor Law Board – with Edwin Chadwick as the first permanent Secretary. This oversaw the efforts of an inspectorate of assistant commissioners – 'Chadwick's young crusaders' – and generally attempted to urge the acceptance of austere programmes. The initial task of the assistant commissioners was to incorporate the parishes into unions, which were encouraged to build a large union workhouse, with the suggested segregation of paupers into seven categories, the first major attempt to divide social casualties by cause, such as infirmity.

The unions were, in turn, controlled by boards of guardians, elected by the rate-payers, in true Benthamic style. By 1838, and against a backdrop of often militant opposition, approaching 14,000 of the parishes had been incorporated into nearly 600 unions, and these were encouraged to appoint professional staff to ensure that the system was rigidly run. By 1846 there were over 8,000 such officers at work, by far the largest and the most important group composed of relieving officers, upon whom fell the day-to-day burden of operating the new poor law. The unions were also given responsibility for the seminal statistical function created by the 1836 Act for the Registration of Births, Deaths and Marriages. This was to become the foundation for the more accurate implementation of social policy from that day to this.

The outcome of poor law reform

There were flaws to dent the neatness of the theory. Parish influences remained, especially in the matter of collecting the rates; the central role was never as forceful as Chadwick had envisaged; and the officials were often the old overseers and workhouse masters under new management. The workhouses, in particular, were viewed with sullen suspicion, especially when, for example, the Andover Workhouse Scandal of 1845–6 exposed the bestial treatment of paupers. However, the main problem faced by the poor law authorities was a basic misunderstanding about the cause of poverty. In spite of a free labour market, there were, both in agricultural work and, increasingly, in the industrial trades, periodic bouts of chronic under-employment, often a consequence of downturns in foreign commercial activity. The workhouses could not be built that might embrace the massive outbreaks of temporary distress of that kind, which had nothing to do with the predisposition of workers to prefer idleness. Moreover, the poor law authorities had insufficiently taken into account those other forms of social casualty – invalids, orphans, lunatics – for whom work could not be found.

The upshot was that outdoor relief was never abandoned. Both institutional and domestic solutions were thus continued. In 1846, out of 1.3 million paupers, only 199,000 were 'in' (that is, 'in' the workhouse) paupers, of whom only 82,000 were the able-bodied adults at whom the law was so stringently aimed. Of the 1.1 million 'out' paupers, 292,000 were able-bodied adults. By 1854, 12 per cent of the population were registered paupers, compared with 10 per cent in 1832. The figure was close on two million, but only a quarter were accommodated in workhouses. And that process was never turned back. The acid test, however, was financial, and here there was some cause for cheer. By 1854 sometimes harsh efficiencies had led to a reduction of the poor law bill from the £7 million of 1832 to £5.3 million, despite a rise in population and a proportionate rise in pauperdom. The per capita rate charge had dropped from ten to six shillings (50p to 30p).

In a sense, the new poor law tried to 'prevent' the wrong ill. As so frequently occurs with poverty, it was the symptoms, not the roots, which were treated, and one is left with the familiar feeling of those in authority, nationally and locally, being anxious chiefly to order 'the abatement or removal of the public nuisance of destitution'.

Approach to ill-health

A flood of government reports betokened the atrocious health conditions of the age, among them the Report of the Select Committee on the Health of Towns (1840), the Report on the Sanitary Condition of the Labouring

Population (1842) and the two Reports of the Commission for Inquiring into the State of Large Towns and Populous Districts (1844/5). In the second 'Large Towns' report, Lyon Playfair calculated, after the macabre manner of Chadwick, that in 1841, 14,000 deaths and some 400,000 illnesses were 'preventable' in Lancashire alone, and that the financial cost of this was £5 million. William Farr, 'the father of vital statistics', had calculated that 'the minimum value' of the population was £159 a head, and with a quarter of the deaths and three-quarters of the cases of sickness 'preventable' across the nation, the drain on resources was exhausting.

The beginnings of public health

Cholera, typhus and, despite vigorous vaccination campaigns, smallpox were the most lethal epidemic diseases; a quarter of the deaths were due to pulmonary complaints; there were all manner of diarrhoeic afflictions, added to which were a whole series of industrial illnesses, to say nothing of the ravages of malnutrition and fatigue. In urban areas a quarter of children died before they reached the age of one; as for the mortality rate, against Farr's suggested norm of 17 in a thousand deaths, the real figure was closer to 40. Among other horrors, the parish graveyards could not cope with the corpses – Bunhill Fields, a four acre London cemetery, was crammed with 100,000 bodies.

Chadwick and his ilk espoused the miasmatic or pythogenic theory of disease, and this held sway until Pasteur and Koch developed the germ theory later in the century. It was 'the poisonous exhalations' which emanated from the filth and ordure – a 'dung mountain' of 25,000 tons was not uncommon in the cities – that caused death and disease. The 'congregation' of too many people in cramped environs led to an horrific assemblage of sewage and waste matter, and a corresponding pressure on frail supplies of water. The 'sanitary idea' urged that water supply and drainage were the keys. This led to what *Punch* magazine called Chadwick's 'perpetual bath-night'. The engineering principle was that of 'arterial-venous' drainage, based on the hydraulic pressure of water. This would drive high-velocity water into the towns and their habitations, and sweep out the refuse and ordure through the new small-bore, egg-shaped earthenware pipes, carrying, in Chadwick's almost romantic but unrealized version, 'rich town guano' to fertilize the country fields.

Much early work was accomplished by municipal initiative: Liverpool appointed Doctor W. O. Duncan as the first permanent Medical Officer of Health and the 1846 Liverpool Sanitary Act was to prove a milestone in respect of sanitation. But there was opposition, as ever, from the vested interests of local authorities (London, for instance, had 300 bodies operating 250 local acts), from the 'contagionist' medical profession, who believed in bodily contact as the cause of disease and advocated quarantine, and from the private companies who plied their inadequate trades in, for example, scavenging, providing water and building flat, large, stagnant sewers. Somewhat inspired by the public health pioneer, Johann Peter Frank, with his endeavour to awaken the German 'hygienic conscience' with his medical 'police' regime, Chadwick and others sought to impose an administrative diktat.

The 1848 Public Health Act

This closely shadowed the poor law concept. The 1848 Public Health Act created a General Board of Health, with, inevitably, Chadwick as its first paid commissioner, its task being to encourage the largely permissive establishment of local Boards of Health, either specially elected or coterminous with a borough council. A local inquiry would, in miniature, calculate how investment in water and drainage would 'secure health with commercial prosperity', and full-time officials were expected to be appointed. By 1855 there were only about thirty medical officers of health, and, indeed, only 182 boards had been formed, with but 13 water and sewerage schemes completed. After 1858, the duties of the General Board of Health were distributed among several government departments. On the brighter side, one must mention the tact and skill of Sir John Simon, who became London's first medical officer of health in 1847 and, through his appointment to the General Board, effectively national medical officer of health in 1855.

Although the 1848 Act was, in practice, feeble, its passage has been hailed as the most significant moment in world public health history, simply because it originated the notion of public intervention. The death rate still remained ominously well over 20 per thousand into the 1860s and, of course, the problem did not stand still. Every extra person added to the population of a town meant a demand, at least, for eight or ten gallons of water a day, and the wherewithal to despatch over two pounds of sewage. The material fabric required by the so-called 'clean party' – municipal cemeteries, reservoirs, sewers, water pipes, taps, wash basins and water closets – was enormous and it was expensive. Manchester's Longdendale water scheme, started in 1847, cost £650,000, but it provided 30 million gallons of water a day, where the private water company it replaced had managed only two million.

There were moves on the medical front. The tales of Florence Nightingale in and after the Crimean War (1854–6) and the growing respectability of the nursing profession are well known, while the 1858 Medical Act, which established the General Council for Medical Education and Registration, demonstrated the growing legitimacy of doctoring. Both reflected the expanding 'health consciousness' of the English middle classes. The crucial issue, however, remains the emphasis on prevention, and this was an environmental rather than a medical model, its motive the removal of what were believed, for whatever explanations, to be the causations of sickness. Whatever the difficulties of civil engineering or the inertia of vested interests, this 'preventative' credo in public health circles was very powerful. For all that the theories in vogue were misleading, the accent on private and civic hygiene was commendable and correct, much more so, say, than the 'preventative' precept in use for poverty. Because the answers entailed vast domestic and public undertakings, they also represented perhaps the most dramatic interference into the everyday life of its citizens that the state had thus far envisaged.

Approach to ignorance

That the tutelary state should act educatively seems wholly appropriate. Ignorance was as much a liability as poverty or ill-health, a barrier to the unrestrained interplay of people's activities. James Mill, father of John Stuart Mill and an uncompromising Benthamite specialist in education, urged 'utility' as the measure of schooling, pressing John Locke's seventeenth-century view that 'practice must settle the habit of doing'. Psychologically, it was believed that the child was a 'little man' or 'little woman', with a mind open to 'facts' in the same fashion that a mug may be filled, in the popular metaphor, from a jug. The most extreme version of this theory, famously lampooned in Charles Dickens's *Hard Times*, was the Hazelwood School at Birmingham, based on the 'chrestomathic' precept (i.e. 'useful learning'), endorsing a heavily competitive regimen. If children could, then, be sufficiently filled with information, they would be the likelier to make the more advantageous choices between pain and pleasure, indolence and work, crime and honesty, and so on.

The Church involvement in schooling

It should be remembered that, by this same period, the religious evangelical movement had done much to cleanse English middle class life of its boisterous crudities. In matters of hard work, keeping healthy and avoiding felonious behaviour, the Anglican and non-conformist Churches were at one with the Chadwickian reformers. This was strikingly true of education. Middle and upper class parents were seeking a more rational schooling for their offspring, and, during the century, the reformed public schools, notably Tom Brown's Rugby under the headmastership of Thomas Arnold, doubled in numbers and improved dramatically in quality.

It was apparent that rectitude of behaviour was identified with religious and moral tuition. Although there was some talk of educating young people so that they would be able to staff a more sophisticated economy with greater efficiency, the primary accent was on maintaining stability. Dr James Kay-Shuttleworth, significantly a one-time assistant poor law commissioner and a disciple of Chadwick, became first secretary to the education committee of the Privy Council. He had few doubts as to the aim of public education. 'The preservation of internal peace', he said, 'not less than the improvement of our national institutions, depends on the education of the working class.' And the prime minister of the time, Lord John Russell, wrote that 'by combining moral teaching with general instruction the young may be saved from the temptations to crime'. There was a strong conviction in the need for what the left-wing education historian Brian Simon was to call 'economic indoctrination', with schooling used to ensure that the future workers would labour hard and long, and deferentially know their place.

Where schools had hitherto existed, they had usually been small of scale and tutorial in approach, that is, what had been learnt was heard singly or in tiny groups by the teacher. The charity school movement was perhaps the most characteristic type, with the Society for the Propagation of Christian

Knowledge, started in 1699, having oversight of as many as 1,500 subscriptive and endowed schools in the eighteenth century, with, on average, no more than 15 pupils. There were dames' schools and private or 'proprietary' schools as well, but the demographic flood of the late eighteenth century left them quite unable to cope.

It was, however, the Church which responded most speedily, retaining its age-old grasp on education. The National Society, associated with the name of Andrew Bell and the Church of England, and the British and Foreign Society, associated with the name of Joseph Lancaster and the non-conformist Churches, developed, with minor differences, the concept of the monitorial system. Sometimes called the Madras system, because of its early use by Bell in India, it was, in brief, a pyramidal scheme, whereby the teacher taught monitors and monitors taught children. As opposed to the traditional tutorial-cum-preparatory approach, this enabled one teacher to handle hundreds of children, and, in fact, it was the basis of the later class teaching system. It was the 'mass' answer to what was essentially a question of quantity.

This voluntary system, cheap and plentiful, met most needs during the first decades of the nineteenth century, especially as it was recognized that a child's labour was often required 'to relieve the pressure of severe and bitter poverty'. Efforts were made to involve the state directly in education, but they all failed, until the Reform Act of 1832 produced parliaments more conducive to change. There were now over 20,000 schools, mostly Church schools, but both the Factory Acts and the poor law reform were to have an effect, giving rise to factory and pauper schools. Furthermore, the registration of births was to offer a better guarantee of exactitude when it came to deciding on school attendance.

The beginnings of state intervention

In 1833, following rejection of the latest of a series of education bills to promote parish schools and/or committees, £20,000 was voted for half the cost of school buildings, to be divided between the two main voluntary societies. In 1839 a committee of the Privy Council was set up to superintend such annual grants and generally to oversee education. From 1856 the Department of Science and Art, supposedly a support of higher education, was added to the committee's duties, and it was, of course, the forerunner of today's Department of Education. By 1858 the grant had risen substantially to £700,000, and from 1847 societies other than the original twosome became eligible. Typically, these subsidies were examined by a group of inspectors, among whom was Thomas Arnold's son, Matthew, the celebrated poet. James Kay-Shuttleworth inaugurated the pupil-teacher programme – a five year apprenticeship – and there were also Church training colleges, so that, gradually, the notion of the properly qualified teacher evolved. It was yet another clear-cut example of the state, chiefly through carefully inspected grants, encouraging private endeavour.

Liverpool experimented with municipal schools from 1827, and Manchester tried assiduously, if vainly, to lobby for a secular, rate-covered scheme. To simplify a complex dilemma, it might be said that voluntary schools could not cope unaided with the full introduction of elementary schooling now sought, but many objected vociferously to rates and taxes being spent on Church schools. The Newcastle Commission of 1861 attempted to resolve the poser, and it provided the first-ever comprehensive review of education. Finding 2.5 million on the rolls, over three-fifths in grant-aided schools, with an average of four years' schooling, the commission concluded (not without controversy, then and since) that the system was working well enough, but needed to be more efficient.

In 1862 Robert Lowe, vice-president of the council committee, therefore introduced the rigorous device of the Revised Code, payment by results based on attendance and testing: 'if it is not cheap', he declared, 'it shall be efficient; if it is not efficient, it shall be cheap.' It prescribed, as he said, 'a little free trade' in place of 'bounties and protection' – and, against the cost of highly mechanical rote-learning and mental drudgery, it worked. Over the next few years the average attendance increased from 888,000 to over a million, and the grants fell from from just over £800,000 to about £600,000. No more lucid application of Benthamite methodology could have been devised.

Approach to crime

As with poverty, sickness and ignorance, the moral aspect of crime was secondary to its practical aspect. Edwin Chadwick, whose initial specialism was law and order, masterminded the lurid Constabulary Report of 1839. Crime was on the march: 40,000 were 'living wholly by depredation' and as many as 120,000 were in some part involved in criminal activity, giving rise to a high prison population. Transportation to the Americas had naturally ended with American Independence in 1783, but Australia and Bermuda remained, while the coastal prison hulks were then the nearest to a national prison system. Local bridewells and jails accommodated the remnants of what amounted to some 17,000 committals to prison each year.

Much has been made of troops been called to subdue working class strikes and demonstrations, like those of the 'physical force' Chartists, campaigning for radical constitutional reform. There is, however, little doubt that it was the niggling, insistent irritation of theft that caused the middle class businessman and shopkeeper most annoyance. Ninety per cent of crimes were crimes of gain. The losses, therefore, were straightforwardly monetary ones, and the 'felicific calculus' was soon in use, pointing up how investment in police would save money. Chadwick wrote that 'the first great object of a police, that to which every practical adoption should conduce, is to prevent the commission of crime'.

The new police

It was fear of 'apprehension', backed up by comfortless punishment, that would 'prevent' crime and make it 'less eligible' than earning an honest crust: hence, incidentally, the wearing of the tall hat or helmet, so that the policeman would be seen; hence the preference for the night-stick or the cutlass over the fire-arm, not because it was less bloodthirsty but because it was more effective for arrests. Crime threatened the interplay of the market, and people must be 'tutored' towards the pursuit of happiness. One police-man to each 1,769 people or 4,403 acres was Chadwick's typically precise formula, and there was a naive faith that this would actually restrict crime to negligible levels.

Again the tutelary state was to be in the van. The Metropolitan Police, established by Sir Robert Peel in 1829, had enshrined the regimental pattern of beats, sections and divisions, and certainly owed something to the ideas of the famous soldier, Sir John Moore. Initially run by an army officer, Charles Rowan, in association with an Irish barrister, Richard Mayne, its 3,000 and more men had as 'the principal object . . . the prevention of crime'. Delighted with the seeming success of this experiment, Chadwick had wanted to set up a national agency, building upon the Metropolitan force and ex-tending the overall authority of the Home Office. In this he was thwarted, but the use of the Home Office as the central control was accepted, complete with, from 1856, inspectors of constabulary to adjudicate as to efficiency and, by that token, state grants.

The existing local authorities were utilized for local development of police-work. The Municipal Corporations Act of 1835 obliged boroughs thereby incorporated to appoint a watch committee and organize a paid preventive police. The 1839 Rural Constabulary Act permitted counties to form con-stabularies under the aegis of the county magistrates, and the 1856 Act obliged them so to do, thereby completing a nationally ubiquitous system of police enforcement. The employment of paid and trained officers was, obviously, all of a piece with the requirement to enact social policy through professional officials.

The effects on crime

It proved to be a slow business. With some honourable exceptions, such as Essex and Suffolk, many areas were slow off the mark. By the 1850s there were still some thirty counties without a regular police force, which is why the leverage of the 1856 Act, with its clauses on an inspectorate, had to be introduced. By this time there were some 12,000 policemen in England and Wales, made up of 5,500 in London, 2,300 in the counties, with Lancashire at 500 the largest shire force, and 4,100 in the boroughs, with Liverpool fielding the biggest force at 900. As with the other local services, recruitment was often from existing cadres, in this case the old day and night watches, and the lowest grade of police constable was paid no more than 16 shillings a week (80p). Drunkenness and indiscipline were rife: suffice it to say than when the 239 forces (59 counties, 178 boroughs) were first inspected in 1857, no fewer than 120 were judged 'inefficient' and failed to qualify for the state grant of 25 per cent for pay and clothing.

Committals for indictable offences in the 1850s were about 28,000 a year, much the same, pro rata, as in the 1830s, and there were some 167,000 men, women and children in prison. According to the spirit and practice of that utilitarian age, inspectors of prisons were appointed in 1835. Although the cost of the police was kept close, in real terms, to the £56 annual expenditure for each officer envisaged by Chadwick, there was also the cost of prosecutions and prisons, and there was little sign of a reduction in crime, in spite of the 'blue-butchers'. As with poverty, the analysis tended to deal in symptoms, forgetting that many 'habitual depredators' might have been driven by want rather than by the perception that there were easier pickings in crime than legal toil. But, as with health, the idea that one should stop it happening rather than respond when it did happen was an attractive one. Unluckily, perhaps, it was not to be a doctrine which long reigned at the courts of social policy.

Comparative features

The European states had primarily remained absolute monarchies, albeit with rising merchant classes vying for power or scope to trade without undue stress. Roman-like in their combine of private property rights with public authority duties, moderated by a monarch, these states continued to be paternalist about social welfare. Their task was to wage war internally against ill-health, disorder and so forth, for the same reason they waged war externally; that is, to protect the safety and increase the riches of the realm.

Social policy in Europe

They were not greatly successful, lacking, as they did, the administrative clout to carry out, for instance, the wholesale 'medical police' reforms proposed by Johann Frank in 1779. It was much more piecemeal. Most had forms of poor relief: Sweden was quick off the mark with the collection of statistics from 1748 onwards; many German states introduced compulsory vaccination shortly after Edward Jenner's discoveries in 1796; Denmark offered free treatment for venereal disease from 1790; both Denmark and Sweden were considering state hospitals as early as the 1830s; and, in 1840, the French *préfets*, controllers of the *départements* through which the French state operated, received their first circulars about state hospitals. The first signs of a recognition that health hazards knew no frontiers was in 1851, when the first of an annual series of International Sanitary Congresses was held. There were attempts, notably in Prussia, to wield authority over education for palpable reasons of state. Many of these somewhat sporadic ideas were spread to the colonies of those absolutist powers, and, through German influence, to Japan.

Britain was in a different position. Its middle classes had begun their assault on the bastions of power earlier and their victories had occurred more smoothly. Consider the condition of France, something of a victim of what has been called its 'amphibious geography'. Wracked by internal revolution and dislocation and eventually defeated, at the battle of Waterloo in 1815, after lengthy, bitter hostilities, it was in no shape to compete with Britain. Stability at home and victory abroad had been, conversely, the prerequisites for Britain's continuing commercial advancement. At the same time, the long Revolutionary and Napoleonic Wars had separated Britain from European influences at this critical time, and a peculiarly British approach to social welfare had emerged. The twin phenomena of parliamentary government and industrialism left Britain variously ahead of its competitors, in terms both of problems thrown up and answers proposed.

The crucial difference, but not the only one, lay in the independence of local decision-making. The clearest example lies in police-work, where the English (less the Irish and Scots) remained profoundly suspicious of national control, and there evolved a system of locally controlled civil police forces, vastly different from the centralized and paramilitary police – the *gens d'armerie* – of the continental brand. It was local authorities who, on the whole, were also presented with the job of resolving the huge question of public health, and here the priority given to the environmental rather than the medical solution must be re-emphasized.

Social policy in the United States

The situation in the United States tends to provide a rule-proving exception. The influence of English colonization was high. The American poor law derived directly from the Elizabethan system, and, when nineteenth-century concepts of free labour battered, as in Britain, the age-old idea that a pauper must be associated with a particular 'settlement', 'less-eligibility' measures were also introduced. Local schooling was also the norm. The USA was assailed with smallpox and yellow fever epidemics, and, as in Britain, there were local health boards – Baltimore in 1798, Charleston in 1815, Philadelphia in 1818 – and there were epochal public health reports – in 1850 the Massachusetts Sanitary Commission Report, associated with Lemuel Shattock, and in 1865 Stephen Smith's New York City Report. The first State Health Board was formed for Massachusetts in 1869.

Localized police-work continued to be the not always satisfactory method of law enforcement until the twentieth century, while American prison reform became something of a reverse influence. The Ghent House of Correction in France (1775) is said to have been the first to introduce the segregation of categories of prisoner, and the Papal Hospice of St Michael, Rome, for errant boys (1703), the first to experiment with solitary confinement – as opposed to the crowded hurly-burly of most prison life at this time. The Americans, in part influenced by Jeremy Bentham's 'panopticon' model prison, variously introduced 'hard labour', 'solitary', 'silent' and 'separate' (that is, with cell-based work) systems, as well as mixes of these methods. The first American territorial state penitentiary was based on Philadelphia's Walnut Street Jail in 1794. The Americans also helped to pioneer more reformative methods – the 'marks' system, for instance, whereby prisoners might gain credits towards early release for good behaviour and hard work. Such methods had been tried out on Norfolk Island, Australia, by Captain Alexander Maconochie in the 1840s and by the Director of Irish Prisons in the 1850s, Sir Walter Crofton. These ideas were later to bear fruit back in Britain and on the continent.

The paradox remains that Britain, the nation that had found such delight in civil and commercial liberties, contrived in the mid-nineteenth century to be the strongest state in Europe and North America; that is, as far as social policy goes. Its peculiarly Chadwickian characteristics of local determination, linked with central invigilation, produced a tutelary state which, in total, managed to interfere quite substantially in the everyday life of its citizens. Moreover, it differed from its neighbours and rivals in its attachment to the 'preventive' ideal, for its European counterparts were far less wedded, for instance, to the sanitary idea or the idea of negative policing, rather preferring the medical or the punitive policing notions.

Special features

Two features might be mentioned, more for what they envision for future consideration than for their then present impact.

The Irish emigration

The first is the Irish emigrations of the 1840s, consequent on the tragic Irish famine of those years. Although the huge majority of emigrants travelled to the United States, many British mainland towns, especially in the north-west, found themselves with an expatriate Irish community. Because of the social and religious differences between them and most of their new-found hosts, because of the threat they sometimes seemed to bring to employment, to good order, to the economics of poor relief and to health (typhus soon became known as 'Irish' fever), one is able to observe the kind of antagonistic responses which would be engendered by waves of overseas migrants into Great Britain in the twentieth century. Although there had been several discrete migrations into Britain and although, technically, Ireland was a region of the nation-state, this was the first large-scale importation into mainland Britain of what was deemed a 'foreign' people since the Norman Conquest.

The treatment of mental illness

The second marker is the one to be placed against disability, especially mental illness, for, just as a rapid population increase threw up 'mass' problems throughout social life, the nation was faced with correspondingly large numbers of disabled and handicapped people. The poor law, the only social service extant, was used as little more than a dumping ground for many such unfortunates. The aged infirm, the blind and the lame were often pushed into the workhouses, fuelling the already extensive misuse of those agencies, with their basic intent being to accommodate the able-bodied as a test of their desire to work. Indeed, one London workhouse in 1861 had only one in ten of its inmates who was able-bodied. In the same year it was reported that many paupers had been in the workhouses for more than five years, almost all of them either aged long-term sick or mentally ill people. Lambeth workhouse had as many patients as Guy's Hospital in the 1860s, at which time the 39 London workhouses housed 22,700 officially sick, infirm or insane inmates, out of a total of 31,000.

Despite the efforts of the Lunacy Commissioners and the 1828 Lunacy Act, which scheduled the process of 'certifying' lunatics, the county authorities refused to build asylums, and so-called insane people found themselves left to the devices of the workhouse. Although there was some attempt at categorization and although one or two places had distinguished records (Colney Hatch asylum for London, for example), there was little treatment and no distinction between, for instance, the feeble-minded and the mad person. In 1870, 11,000 'in-paupers' were classified in England and Wales as being 'idiots' or 'lunatics', with a further 6,000 on out-relief. The negative characterization, the shutting away, of mentally ill or handicapped people in particular, and of disabled people in general, was largely shaped by these insensitive devices.

Conclusion

The baleful shade of Sir Edwin Chadwick watches over the results of early Victorian reform, whereby the administrators of the day grappled with the novel 'mass' slant of old problems. They were confident and abrupt in manner, rarely suffering gladly the fools of diffident questioning, riding roughshod over the arguments of enemies. For the future, it was probably the construction of forms of administration, in particular the peculiarly English device of central/local balance, and of forms of institution and delivery of services which were to be most influential. The next chapter traces the gradual, seventy year build-up towards the welfare state of the 1940s, when those same salient features – the sharing of central and municipal responsibility and the deployment of insulated institutions, but not, alas, the welcome element of prevention – grew in significance.

Advice on further reading

As we enter the modern period, and the studies become more specialized and distinct, the reading follows suit. First of all, there are two valuable books covering this formative time. These are:

Bédarich, F. (1991) *Social History of England 1851–1990*, Routledge, London (also useful for succeeding chapters).
Hobsbawm, E. J. (1968) *Industry and Empire*, Penguin, Harmondsworth (3rd edn 1990).

Two other books offer the essential detail of welfare and allied policy matters:

Finer, S. E. (1952) *The Life and Times of Sir Edwin Chadwick*, Methuen, London.
Roberts, D. (1960) *The Victorian Origins of the Welfare State*, Yale University Press, New Haven, CT.

For more specialized attention, students might consult:

Armytage, W. A. G. (1965) *Four Hundred Years of English Education*, Cambridge University Press, Cambridge.
Deane, P. (1965) *The First Industrial Revolution*, two volumes, Cambridge University Press, Cambridge (10th reprint 1992).
Hart, J. M. (1951) *The British Police*, George Allen and Unwin, London.
Howard, D. L. (1960) *The English Prisons*, Methuen, London.
Lambert, R. J. (1964) *Sir John Simon*, MacGibbon & Kee, London.
Steintrager, J. (1977) *Bentham*, George Allen and Unwin, London.
Webb, S. and Webb, B. (1929) *English Local Government*, Cass, London (reprinted 1963). Especially volumes 4, 6 and 8 of this large series.

5

Piecemeal collectivism: Precursors of the welfare state

Summary

Britain sustained its place in the international economy and maintained a vast empire, and there were material improvements in the life of most citizens. None the less, in the period from about 1870 to the outbreak of the Second World War in 1939, the struggle continued to keep social need and social welfare in some form of equilibrium. The state intervened more forcefully and was much more proactive: the emphasis became much less 'preventative' and much more 'curative'; in municipal housing, for example. Such changes were driven by pragmatic, rather than by ideological, forces, and were correspondingly piecemeal, but there was a bunching of activity in the 1870s during the high days of Gladstonian Liberalism, and again in the years before the First World War, associated with Lloyd George and the last Liberal government. Next, the methods used often had common elements, notably the furtherance of the large-scale institution – the school, the hospital and so forth. The period was also marked by the completion of the bipartite arrangement of central and local government in some form of partnership. Certainly, by the beginning of the 1939–45 War, there was a substantial tranche of public social provision in place. This included: old age pension and illness insurance; fairly positive public health and housing legislation; a developed system of policing and prisons; and a full-run network of elementary schooling.

> There are a number of terms from this chapter that can be found in the glossary: collectivism – Marxism – Fabianism – idealism – Christian socialism – Tory philanthropy – factory formula – functional/acquisitive society – curative principle – imperial preference – prescribed qualification – contributory principle.

Social and economic background

The momentum of industrialism continued. Britain remained a heavily industrialized and urbanized nation-state, governed by a form of parliamentary democracy. In a basic sense, the social and economic background was bespoke, and was not to alter again. Of course, the internal characteristics were subject to substantial change. Where steam had been the originating power source of the Industrial Revolution, other kinds of energy – gas, oil, electricity – were to grow in importance, and technical advance was often bold and imaginative. Britain built and ruled over a larger empire than any other nation, and because of this and as a counter to the rising competition of rivals, moved away from the classic free trade principles of the mid-nineteenth century to something closer to imperial preference, that is, tariffs used to protect the home and empire market.

The economy 1870–1940

The period from the last faltering steps of the 'tutelary' state to the outbreak of the Second World War – from about 1870 to 1939 – is a lengthy one and, because it touches dearly on the memories and folk-memories of those alive today, it appears to teem with detail. Certainly there were deeply significant events. There was the challenge to Britain's industrial leadership, as other nations developed an industrial potential, and this meant that, for instance, there were downturns in the trading cycle at some point in each of the last three decades of the nineteenth century. The 1914–18 War was a calamitous conflict, the horrors of which require no further rehearsal, while the slump of the late 1920s and the 1930s, following a bright, brief post-war boom, is another example of Britain finding itself economically distressed in a world context.

Throughout the period, however, and having made due allowance for such disastrous events, there were the compensations of, in general, a rise in the real value of wages and some overall improvement in living standards. Population continued to increase, but not perhaps so dramatically: it was 32 million in 1871, having doubled since 1801, and it was 46 million in 1939. In other words, that second phase of seventy years added a third, rather than as many again. Urbanization remained, needless to say, a major key. In 1801 only a third of the population lived in towns; by the end of the century that fraction had reached four-fifths, and it was destined to rise still further. In the short phase from 1871 to 1901 the number of towns of more than 50,000 inhabitants jumped from 37 to 75. The word 'conurbation' was coined in 1915 by the town planner Patrick Geddes. By the end of the century Greater London housed a fifth of the population of England and Wales.

As the population at large and the towns in particular grew, so did productivity soar in even more geometric progression. Throughout this period the staple products remained much the same – textiles, coal, steel and shipbuilding – although they were all to receive a battering during the 1930s depression. For example, and to take a middle point just before the start of the First World War, Britain then manufactured almost two-thirds of the world's ships, its maritime marine sailed a third of the ships afloat and carried a half of the world's sea-borne trade. Yet, in 1932, all but two of Tyneside's 72 shipbuilding berths were empty, as a fifth of world shipping lay idle. Similarly, Lancashire had only half the spinning and weaving capacity, with a corresponding reduction in the workforce, in 1939 as in 1920.

However, despite such inroads, the socio-economic landscape was much the same: it was reduced in busyness, rather than transformed. The railways, for example, remained the principal means of passenger and freight transport, although, as time drew on, motorized road vehicles – their manufacture as well as their deployment – played a larger part. Public transport reached high levels – and the success of municipal action in this field probably helped to cushion the introduction of further local provision of a more social brand. It lowered suspicions of such public interference. By 1913 there were, annually, some 700 million train and some 1,500 million bus and tram journeys in Greater London alone.

Society 1870–1940

From the viewpoint of social welfare, the significant factor is that the national social pattern was not much altered over these late nineteenth century and early twentieth century years. The political system and the economic methods were virtually unchanged. Most strikingly, the social divisions, bearing their differing monetary rewards, were constant. It might be estimated that, in 1870, approximately 80 per cent of the population were working class, and earning something between £10 and £73 a year, leaving an upper and middle class echelon of some 20 per cent, some of them earning a little under £100, but most of them over that figure, with 2 per cent earning over £1,000 a year. The 1930s saw little shift in that position in terms both of proportions and differentials, although, naturally, the actual sums were a little higher, with the average manual worker's wage about £150 a year. Just before the First World War about 1 per cent of the population took a third of the available income; just before the Second World War 1.5 per cent of the population enjoyed a quarter of the aggregate national income.

It follows from what has been said about industrialism that the British working classes were the most heavily proletarian in the world. As the century turned, almost half the labour force were in the staple mining and manufacturing industries, with a further fifth in trade and transport jobs. Fourteen per cent were in domestic and personal service, and that figure continued to drop over the succeeding years, while as few as 9 per cent remained in agriculture (plus forestry and fishing), once, of course, the leading occupation by far. At the outbreak of the Second World War, agricultural and similar workers numbered about 5 per cent – at a time when no less than 11 per cent of the German labour force was thus employed.

In broad terms, therefore, the canvas apropos social provision was relatively constant over this long and politically volatile era, with a commonly recognizable distinction between an industrial working class outnumbering a much smaller middle class in the ratio of something over 7 to 3.

Common factors of social provision

The period roughly marked out by 1870 and 1940 is one of creeping collectivism. Early endeavours to hold up the tide of social suffering had barely
kept pace with the accelerating surge, the consequence of increasing
population and other elements. Indicators, such as infant and general mortality figures, demonstrated that truth starkly enough. What the pre-1870
phase of negative or 'tutelary' state interference provided was, first, a chance
to experiment with some administrative models and, second, a lubrication
of the public's willingness to accept hefty doses of state action, all of which
had to be paid for from heightened taxes and rates.

Collectivism defined and examined

Collectivism might be defined as a belief in the communal protection of
individuals from social ills, in an attempt to create opportunities for them
to lead productive and constructive lives. Several theoretical and, indeed,
pragmatic strands were enmeshed in this concept. It was but a step, a bold
one, but no more than a step, from the position of civic Benthamism, with
its stress on legislating for an 'artificial' harmony of self-interests, to a mild
collectivism. John Stuart Mill, son of a Benthamite purist and the classic
liberal thinker of Victorian England, agonized over the shifting borderline
between that which primarily concerned the individual and that for which
the community must take responsibility. He advocated liberty in all that
concerned the individual, qualified by discipline in all that concerned the
community, a rule of thumb useful for collectivist action, despite –
sometimes because of – the blurred boundary between the two.

There were other influences. There was the modernization of electoral
procedures and the expansion of the suffrage: the Reform Acts of 1867, 1884,
1918 and 1928 gradually extended the vote to all men and women over 21.
There was the growth of respectable trades unionism, with the Trade Union
Act of 1875 the first of several pieces of legislation which, in spite of con-
flicting setbacks, helped to establish the credibility of the labour movement.
There was a corresponding rise, through limited liability and other devices,
of large corporations in the world of capital, rather than the small-scale self-
made businesses of yesteryear; and these were subject to parliamentary scrutiny
and oversight – capitalists were becoming accustomed to a major role for the
state.

There was the contribution of 'Tory philanthropy', associated, for instance,
with Lord Shaftesbury, 'the complete beau-ideal of aristocracy', with its
humanitarian form of *noblesse oblige*: this was shrewdly exploited by Disraeli,
and has remained a significant aspect of Conservative politics ever since.
There was, in alliance with this approach, a greater sense of social commitment
in the established Church, with the 'muscular' Christian socialism of men
like Thomas Hughes, author of the semi-autobiographical *Tom Brown's
Schooldays*, having some sway. There was, alternatively, the vigour of non-
conformity, especially of Wesleyan Methodism, with its particular contribution
to the 'Lib–Lab' axis of British politics towards the end of the last years of

the nineteenth and the early years of the twentieth centuries. There was, from Charles Dickens and Elizabeth Gaskell to George Bernard Shaw and H. G. Wells, an outpouring of powerful literature, part polemical, part analytical, which seized the public mind.

There was the Oxford school of philosophy, with T. H. Green, in the wake of the German philosopher, Hegel, enunciating the exalted 'ideal' of the individual 'free', in the positive sense of dependence on the community's securing for him the necessary conditions for the good life. There was the more orthodox collection of telling facts and figures by the likes of Charles Booth, the Liverpool businessman who was especially influential in the closing decades of the nineteenth century. There was the Anglo-Saxon variant on continental social democracy in the form of the Fabian Society, preaching, through protagonists such as Sydney and Beatrice Webb, the notion of 'socialism by instalments' and 'the inevitability of gradualness'.

All these influences were busily propagating the plant of collectivism. They certainly assisted in ensuring that the ground was prepared and the soil conducive to its growth. At one level it added up to a return to – in the concepts of R. H. Tawney, the leading socialist thinker of the English scene – the more 'functional' society of Tudor and Stuart times, after the 'acquisitive' interregnum of the *laissez-faire* state of the late eighteenth and early nineteenth centuries. It is proper to keep this see-saw notion in mind, for it is facile to believe that state intervention, in purpose, if not always in effect, is a recently initiated and then ever-expanding condition. The phenomenon of state interference is best seen, historically, as a thing of swings and roundabouts.

It is equally certain that the contributory influences, for all their apparent diversity, were all responses to the stark fact of the social fall-out from the industrial experience. Charles Booth, for instance, on the basis of his careful investigations, was able to relate poverty to the economic environment, rather than to personal turpitude, and to press the case for 'limited socialism' (as he perhaps riskily termed it) as a defence against more desperate social perils. It was, then, the sheer volume of pathetic suffering and simmering unrest which continued to alarm the late Victorian and early twentieth century head, where its heart may not have been so simply touched.

'We are all socialists now' went up the ironic cry, as the old century faded on a nexus of state or municipal controls; but it was ever a misleading conclusion. Collectivism, especially as advocated by the newly born Labour Party, became synonymous with socialism, and may indeed have been inspired by the more pyrotechnic versions on the continent. However, Karl Marx, and other socialist thinkers of the nineteenth century, actually regarded the state as the prior evil, and were as wishful for its demise as the most ardent protagonist of *laissez-faire*. This anti-state view, this revolutionary hope that the 'administration of things' would replace 'the government of persons', was far removed from the stealthy collectivism of this period, which revered the state as saviour. The true Marxist scorned collectivist amelioration as a sop to the working classes and an inoculation against rebellion – and it is worth adding at this point that, whatever sort of societies were produced by Russia and its Eastern European satellites after 1917 and 1945, the last descriptor that should have been applied to them was 'communist'. It is the collectivist or, as it later became called, especially in the continental political context, the social democratic, tradition which espouses the emphatic use of the state.

The state apparatus

Much as the state might wish to propose and dispose, the crucial element was the administrative equipment for such widespread social engineering. It was a gap filled by the kind of organizational mechanics beloved of Edwin Chadwick and his colleagues. This was the critical piece in the jigsaw. However much previous authorities, as far back as Henry VIII and even Henry II, might have huffed and puffed about powerful government, it was not until late in the nineteenth century that the apparatus existed to guarantee its implementation.

Parliamentary sovereignty remained the key, and this was a parliament which went about its business a good deal more tidily, with the thrust of largely two-party government, and with usually well-disciplined parties at that, enduring from 1868 to the present day. The dichotomy, pioneered by the Chadwickian fraternity, of the central government department inspecting and advising mainly autonomous local agencies also persisted. From lunacy to burial, there was a whole string of national commissions and locally elected boards, with the inspector a ubiquitous figure.

The inspector exemplified a further ramification of bureaucratic reform, in that great play was made of the official, preferably with the 'prescribed qualification'. This period watched benignly over the specialized endorsement of the relevant professions: school teachers, sanitary engineers and all the other purported experts were subject to training and essential qualification. Nowhere was this more telling than in the civil service. Starting with the well-known historian Thomas Macauley's introduction of examination for entry to the India Office in 1853, and boosted by the civil service reforms of the 1870s, this was to have an enormous effect on the integrity and competence of this now vastly expanding body of public officials. Incidentally, the competitive 'rivalship', implicit in examination, was widely lauded by the admirers of free trade and the opponents of patronage, in education as well as in the civic professions.

Local government was also undergoing something of a transformation. The 1835 Municipal Incorporation Act, which provided for the management of boroughs, was updated in 1882, while the seminal 1888 County Councils Act created the long-lived system of properly organized shire government, with larger cities and towns designated as county boroughs, and having much the same raft of responsibilities. In 1894 the parish councils were given something of a face-lift, while the urban and rural district councils were inaugurated to act as the subsidiaries of the county councils. By these means, the whole of England and Wales was covered systematically by a consistent pattern of local authorities, while Scotland developed a similar network on its own account, with elected county councils from 1889 and its system of shire, town and district councils refurbished in 1929.

Since the 1850s, the various local authorities had successfully widened their scope, and municipal trading became all the rage, in such diverse areas as markets, transport, libraries, gas, electricity and recreation. The acclimatization of the public to the idea of the strong municipality was very effective. As the reforms took shape, the local authorities adopted many of the tasks of the specialist 'boards', be they for education, burial, health, education or, eventually, poor relief. Thus evolved the concept of the multi-disciplinary local authority, the generalist, all-purpose model of local control. It had its virtues – the collection of one rate, the opportunity to interlace activities for the common good. It had its vices – the specialist 'board' offered a singular focus on an important subject, and allowed enthusiasts chance for fervent effort. By the 1930s, it is safe to say that the entire gamut of local public services, including all those directly concerned with social provision, were in the hands of the same authorities across the nation, with, in the case of each service, a regular connection with an appropriate central government department.

Finally, on this topic, one must not underestimate the silent and humdrum support afforded both central and local government by technical means. History often tempts with the colour of vivid political rows or military rivalries, but it is often the mundane which really matters. The mechanization of offices may seem a dry item, but there would have been no administrative possibility of collectivist encroachment without such artefacts as the typewriter, the post office, the telegraph and telephone systems, and all those other bureaucratic instruments.

The character of collectivism

Although piecemeal and sporadic in origin and incidence, the collectivist trends in this 1870–1940 period did have some common characteristics. Two, in particular, should be addressed, the one in respect of approach, the other in respect of method.

In the first place, the 'preventative' principle yielded pride of place to what might be labelled the 'curative' principle – and, were the ancient proverb about prevention and cure to be accurate, it was a change for the worse. This is a twosome difficult to divorce. The introduction of curative measures naturally creates the condition which might prevent more of the same ill: for example, a grant to an already impoverished person might enable him or her to struggle through to solvency. Then again, it might not. It is true that the 'preventative' principle, especially in regard of the poor law, was implemented with severe abrasiveness, but it was just as lacking in an appreciation of the fundamental causes of poverty as its eventual replacement by way of monetary benefits. To project the medical metaphor, collectivism, no less than preventive tutelage, treated the symptom, rather than the disease.

The collectivist approach to both health and law and order epitomized this tendency. Although the narrowly 'public health' aspects of the former survived and were even, on occasion, extended, the 'medical' model superseded the 'preventative' approach in high degree. The emphasis became, in simplistic terms, on making people well after they had fallen ill, rather than on guaranteeing them immunity from disease in the first place. Similarly, and dramatically, with police-work: in short order, the 'preventative policing' of Chadwick's well-intentioned dream was replaced by the 'detective' mode, with its underlining of catching criminals once offences had occurred.

Admittedly, the state was overwhelmed by the galloping stampede of ignorance, illness and crime, and defensive positions had to be erected. None the less, it was – and is – a pity that the 'preventative' argument was not allowed further development, particularly as the investment in clean, regular water supplies and efficacious sewaging had been deemed so successful. In the event, then and thereafter, the state, nationally and locally, adopted what is sometimes adequately described as a 'fire brigade' mentality. It was more concerned with dowsing the fires of social casualty, once ablaze, than with stopping them from breaking out initially.

In the second place, this phase of piecemeal collectivism is noteworthy for its continued and expanded use of the 'institutional' answer, rather than for its reliance on more individual, perhaps cash-based, responses. It was as if the four 'Ps' of late Victorian social casualty – paupers, patients, prisoners and pupils – must be corralled away from the community and isolated in cloistered seclusion. I have elsewhere named this tendency 'the factory formula', indicating how the social reformers, observing the efficient management of the large-scale factory, cast or recast their social agencies in the same mould as this one hugely successful device. The large union workhouse and its near relative, the large lunatic asylum; the sizeable general hospital; the national prison; the big school – the inmates of these were walled in, just as all-embracingly as their fellows were subjected to the severe disciplines of the mill or the mine or the foundry. The military barracks, particularly perhaps in regard of hospitals and prisons, was another, if similar, model.

The analogies are endless. The works manager controlled the domain of the factory, divided into workshops supervised by foremen or overlookers, each workshop providing a special function or part of the product. The same format was to be found in the new social agencies: hospital matron/sister/wards, by type of illness; prison governor/warder/wings, by type of offence; workhouse master/assistant overseer/dormitory, by type of pauper 'category'; headteacher/assistant teacher/class, by age and/or aptitude. And it is too easily forgotten, as we inherit such agencies and attempt to make them work to our modern wishes, that their progenitors knew exactly what they were doing, and that theirs was often a conscious act of 'factory' replication.

This rather grim dependence on insulated, almost embattled, citadels of social provision was, in reality, the outcome of accepting the 'curative' mode, for these were essentially locations for those who, in some way, fell short of the social norms and required treatment. In contrast to the cheerful and bustling traits of Victorian commercial 'institutions' – the department store, the football ground, the seaside resort, the music hall – these were forbidding places, and their harsh demeanour still casts a doleful shadow over their present-day successors.

Perhaps the newest and the most abiding illustration of this combine of the curative and the institutional was the decision to build public housing for letting. Although poverty was an obvious determinant, it cannot be over-stressed that this initiative emanated primarily from the public health sector, and, as such, is considered under the 'health' sections of this and subsequent chapters. Because deleterious housing so undermined health, the public weal had to undertake what, over the years, became a massive building programme, embracing new towns as well as municipal estates. These have been, without a doubt, of major benefit to successive generations of people, but it remains a moot point whether they have rendered those people more or less dependent. At root, public housing arose because the economy did not reward many of its workforce with sufficient funds to purchase reasonable accommodation of a healthy and pleasing sort. Again, there is something of the treating of the symptom. That said, the move into state housing was well-nigh unprecedented, and was an impressive step in the collectivist march forward.

The collectivist advance

It was a story of collectivism by stealth and by haphazard degrees, and, although there were common features, these often were a matter of accident rather than design. Certainly there was rarely a time when some kind of blueprint was prepared and issued. This means that, whatever government was in power, from Gladstone's Liberals in the 1870s to Chamberlain's Conservatives up to 1940, there was always some likelihood of finding collectivist legislation entering the statute book. There has been a tendency in the literature on this subject to note only the more cavalier dashes of public extension, but scarcely a year was to pass without one or two extra laws of this type being passed. None the less, there are two overt and more deliberate exercises in collectivism and, given that this study advances thematically rather than chronologically, these are worth noting before that more topic-based analysis. The first of these was during the 1870s, and it was clearly associated with the reforming zeal of Gladstone's first administration, but with some follow-up activity under the aegis of his colourful competitor, the Conservative leader Benjamin Disraeli. The second was in the Edwardian years before the First World War, and the name of Lloyd George is naturally the one to catch the eye.

In each of these short periods one may find important reforms, usually in all the four areas of social provision here reviewed. By the same token, they were both times of other kinds of reform – the army reforms of Edmund Cardwell under Gladstone, for instance, or the fiscal reforms for which both administrations were famous. That overall reforming zealotry is typical, at least of modern British politics, with social change but one component of the whole. By the same token, it has to be said that the inter-war years, although never free of collectivist action, appear a little dead and dull by comparison. In spite of the swingeing horror of the 1930s depression, there was no political riposte of vital swagger.

Before looking more closely at each of the sections of public provision during this era, it might be timely for us to consider this extract from Sidney Webb's *Socialism in England*, published in 1890, with its wry acknowledgement of the imperceptible advance of collectivism. It reveals much about the psychology of so-called 'gas and water' socialism, and the bounteous pride that local worthies developed in their grandiose institutional buildings:

> The practical man, oblivious or contemptuous of any theory of the social organism or general principles of social organisation, has been forced by the necessities of the time, into an ever-deepening Collectivist channel. Socialism, of course, he still rejects and despises. The individualist town councillor will walk along the municipal pavement, lit by municipal gas, and cleansed by municipal brooms with municipal water, and, seeing by the municipal clock in the municipal market, that he is too early to meet his children coming from the municipal school, hard by the county lunatic asylum and municipal hospital, will use the national telegraph system to tell them not to walk through the municipal park, but to come by the municipal tram-way, to meet him in the municipal reading-room, by the municipal art gallery, museum and library, where he intends to consult some of the national publications in order to prepare his next speech in the municipal town hall, in favour of the nationalisation of canals and the increase of government control over the railway system. 'Socialism, sir,' he will say, 'don't waste the time of a practical man by your fantastic absurdities. Self-help, sir, individual self-help, that's what's made our city what it is.'

Approach to poverty

For the bulk of this period the symbol of the treatment of poverty remained the workhouse, although these times were also marked by a widening spread of money benefits, notably the old age pension and national insurance. Although austerity ebbed and flowed from place to place and decade to decade, the overall effect was a gradual slackening of severity. In a word, the workhouse became a refuge rather than a test-bed of idleness. There was civic pride in these dour emblems of local regard: the Preston Workhouse, for instance, was ceremonially opened in 1868 at a then huge cost of £90,000. While the pauper funeral remained the fate to be dreaded, the poor law registry office marriage became rather more 'respectable'.

The last years of the poor law

Administration was tighter. Befitting the rise of a collectivist mode in the last years of the nineteenth century, the number of assistant commissioners doubled to twenty, the entire country was 'unionized' by 1869 and the Poor Law Board won total control over the finances of the unions by 1868. The Union Chargeability Act of 1865 made the 'area of administration and expenditure the same', thereby sweeping aside the ancient obstacles of parish interference in both the collection and spending of the poor rate. This more efficient construct, with the workhouse still important, remained the chief social service until well after the First World War. For instance, in 1889 there were 820,000 paupers receiving out-relief, with 192,000 workhouse inmates, and this figure of about a million paupers was to remain constant certainly up to the start of the Second World War. Increasingly, these numbers reflected several categories of distress. Of the one million paupers registered in 1889, 260,000 were under 16 years of age, while in the 1920s the poor law authorities catered for over 100,000 lunatics, as they were still called. A portent of 1990s discussion of care in institutions or in 'the community' is revealed in the fact that, over this era, the cost of 'indoor' was three or four times the cost of 'outdoor' pauperism.

Unemployment and underemployment continued to be the root cause of poverty, rather than indolence. Thus harsh economic difficulties upset the poor law apple-cart considerably. During the time of the 1926 General Strike, the number of paupers doubled abruptly to two millions, and similar figures were recorded during the abrasive days of the 1930s depression. By this time, however, there had been a major organizational change. In common with similar tendencies elsewhere, the local authorities (more especially, their public assistance committees) took over the specialist work of the poor law under their powers in the 1929 Local Government Act. The unions and the boards of guardians were no more, and the Local Government Board, established in 1871, took over the central responsibilities from the Poor Law Board, thus continuing the bipartite method of control. Lest one feels that this was automatically beneficial to paupers, it should be added that some boards of guardians had grown quite generous, especially where controlled by Labour Party representatives, and the new regime was often more stringent.

The coming of the old age pension

The complementary development of monetary payments became rather complex, but, in essence, it heralded a recognition that poverty was intrinsic to an industrial economy, and that cushions against it must be ensured. The long campaign for pensions reached its height in 1908. Many schemes – as many as a hundred – had been proposed, while the 1895 Royal Commission on the Aged Poor played an influential role. The non-contributory proposal of Charles Booth, promulgated in his *Old Age Pensions and the Aged Poor*, initially won the day, and his ideas found support from both the left (organized labour, the friendly societies and the Fabians) and the right, where the employers were beginning to shed workers earlier, in part because the 1897 Workmen's Compensation legislation left them, they felt, open to payments for accident-prone, ageing employees.

Certainly, a key factor was the perceived need, as techniques grew more sophisticated in the workplace, to syphon off older workers, and it it is no coincidence that the same period witnesses an extension of occupational pensions. Following the famous Superannuation Act of 1857 for civil servants, such pensions were offered to school teachers, policemen and other public employees, and those employed by large, paternalistic concerns, like the railway companies. Their lineage – the allotment of monies to public and allied officials – is basically distinct from that of the state pension, which is in direct line of descent from the poor law.

Nor should it be forgotten that, until the civic registration of births had sufficiently advanced, it was not readily possible to administer grants on an age basis. It was 1890 before ages were officially recorded for poor law purposes. In the end, and after many enquiries and debates, the 1908 compromise was attained, with 70 – exaggeratedly thought by some to be five times cheaper than 65 – arbitrarily determined as the threshold. The pension was five shillings (25p) and there was both a morals test and a means test, with £21 a year the bottom line for the full amount. Some 490,000 people received the first old age pensions in January 1909, about a third of Britain's over-65s. It is worthy of note that, ever since the end of the eighteenth century, about a third of Britain's over-65s had been in receipt of poor law subventions. Furthermore, the usual weekly grant at the turn of the nineteenth century had been around five shillings, and, contrary to the propaganda which suggested that the aged poor were heavily concentrated in workhouses, only about a quarter of aged paupers were institutionalized, including those in the infirmaries on health grounds. Incidentally, this meant that about 5 per cent of the actual age-range were in what now would be termed residential care, roughly the same proportion as the present day.

It cannot be said too forcefully that the inauguration of the old age pension was, in practice, the 'nationalization' of outdoor relief for old people. The number of 'aged paupers' fell dramatically, and financially the scheme demonstrated little more than a transfer from local to central taxation. Although it was less stigmatic – the use of the post office for distribution was a benign brainwave – that degree of continuity should always be recalled when the origins and thus the evolution of state pensions are analysed. This particularly applies to the root sum involved, for five shillings then was approximately a fifth to a quarter of the annual manual weekly wage – and so the ratio has, by and large, remained.

Clerical frustrations – there were 10,000 appeals in the first three months – led to a slackening of the regulations but, conversely, on grounds of both cost and merit, the grand 'universal' proposition of Charles Booth and others was compromised after the First World War. By 1922 the cost of pensions – they were now ten shillings (50p) a week, against an average wage of £3 – was over £24 million, a large increase from the initial outlay of some £7 million. The 1925 Old Age and Widows and Orphans Contributory Pensions Act introduced a contributory pension for insured workers and their wives, to carry them through from 65 to the state pensionable age of 70. Ten shillings remained the pension, as it also became for widows, with five shillings for orphans: this was extended to lower middle class workers in 1937, and the age of payment for women was reduced to 60 in 1940. The non-contributory pension more or less collapsed.

The coming of national insurance

The progressive Liberal government, which initiated the old age pension, was likewise active in the major field of impoverishment, namely unemployment.

The friendly societies (and in 1900 these mutual aid groups, such as the Foresters and the Oddfellows, had six million members, compared with the trade unions' 1.3 million) and charitable assistance had made a good contribution, but there were calls for more systematic cover. Labour exchanges were introduced in 1909 – there were over 400 of them by 1914 – and in the same year the Trades Boards Act was passed for the fixing of wages. The cornerstone of the social legislation of the Liberal government was, however, the 1911 National Insurance Act.

This instituted the pattern of mixed contributions – worker 7 old pence, government 2 old pence, employer 3 old pence – for workers on more than £160 per annum, against ten shillings (50p) a week benefit for thirteen weeks, then five shillings (25p) for a further thirteen weeks, in the event of loss of earnings through ill-health. It also paid for the use of a so-called 'panel' doctor. The scheme was administered at first by 'approved societies', such as friendly societies and insurance companies, and overseen by the new National Insurance Commission, with the famous civil servant Robert Morant as its first head.

As for unemployment of itself, seven shillings (35p) per week was made available for fifteen weeks, and the notorious 'dole' was hereby invented. This initially covered 2.5 million workers, but it excluded poorly paid workers, on the simple grounds that they would have difficulty paying the contributions. None the less, the numbers involved sprang remarkably after the First World War, and from 1921 came to include dependants. The troubles of the 1930s saw cuts in the benefits as unemployment soared to 14 per cent of the workforce, and means testing had to be used to assess for 'uncovenanted' dole beyond the fifteen weeks statutory period. Many were flung back on to the poor law from which national insurance had supposedly saved them, and it was this kind of pressure which led, in part, to the abandonment of the 'poor law guardians' set-up in 1929. In 1934 the Unemployed Assistance Board was founded to deal with those who had run out of benefit, and in 1940 the Public Assistance Board took over the work of the Public Assistance Committees. This meant that the poor relief was now a central, not a local, responsibility, as was already the case with the old age pension.

By the 1930s nearly half the population enjoyed national insurance cover, with the 'dole' beginning at fifteen shillings (75p) for a male worker, and the costs involved, in some years as much as £37 million or a quarter of all social service expenditure, raised the expected squabbles and cries of 'scroungermania'. There can be little doubt that the various economic upheavals, with organized strike action a dreaded factor, seriously concentrated the minds of politicians and indeed employers over the seventy years before the Second World War. Unemployment, often of longer duration than was expected, obviously fuelled any existing discontent, and it remained in the best interests of those controlling the state and the economy to sustain the stability of the workforce, despite the heavy financial costs.

Two final points might be made. First, the notion that unemployment could be 'prevented' was dead, even among those who nursed the acid grievance that too many idlers abounded. The whole structure of paying subsistence grants to those out of work or, as pensioners, no longer required for work was predicated on this acceptance that full employment was not the norm.

Second, the pre-1914 format of health, unemployment and old age benefits removed a huge swathe of chiefly able-bodied people from the grasp of the poor law, and ensured that, by 1940, these money benefits, with most of them involving the contributory principle, were controlled by central government. The local authorities maintained whatever residential and other services in kind might be on offer, together with some residual tasks, but the antique function of the locality to raise and distribute money for social casualties was virtually ended. When the welfare state arrived in full pomp, the accent would be on the central state.

Approach to ill-health

Nearly 15,000 died in the cholera epidemic of 1866, a timely reminder to the Victorians that, for all their valiant endeavours, the scourge of ill-health was not easily vanquished. Before and during the first Gladstone administration, there was a flurry of legislative activity: an Act of 1866 enforced the removal of 'nuisances' and insisted on clearer local action; the 1869–71 Royal Commission on public health created much attention; the Local Government Board (1871) attempted to draw together the threads of public health work done by varied agencies; and the 1872 Public Health Act mapped out the nation into Urban or Rural Sanitary Authorities, each with a medical officer of health.

Public health measures

The crucial statute was the 1875 Public Health Act, associated with the name of Slater-Booth, President of the Local Government Board, under whose provisions, it has been said, 'all the cities and towns in this country have become places fit to live in'. Its protagonists urged the furtherment of a 'national sanitary minimum', and this 'model enactment' guaranteed a most comprehensive set of environmental provisions. These included food inspection, street lighting, burial and the notification of diseases, as well as water supply and sewage removal. Throughout this time, the local authorities gradually improved and completed basic water and sewerage amenities, with much advanced civil engineering obviously making a major impact.

More than in other sectors of social policy, the preventative concept was kept to the fore: these were definite attempts to erase the causes of sickness and pestilence. They were, of course, driven by the need to preserve the health of the labour force, that the economy might be well-served. It was all a question of what was termed 'national efficiency', and this embraced the issue of military security. Forty per cent of the recruits for the Boer War around the turn of the century were rejected on medical grounds, a dispiriting blow to national pride and resolve, especially as Britain was becoming concerned about the growth of Germany's strength and the risk of a continental war. There was little solace to be found with the outbreak of such hostilities in 1914 – an even higher proportion of First World War recruits were rejected for health reasons.

Politicians and tax-payers bit on the bullet of increased taxation, local as well as national. There was much attention paid to the needs of children, for, however individualistic one's political creed, it was hard to argue that children could care for themselves. In 1904 the grimily titled Inter-departmental Committee on the Physical Deterioration of the Young was set up; the 1902 Midwives Act sought to register and supervise that critical profession; and the 1936 Midwives Act ensured it was a full-timed salaried service. In 1906 meals and milk were encouraged at school level (following the example of about 300 voluntary 'feeding associations' and the arrival of the first 'hygienic milk depot' in 1899) and in 1907 school medical inspection was introduced. The Children's Act of 1908 consolidated the legal protection of children as minors, and they were gradually removed from the stern clutches of the poor law. The Maternity and Child Welfare Act of 1918 established a network of local authority clinics and allied services; and, very importantly, the office of health visitor was generally promoted. Their numbers sprang from 600 to 1,335 during the First World War.

Housing

Nowhere is the bridge from Benthamism to collectivism more clearly viewed than in housing. That most personal of possessions, the notion of the private house – 'the Englishman's castle' – was embedded deeply in the political psyche, but such was the terror of disease and filth that it succumbed to the public credo. From encouraging house-holders to create clean conditions for themselves, that they might preserve good health and work hard, to insisting on certain high standards of hygiene and amenities, all the way to building the actual houses – such is the narrative of housing policy in a nutshell. It is, then, important to grasp that, initially, public housing was the child of public health, and not directly – despite the self-evident links – of poverty.

The slums were feared because they were the source of sickness, of low economic productivity and of likely violence. They also stood, often (and railway development is the key example), in the way of capitalist progress, and thus the policy of 'search and destroy', as it has been gruesomely called, was practised. The housing acts of 1868 and 1875 – the second associated, like the Public Health Act of the same year, with Disraeli's essays in wooing the newly enfranchised urban voter – gave powers to local authorities to demolish but also to rehouse. These did not, according to the 1884–5 Royal Commission on Housing, have much effect, although there were some philanthropic 'model dwellings' constructed by the likes of the Peabody Trust and the Guiness Trust, and three local authorities, Liverpool, Devonport and Nottingham, had built a few council houses. The urgings of reformers like Octavia Hill led to further legislation, notably the 1890 and 1900 statutes, which provided for the clearance and replacement of unfit accommodation.

These early forays into the sacrosanct field of housing prefaced the mighty array of municipal housing of the twentieth century. Population grew, and unhealthy overcrowding was not stemmed; in London in the 1900s there were seven or eight persons in each dwelling. The London County Council, established by the 1888 County Councils Act, took the lead. By 1914 London had erected half the nation's 24,000 council houses, and had developed estates at Tottenham, Acton, Tooting and Croydon. To put that in perspective, the whole sum amounted to no more than 1 per cent of the housing stock. The crux of the question was that the private sector was unable to produce decent housing at a price affordable by working class families. Moreover, until public subsidies became available, local authorities could barely afford such investment either.

The years following the 1914–18 war, when unrest simmered as 'the homes fit for heroes' resolutely failed to materialize and the nation's leaders watched the 1917 Russian Revolution with fearful trepidation, saw some changes. Addison's Housing and Town and Country Planning Act of 1919 introduced state subsidies for municipal housing, and 170,000 houses were quickly built under its auspices. In 1924 John Wheatley was responsible, during a minority Labour ministry, for the Housing Act, which doubled the subsidy and established the National Housing Building Committee. Over the next eleven years, no less than half a million houses were constructed, by far the largest degree of public housing thus far. There was a tendency to revert to slum clearance and replacement thereafter, a swing from the broader view of overall housing needs. Alongside these activities, the ribbon development of owner-occupied suburbia was growing even faster. In the years prior to the Second World War, a quarter of a million private houses were annually built, and weekly mortgage repayments were as low as eight shillings (40p), only slightly more than a council house rent.

In total, four million houses were built between the wars, a million of them by the local authorities, but this still left, it was estimated, a million families in overcrowded and slum conditions. Just as the first tranche of national insurance participants were reasonably paid artisans, so were the first residents of municipal housing, who had to find six or seven shillings a week (30p/35p) rental. The lower working class of unskilled labourers, agricultural workers, domestic servants and the like were still rather left out of the picture. In any event, it remains a moot point whether cheap state-subsidized housing is the most massive dosage of socialism, or whether, by guaranteeing accommodation in that fashion, it merely underpins the sort of economy in which men and women are not paid adequately enough to purchase their own homes. Putting that philosophic speculation on the shelf temporarily, the pragmatic fact to conclude with must be that Great Britain was already rapidly moving from the 1914 position, where 90 per cent of houses, rich or poor, were privately rented, to one where owner-occupation and public rental were more the norm. Moreover, it was a society where, given the private business examples of the Bourneville (1876) or Port Sunlight (1887) housing developments, there were also initial moves – in the acts of 1909, 1919 and 1932 – towards effective town planning. As if as proxy for the link between social environment and disease, the Ministry of Health took over all health responsibilities from other central departments in 1919, including that for housing and planning.

Medicine

The great medical shift after the 1860s was the success of the 'microbe hunters', such as Louis Pasteur and Robert Koch, and the development of the germ theory of disease. Bacilli were identified and medicines correspondingly manufactured; Lister first used his antiseptic technique in 1865 and the pasteurization of milk was invented in the 1880s. Whatever else, this gave the medical profession a generally accepted scientific base, and, assisted by the 'panel' mechanism, their patient numbers widened considerably. Although there are obvious ways in which one helps the other, it may be argued that, as a consequence, 'cure' came to outweigh 'prevention', as calling in the doctor once illness threatened became the cultural norm. Certainly, the hopes that large-scale environmental measures would actually sweep away disease were no more well-founded than aspirations to prevent unemployment by stringent poor laws. None the less, something of the preventative momentum was lost: fitness became a more individualistic affair; people thought more in terms of 'personal' than of 'public' health.

The emblem of this approach was the hospital, and it was over this period that, from their joint origins in the charities and in the poor law, the huge hospitals arose as further urban monuments to institutionalism. It was, needless to say, antisepsis which, as much as anything, allowed the collection of many patients together without undue danger. By 1891 there were 113,000 hospital beds in Britain; by 1938 that figure had more than doubled to 263,000. At that latter date, the voluntary hospitals still held some sway, owning a third of those beds, but there had been, via the local authority take-over of poor law tasks, a switch to municipal control of a half of the beds. This still left a fifth in former poor law infirmaries and workhouse wards. It also represented a major building programme, usually with larger municipal hospitals and smaller voluntary 'cottage' hospitals the norm. There were also illustrations of specialism, not only by ward, but also by separate building, with maternity and tuberculosis (a thousand a week died of TB around the 1900s) instances of this.

All in all, this complex of environmental and medical elements, in whatever degree, helped to improve the health of the nation. The death rate slowly dropped from 230 per thousand in 1850, to 170 per thousand in 1900, to 120 per thousand in 1939. What was, rather coldly, referred to as 'human capital' in the 1930s was rather fitter, although fears that economic recovery was put at risk through the continuing poor health of that 'human capital' were not altogether allayed.

Approach to ignorance

The 1870 Education Act co-stars with the 1875 Public Health Act as the lead measure of early collectivism. It was the work of W. E. Forster, a key member of the first Gladstone ministry, and it foreshadowed the centralized state system of the present day. It was an attempt, in Forster's words, 'to fill up the gaps' left by the idiosyncrasies of the state-subsidized and inspected system. Population had continued to boom, so that, rather as in the public health field, existing agencies could not even maintain provision. As British industry was challenged by foreign rivals, it was urged that education in France, Germany and the United States was a contributory factor to their commercial success. While that view has been challenged by commentators, who claim that superior technology was the key to these achievements, there is no doubt that it was a plea strongly felt at the time: 'upon this speedy provision of education depends also our national power', thundered Forster to the house of commons.

Less well-documented, but probably as vital, was the havoc caused by children who had neither work nor school to attend. As industry became more mechanized and as child labour was required less, and as, in a somewhat cynical view, the Factory Acts forbidding categories of child labour took complementary effect, the streets were filled with hordes of children. In many towns almost half the children of usual school age roamed at enforced leisure, and their potential for social disturbance was a grave source of uneasiness among the middle classes. In a society where, increasingly, home and work were on separate sites and, consequently, parental control of older children was difficult, the school must be seen as a necessary agent of social rather than merely economic needs.

The terms of the 1870 Education Act

The act was a 'hard compromise' between the secularists, headed by the National Education League, who were opposed to Church schools and wanted a non-sectarian, national system, and the religionists, led by the National Education Union, who wished the voluntary Church schools to continue with augmented government funding. The medieval and early modern influence of the Church on social policy remained at its fiercest in the world of education, and the bitter debates were only resolved in the famous Cowper-Temple 'conscience' clause, which allowed parents to withdraw their children from religious teaching. Forster allowed the churches six months' grace, during which they increased their school properties by a remarkable 30 per cent, and then, following surveys, the Privy Council Committee on Education was empowered to request the establishment of local and popularly elected school boards. Both Church and board schools were to receive public funding, and the school boards, while in one sense a throwback to the 'tutelary' device of single-purpose agency, had a wider franchise than the town councils.

Predictably, neither side was happy, the one angry at the continued financing of religious schooling, the other fearing the loss of Church influence on the new 'godless' schools. Nevertheless, the practical outcomes were sound enough. Over 300 school boards were quickly and often enthusiastically formed, and by 1874, when Gladstone's ministry fell from office, 5,000 new schools had been added to the existing 8,000, giving an additional 1.5 million places, a third of them in board schools.

Lord Sandon's Act of 1876 established school attendance committees under the control of the poor law in non-school board areas, and advanced the cause of obligatory attendance. It outlawed child labour under the age of ten. Anomalies and evasions remained legion, as families were often needful of income from children and suspicions remained as to the value of schooling. Eventually, in 1880, A. J. Mundella's Compulsory Attendance Act was passed, which obliged authorities to submit attendance by-laws for all children between five and ten. By the 1890s the school-leaving age was effectively eleven, and education was well-nigh free, with H. A. L. Fisher's Act of 1918 formally abolishing elementary school fees. There were then over 20,000 schools and the state, in taxes and rates, found £14 million for their upkeep, a notable increase from the £1 million of 1872.

The terms of the 1902 Education Act

The next move in the complicated educational game was the Conservative Education Act of 1902. This eliminated the boards (of which there were now over 2,500, together with 700 school attendance committees), partly because some were tiny and derisory, partly because some were large and avid. The Board of Education had replaced the Department of Education, still under Privy Council reins, in 1899, and Robert Morant, its first permanent secretary, whom we have already met wearing his national insurance hat, was 'the assassin of the boards'.

In Liberal-controlled urban areas, the boards had sometimes overstepped the mark, occasionally illegally, in terms of technical and post-elementary education, and there were political motives, chiefly an eagerness to succour the church schools, behind the 1902 decision to hand over education to the new county councils and county boroughs. (Larger boroughs and urban district councils, known as Part III authorities, to distinguish them from the Part II county/county borough ones, clung to control of elementary schooling.) However, this, of course, was in line with what was happening elsewhere, with a state department in liaison with one of the now many departments of the local authority.

The board and voluntary elementary schools, now labelled 'provided' and 'non-provided', alike became the responsibility of the novel 328 local education authorities or LEAs, which also had to consider post-elementary education. Robert Morant's rather arid 1904 regulations for the new county secondary schools were couched in traditionalist terms, with vocational education, favoured by some of the boards, at a discount. There was a resurgence of the grammar school, long decayed after its sparkling beginnings in the Elizabethan period. There were only 491 such schools in 1904, but by 1925 there were 1,616. In many ways, it aped the values of the public schools which, during the second half of the nineteenth century, had become models of upper crust propriety. That serves to remind us that, as with medical care, the advance of the British state was by accretion on an existing private base. With schools, as with medicine, this commercial sector was never obliterated. Two-tier public and private systems were built into society.

Again like the medical profession, the teaching profession was by now in much better heart, with training colleges, clustered around the universities, the usual route to the 'prescribed qualification'. Under the 1902 Act, teachers became officially registered for the first time, and the National Union of Teachers, founded in 1870, was growing in strength. In the inter-war years there was a concentration on secondary education, with several enquiries and commissions discussing that topic, and, one way or another, most children stayed at school until they were fourteen, with plans laid, but aborted because of the Second World War, to raise the school-leaving age to fifteen.

In one real sense, it was the mixture as before, with that combine of municipal and Church schools embedded together, the religious question still extant and a sometimes awkward partnership of central supervision and local responsibility. A good example of this is the Conservative government's suspicions, revealed in the 1902 Act, of the often Liberal-dominated local school boards.

In another equally real sense, there had been a cultural sea-change, for the old resentment had, by and large, died, and the notion that parents should legally ensure that their children attended school was taken for granted. It was a triumph for collectivism, this bland acceptance that individuals were not necessarily the best judges of their children's well-being. The final point carries echoes from other parts of the field of social welfare, for the often large school, including many all-age examples, loomed large on the urban landscape. The London School Board alone built nearly 400 schools, often of the 'central hall' variety, with abutting classrooms, and often the work of E. R. Robson, most noted of Victorian state school architects.

Approach to crime

Law and order, always a foremost anxiety in the political mind, had more or less completed its re-examination by and in the 1856 Constabulary Act, but, of course, there were to be changes in both the police and prison services, as population grew and social conditions altered.

The police up to the Second World War

In 1874 exchequer grants for 'efficiency' were raised from a quarter to a half, and new boroughs of less than 20,000 inhabitants were stopped from having a separate force, as the state tried even harder to seize sufficient control. Once again, however, it was the 1888 County Councils Act which provided a unique opportunity for reform. That statute abolished all forces where their catchment population was less than 10,000, and this reduced their number from 231 to 183. There were ups and downs over the years, as new boroughs and thus new forces were formed, but in 1939 there were, curiously, still exactly 183 forces in England and Wales. The borough forces were overseen by the watch committees, and the county forces by standing joint committees, with both inclusive of justices of the peace representation.

There were police strikes in 1918–19, very worrying to the establishment, and the 1919 Desborough Committee led to a further Police Act in the same year. This strengthened the Home Office role through its Police Department, instituted the Police Federation (a kind of staff association for police officers, as a sweetener for the act having made trade unionism illegal) and generally stiffened standards. It also abolished forces where there were less than a 50,000 population, and, in effect, the counties and county boroughs remained the ambit for policing.

As for prevention, that hardly survived the opening years of the reformed police forces. As early as 1842 the Metropolitan Police had formed a detective department, the forerunner of the CID, and, elsewhere, the emphasis on detection, on finding offenders rather than forestalling them, became the motif. This is probably the most dramatic example of the abandonment of the optimistic creed of prevention and, as with medicine, the cultural and popular aspects – the solving of the gruesome murder, the mercy dash and the emergency operation – favoured the curative elements at the expense of the less colourful demands of preventive action.

As with poverty, disease and ignorance, the problem of crime refused to dwindle in the face of greater commercial prosperity, not without consternation among the baffled ranks of Victorian social commentators. It was believed that the ending of both transportation and capital punishment for minor offences might have augmented the ranks of habitual criminals, but, overall, it seemed that the spur of relative want was sharpened as much by prosperity as by impoverishment. After a minor lull in the 1860s, the amount of crime, with theft still by far the biggest offence (but with violent crime nudging aside drunkenness at the next level of criminality), climbed to its old proportions by the end of the century.

Although there were the Trafalgar Square Riots of 1887, the Tonypandy mining troubles of 1910 and the General Strike problems of 1926, with military aid occasionally required to eke out the civil arm of the police, the fear of a proletarian rising had vanished, save for those of very morbid imaginings. Despite the levels of crime, the degree of public discipline and community peace was possibly higher than it had ever been, or was to be again, in the period from about the 1870s to the 1950s.

The prisons up to the Second World War

The prisons, where the numbers refused to drop, were an odd mix of the preventative and the curative. Prison life, although it became more hygienic and disciplined with its Bentham-like 'cellular' approach, was about separation and solitude, directed to turning the face of men and women from their criminal intentions. Yet it was also about punishment; it was about keeping offenders out of view of the populace and away from opportunities to commit further crimes.

As for their supervision, Sir Robert Peel, as Home Secretary, had as early as 1823 attempted to gain some control over the prisons, while from 1835 inspectors of prisons had continued to oversee the work of the magistrates and corporations who ran the local jails. As the century wore on, the 'huge castellated structures' of Pentonville and Strangeways and Walton prisons and their like came to lour over the urban scene. Scandals over undue cruelties, especially at Birmingham prison under the severe regime of Governor Austin, led first to the Carnarvon Committee, and next, in 1865, to the Prisons Act and a typical tightening of central powers.

The haphazard collection of jails was reduced from 193 to 112, and, with a view to cutting the shire rates, the prisons were nationalized in 1877, with Edward du Cane as the first Chairman of the Prison Commission. It was a clear piece of collectivist legislation, the very word 'nationalization' seeming socialistically alien in that Victorian context. By the end of the century there were just 61 main prisons, many of them newly built, many of them of large size, compared, that is, with the ramshackle town bridewells and shire jails that preceded them.

Thus there was little or no change in the basic structure of either the police or the prison service before the Second World War. Like the other welfare and allied services, they responded, if a little tardily, to social changes at large and the general amelioration of the human condition in the United Kingdom. The construct of central/local authority division of police powers, with the culprits, once convicted, feeding into a national network of large prisons, was to be maintained. In many of its qualities – grants, subject to central inspection; local powers in the hands of democratically elected, multi-purpose authorities; ever tighter Home Office reins – it thus retained a similarity with each of the other social agencies.

Comparative features

By 1939 there were many other European and North American nations with industrial economies and heavily urbanized communities. In spite of differences of a political and geographical character, they had perforce to experiment with social welfare schemes, a sure indication that all were driven by economically determined situations rather than by ideological creeds.

The German Chancellor, Bismarck, famously introduced sickness insurance (1884) and old age pensions (1889) into Germany, aimed at the loyalty of the respectable working class. With the Social Democratic Party banned at this time, Bismarck was anxious to immunize against subversive rebellion and, partially, his format was adopted by Lloyd George for the British pre-1914 reforms. In 1911 social insurance was extended to white collar workers, small farmers and shopkeepers. At much the same period, insurance schemes were begun in Austria, France (where a public network of medical clinics was well established by 1914), Italy, Holland (old age pensions from 1913) and the Scandinavian countries. Denmark began unemployment grants in 1907 and Finland started workers' compensation in 1889. By the 1930s, Sweden, secure and at peace for many years, had developed notions of civil rights, which, guided by the radical politicians Alva and Gunnar Myrdal, led to great social strides.

The United States had to consider social protection. In the so-called 'progressive era' of the 1900s there was the 1906 Federal Employee's Liability Act, and a flurry of welfare programmes in several of the industrialized states. But it was fairly mild stuff, in Canada as well as in the USA – in 1913, when 10 per cent of British public expenditure was devoted to welfare, the corresponding American figure was only 1 per cent. In the 1930s, in response to the dreary suffering of the depression, President Roosevelt introduced the 'New Deal', founded in public works and legislation such as the 1935 Social Security Act.

There was some activity in Australasia, where individual states initiated varied schemes, while a judicial decision about 'appropriate' payment in Australia in 1907 served to act as a kind of minimum wage. Japan enjoyed what is known as the Meija era from 1868 to 1912, when, opened up to western influence, its commerce and manufacture blossomed. The doctrine of 'social instrumentalism', pursued into and through the inter-wars years, called for a rapidly expanding economic and military machine, but with a layer of social protection as the necessary cushion. In the forty years before the First World War, literacy in Japan improved from 30 to 70 per cent.

As for Russia, it is interesting to observe that there were social reforms prior to the Bolshevik Revolution in 1917. Accident and sickness insurance for industrial workers, limited working hours and the beginnings of an elementary system of education – these were in place in Tsarist Russia, simply because factory and town life demanded some such answers to the welfare problems posed. There were major advances in education and health care – school attendance quadrupled and hospital beds doubled in the twenty years after the Revolution – but it would be a mistake to believe that the Leninist/Stalinist administrations began from a standing start.

Here and there one spots a sense of unified national action – Sweden, Japan, post-1917 Russia – but, in the main, it is the absence of a rationale which is the more evident. As in Great Britain, the responses are coloured by local circumstances, such as the overt militarism of Japan, or subject to typical organizational devices, such as much centralism in France and much regionalism in Germany or Australia. The common element is a world of burgeoning industrial nations, each committed to a moderate and usually sporadic dosage of public welfare intervention, and obliged so to commit themselves because of the malign pressures of industrial and urban existence.

Specific features

During this lengthy prelude to the Second World War, there was some emphasis on special categories among social casualties. Administrative, legal, technical and medical tools were more sophisticated, and that helped avoidance of some of the blanket strategies of previous generations. Individual case work, pioneered in Britain by the Charity Organisation Society and others, was to spread overseas, as well as being accepted as a proper formula in the public sector. There were moves to improve the education of handicapped children: in 1893 school boards were given permission to build special schools for blind and for deaf youngsters, and more was done in this line between the two world wars. Attempts were made to treat mental illness more fairly. The Lunacy Act of 1890 and the Idiots Act of 1886 were more concerned with the legal definitions of these conditions, but at least it was a recognition, however chilly, that problems existed. The Mental Deficiency

Act (1913) and the Mental Treatment Act (1930) were more responsive to the social and medical needs of those involved.

As we have seen, substantial essays in medical care for children had been tried, and there were other instances of an acknowledgement of the child-like-ness of children. The 1854 Reformatory Act was one of the first attempts to separate the child offender from the adult offender, and it was followed by moves to remove those aged under fourteen from ordinary prisons, and to develop juvenile courts. The National Society for the Prevention of Cruelty to Children was formed in 1884, although some may regard it as characteristically English that the RSPCA was then already celebrating its sixtieth birthday. Adoption was another matter for concern, and in the Adoption Act of 1926 the foundation was laid for the present regulations in this regard.

Women obtained the franchise in the parliamentary reform Acts of 1918 and 1928, but before that they had already made local political headway, especially in educational administration. Against this background, and given their sturdy efforts on the home front in the 1914–18 war, there were some glimmers of gender equality. They were but glimmers. Women obviously benefited from the increased medical attention paid to children, especially infants, but they remained largely disenfranchised economically. Most of the insurance and pension legislation excluded married women, the assumption being that their husbands would support them, although the Unemployed Women's Act (1905) did permit of the formation of distress committees.

The chief feminist issue between the two world wars revolved around child or family allowances. The Speenhamland system (described in Chapter 4) had, in practice, offered poor relief on a family basis, and after 1908 allowances for widows and for the wives and children of servicemen or the unemployed became normal. The argument was not all one way. Many women rightly objected to the 'domestic tabby-cat' image, with the implication that women should only receive rewards for child-bearing. It was also urged that family benefits undermined the negotiation for a living wage for men, just as the Speenhamland system had been used as an excuse for lowered pay. There was also an inference that men required a family wage, for the wife and offspring, and that women required but a personal wage, a none too subtle way of keeping an unequal wage structure. Nevertheless, there were worries about the lower birth rate and the continuance of child poverty in the 1930s, and, in general, the scene was being set for a new look at the whole question of such benefits.

One way in which women perhaps prospered a little during this period was in the very service they provided to the new services. As the social welfare industry painfully grew, many women were to find careers within it, whereas in other professions and businesses they were still, in effect, denied entry. Nursing, social work and education are self-evident examples of this tendency, and, at the top of those trees, were to be found quite a number of matrons and headmistresses. Even the masculine bastion of the police yielded. The first policewoman was recruited in 1918; there were 230 policewomen by 1939. It was just a tiny step, and it would be hazardous to suppose, from these isolated instances, that the woman's lot, anymore than the Gilbertian policeman's, was a happy or, at least, an equitable one.

Conclusion

The seventy years before the Second World War were thus crowded with much detail of a collectivist character, with, for instance, municipal housing demonstrating a major change of political accent. Whatever that amount of intense and varying detail, and despite its bisection by the tragedy of the 1914–18 war (which is so often utilized as a break-point in studies of this kind) it is a period which stands reasonably discretely. The Industrial Revolution had created a new urban society, based on factory production and a large working class. That scenario was to persist, certainly up until the Second World War. As a significant part of it, piecemeal efforts were made to shore up its social downside with state action, much of it of an 'institutional' nature. These manifold endeavours were the precursors and heralds of the conventional welfare state of the 1940s, a social programme occasioned perhaps by 'war socialism', but owing a considerable debt to the pilot efforts of that long seventy-year travail. An analysis of the arrival and content of the welfare state is the subject of the next chapter.

Advice on further reading

As the years draw nearer the present day, the literature 'hots up', in the sense that many more studies have been made of the more modern scene. Another slight difficulty is caused by the fact that, from this point onwards, many of the recommended books cover more than one chapter of this study – a natural consequence of each chapter itself dealing with a relatively narrow period. Readers should remember that a select bibliography of in-print literature is provided at the end of the book. First, there are some books which might be referred to, if possible, apropos this chapter:

Barnard, H. C. (1947) *A Short History of English Education, 1760–1944*, University of London Press, London.
Burnett, J. (1978) *A Social History of Housing 1815–1970*, Routledge, London (2nd edn 1980).
Frazer, W. M. (1950) *The History of English Public Health, 1834–1939*, Ballière, Tindall & Cox, London.
Gilbert, B. B. (1966) *The Evolution of National Insurance in Great Britain*, Michael Joseph, London.
Halliday, R. J. (1976) *John Stuart Mill*, George Allen and Unwin, London.
Reith, C. A. (1956) *A New Study of British Police History*, Oliver and Boyd, London.

Next, students should turn to the end of Chapter 6, where another lengthy list of books is appended which covers the events leading up to, and the establishment of, the modern welfare state. These fully cover the material laid out in both Chapters 5 and 6.

6

The silent revolution
of the 1940s

Summary

In the wake of the purported 'wartime socialism' of national planning and purpose, and given a general mood favouring 'reconstruction', the Labour government
(1945–51) was able to construct something closer to a programmed welfare
state. Its salient features were the National Health Service, the attendant social
insurance schemes of Beveridge Report minting, the continuation of new town
and municipal housing, and a determination to offer all children access to secondary education. This came closer to an integrated social policy than at any
time before or since, but the continuities with the past were still apparent – in
many ways, this 'silent revolution' was a consolidation of existing mechanisms.
From the standpoint of organization, all the old devices – central department,
local government, specialist authority – were brought into play, and this added
to the continuing sense of still somewhat piecemeal activity.

It was all undertaken against a backdrop of war and cold war, of Britain
struggling to find a place in the international scheme of things, both politically
and economically. Thus, from the beginning, there was a financial tension between welfare aspirations and other priorities, especially defence. However, most
commentators agree that the national mood in favour of a more equitable
approach was probably stronger than at any other time.

> New terms tend to become fewer the nearer one approaches the home
> stretch, with modern usages being more familiar. There are still a few,
> however, including: fascism – Keynesianism – power state – dependency
> – universalism.

Social and economic background

It has been the practice to treat 1945–51 as the period in which the modern welfare state was established, and that has some political logic. It was, after all, the socialist-inclined Labour government, with Clement Attlee as premier, which came to power in 1945, just after the end of the war in Europe, with a set of social proposals that they (perhaps more convincingly than most administrations) actually carried out. However, the longer retrospect suggests that it makes more sense to treat the whole decade, that is, embracing the 1939–45 war, as the critical era. Much of the thinking and the action was war-oriented, so much so that citizens saw re-established in peacetime what they had become used to in wartime.

War socialism

What became known as 'war socialism' was the order of the day. In any assessment of the extent of state intervention into private life, the period of the Second World War emerges without rival. Although always subject to parliamentary critique, the 1939 Emergency Powers (Defence) Act permitted a most intrusive range of regulation over personal lives. The people and resources of the 'India-Rubber Island' were exploited to an astonishing degree, as a state-directed siege economy was fashioned. It is not always recalled that this efficient utilization of productive energies was handled substantially better by the British than the German government, despite the totalitarian zealotry of the Nazi machine. For example, the direction of labour, including that of women, was much more efficacious in Britain; in respect of productivity, less than 5 per cent of the home labour force was employed in the vital task of agriculture, whereas the German equivalent was 27 per cent.

Rationing, which persisted into the 1950s (and which, in some ways, became worse after the war, with a liberated and starving Europe to feed) was a brilliant *tour de force*. With public relations techniques of high order and with a huge level of popular acceptability, it shelved market forces and created a system of nutritional equity which, in practice, puts any later attempts at welfare statehood in the shade. It was pretty well recognized by the authorities that this degree of control was only viable in so far as people perceived its necessity and, equally significant, its fairness.

Social and medical schemes, especially necessary for children or with the onset of bombing, were an adjunct of this, and although the scene was never wholly pure – there was a black market and there were local authority deficiencies – morale and solidarity remained sound. A. J. P. Taylor has judged, without sentiment, that in this 'people's war in the most literal sense', the British citizenry 'came of age'. They were, then, exceptionally attuned to the value of 'fair shares' and to planning, and there was considerable expectation that such values would inform the peace as well as the war.

From an entirely practical angle, however, the crucial factor in the 1940s was the experience of full employment. The effects of the 1930s depression lingered long, and it is sometimes forgotten that Britain entered the war still with high levels of unemployment. It was not until well into 1940 (such is the slowness of administrative diktat) that more or less everyone had a job. At a stroke, the principal cause of poverty, particularly temporary poverty, was swept aside. Full employment was to be maintained after the war, almost to the point where it was taken for granted. Certainly, it is no accident that the high-tide of welfarism goes hand in hand with the existence of full employment, for the latter both obviates a major need for the former, and, through the taxation, direct and indirect, of all those workers, proffers a decent source for its upkeep.

During this decade, and for some time afterwards, Keynesian economics held sway – and John Maynard Keynes was himself an active participant in the events of these years. In a brief phrase or so, Keynesianism might be described as using budget deficits to stimulate demand in recession, and budget surpluses to quieten demand in boom. It envisions a rule of demand management, with full employment a prior objective of that hand on the fiscal tiller. William Beveridge himself was to assume full employment as a given, although the institutions he had in blueprint to assure this happened were not required. Unemployment barely rose above 1 per cent throughout the 1940s, whereas in 1921, for instance, it had stood at 11 per cent.

That other cause of poverty – low pay – also came under attack: in general, because of the same need to sustain the physical and mental vigour of a workforce under stress; in particular, through the efforts of Ernest Bevin, the trade union boss, who, as Minister for Labour, deliberately ensured that, in exchange for their sterling endeavours, British working people should not be treated as inferiors. This acknowledged place for the trade union movement as an active partner in the matter of wages and conditions was to last for three decades before it was challenged.

Of course, it would be folly to dress the Second World War in garments of joy. The attrition was debilitating: 440,000 military and civilian deaths were suffered; three-quarters of a million houses were destroyed or badly damaged; direct taxation rose three-fold; and, apart from untold losses of assets, a debt had been incurred estimated at £3.5 billion. The life-line of American lease-lend, which had provided about two-thirds of the external deficit of some £10 billion accumulated during the war, was abruptly stopped with the unexpected end of the Japanese war in the August of 1945. In exchange for the market convertibility of sterling (which hitherto had been tightly controlled by the Treasury) to dollars, Britain did negotiate an easy interest loan of £3.5 billion from the United States, but it was an onerous beginning to the post-war struggle.

Post-war socialism

As so often happens, the emergent picture was a mixed one. The newer industries – the motor and aircraft industries, electrical, eventually electronic, engineering, oil-based chemical manufacture – were in good heart, while some of the older industries, like shipbuilding and textiles, had enjoyed something of a revival. Agriculture had been transformed by the internal combustion engine: the number of tractors in use leapt ten-fold from 1925 to 1939, that is, to over 50,000, and then quadrupled during the war. There were major dilapidations of machinery, apart from the wear and tear of total war itself, and there were antediluvian practices on the part of both management and labour. There were also shortages of fuel and raw materials with which to contend, and the transport networks were creaking. But the war had been won, and the economic fabric of the nation was much less shattered than those of other European countries. Despite fiscal and other setbacks, such as the dreadful winter of 1946–7, there were signs that the economy might mend itself.

The Labour government sought to exert even more economic control through its nationalization of often ailing staple utilities, such as the coal mines, iron and steel, the railways and road haulage, and the gas and electricity concerns. These were accomplished on a centralized managerial pattern, labelled 'Morrisonian' after Herbert Morrison, famed for his socially aware rule of pre-war London and for his work on the home front throughout the war – although it is reported that Morrison himself had rather lost faith in such giantist approaches to social planning by the time of his death. These seldom tried to involve the worker, let alone the consumer, in their oversight, but they were testimony to a view that one cannot deliver social benefits without substantial control of the economic levers.

Such conscious planning was never to be as effective or as systematic as that accomplished in the post-war years by Germany under the chancellorship of Konrad Adenauer, or indeed France under the shrewd guidance of Jean Monnet. Nevertheless, Britain showed distinct signs of an export-led surge into economic prosperity towards the end of the decade. What barred the way, and what, by that token, prevented any mainline augmentation of welfare policy, was the impasse between the United Kingdom's internal hopes and external aspirations. In a nutshell, the nation was now in the position of the man with champagne tastes and beer pockets.

As A. J. P. Taylor has ruefully noted, the moments when Hitler invaded Russia and Japan attacked Pearl Harbor mark the end of Britain as a world power. The arrival into the war of the two superpowers, the United States and the USSR, transformed it into a global conflict of far-reaching implications, with Britain now very much the junior player. Add to that the exhaustion factor: like one of its own heroes – a Wolfe on the Heights of Quebec or a Nelson at Trafalgar – Britain was, metaphorically, slain at the point of its supreme victory. Courageously, it not only rallied, but determined to battle against social evils, to the admiration of many other nations.

Unluckily, it was not so simple to evade the past, and Britain found itself still involved in what has been termed the 'three-ring vision' of its foreign destiny. It felt it had to remain at a tangent to three circles of world influence. There was Europe, although it avoided the early mustering of European, largely, then as now, Franco-German, cooperation. There was the Empire and Commonwealth, although, starting with the granting of Indian independence in 1947, this began to unravel swiftly. And there was the United States, with whom, other considerations apart, economic ties were restrictively tight. The realities of the then present were such that one should avoid being too pontifical about how some or all of these snares might have been dodged. Suffice it to say that Britain either could not or did not see its way to becoming another Austria or Switzerland, a second-grade power in world terms, happy to look chiefly and solidly to its own affairs.

All this was exacerbated, needless to say, by the alarums and excursions of the cold war, and the adoption of sharply defined positions of belligerence. In 1947 Marshall Aid served formal note of the United States' desire to bolster the European economies as an essential antidote against the communist infection, and in 1949 the North Atlantic Treaty Organization (NATO) cast that view in avowedly military terms. It is true that welfare was frightening more timid spirits among British administrators with its costs: the National Health Service had, by 1950, exceeded its annual estimates of about £130 million to the tune of some £270 million, more than double. None the less, it is almost certain that the expenditure involved in retaining the kudos of acting as America's senior partner in the cold war inflicted, whatever its rights and wrongs, the greatest damage to the cause of welfarism. The crucial event was the Korean War, which broke out in 1950, which involved the nascent Chinese communist regime and which was widely believed to be a feint preceding major invasion by the USSR in Europe. There was a rapid agreement to a vast burgeoning of defence expenditure, to something like £5 billion over a three-year phase.

A graphic illustration of its effects is the dramatic switch from a balance of payments surplus of £300 million in 1950 to a balance of payments deficit of £370 million in 1951. At once, the sinews of the welfare state came under strain, politically as well as economically, and, although there may have been other reasons why no British 'economic miracle' occurred, this was the most fundamental. It meant that the will for and the design of a progressive and coherent welfare state would never again take centre stage, and that the demand for public provision of social remedies would always be in contention with economic and defence imperatives.

Common factors of social provision

The 'welfare state' was the coinage of the Oxford academic Alfred Zimmern, who used the term in 1934, as did Sir George Schuster, the economist, in 1937, and it was widely popularized by William Temple, the Archbishop of Canterbury. All of them counterpoised it against the 'power state', then common in the totalitarian countries of Europe, and not, as is sometimes supposed, against the free enterprise or capitalist state. It was couched, then, as a benign attempt to moderate the excesses of the market economy with a civic code of social amelioration. As William Temple's concern betokens, much of the moral fervour was Christian in tone, a reminder that Labour Party antecedents are, as has often been said, more Methodist than Marxist. There lies the first strand of continuity: since medieval times, the practical teaching and example of, at least, some elements of the Church have been a constant. Such doctrines have added a psychological cement to the edifice of essential responses to harmful social ills.

The welfare 'state'

'State' is as meaningful as 'welfare' in this seminal phrase. The 'power state' of fascist Germany, Spain and Italy, or of communist Russia, might claim to provide succour, through dictatorship, for all its members. This offered some threat to the parliamentary democracies, where untrammelled market forces were leaving too many people on the scrap-heap of social life. Once more we face the unwritten contract of society with its membership: that unspoken obligation to preserve the essential fabric of everyday life, lest the whole falter. Imagine, therefore, how powerful this emotion became in total war, when some of those very 'power states' clashed in hostile conflict with Britain. There was an intensification of the desire to protect and assist every citizen, so that each, in heart, body and mind, would be properly prepared for the fray. And this form of public obligation was to inform the immediate post-war mood, with its marked consensus in favour of state planning for the collective good.

It harked back to the days of Chadwick and before, if less starkly and more benevolently, with the acceptance that the effectiveness of the state lay largely in the efficiency and happiness of its citizenry, as its constituent members. In a real sense, the welfare state is more about patriotism than socialism; more about having a solid, peaceful and strong nation-state, rather than, for its own sake, an egalitarian community.

It is, then, scarcely surprising that there are continuities. The scenario of the 1945–51 welfare state as novelty – the sudden, bright golden dawn of positive equality for the political left, the abrupt dark dusk falling on personal independence for the political right – is a false one, the contrivance of myopic politicos. It is the strength of consolidation which should be stressed. Building on the insurance, welfare and medical services which already existed, and which had been – the Emergency Hospital Service, for example – further reformed and strengthened in the war, it was the welcome task of the Labour government to rule out anomaly and seek for coherence. It is likely that, in the 'reconstruction' post-war climate, a Conservative administration would have done likewise, if with less elan and commitment: indeed, the educational and family allowance statutes were achievements of the wartime coalition and 'caretaker' administrations. What is impressive is that, in massive numbers, the electorate looked to the party which had most lovingly embraced the concept of social benefits across the board.

The devices utilized to develop these peacetime reforms were, usually, well-tried ones. Education, social work and welfare, housing and police-work remained, however redefined, at the behest of the local authorities. The contributory principle of national insurance, first promulgated by the Reverend William Blackley as long ago as 1878, remained the base for the revised and expanded system of benefits, most still obtainable through the ubiquitous medium of the General Post Office. The near-exception was the National Health Service, where the prevailing mixture of municipal and voluntary hospitals gave way, not without much anguish, to a nationalized pattern. But the management of these by a network of district and regional bodies was reminiscent both of the Victorian affection for single-purpose authorities and of the wartime use of similar bodies for civil defence, fire brigade and food rationing, as well as hospitals themselves. In the human political journey, it is but a short step from the National Fire Service (created during the war to meet the needs of widespread fires caused by enemy action) to the National Health Service.

In terms of the traditional pairings of central/local dominion or cash/kind benefits, there is no doubt that, in each of those cases, the former triumphed. Apart from the hospitals, and although there were other compensatory jobs to do, the local authorities also lost to state control whatever gas and electricity installations they owned. There was less permissive legislation as well, which meant that the central authority insisted on local action, where once it might have merely offered the possibility. Hand in hand with this tendency, the proportion of money spent locally which emanated from the national exchequer as opposed to local rates grew, so that, all in all, the period marked a huge increase in central, not just in public, control.

Equally, the accent was on payments in cash through a whole series of benefits, with much less delivered in kind, although school milk and dinners and meals on wheels remained popular. The resort to institutional agencies, such as the workhouse, was also much less, certainly in cases of poverty and distress, even if residential care for some groups, such as dependent elderly people, remained. The major exception to this was the extension of municipal housing and new towns, in so far as that may be judged an 'institutional' solution. Most of the treatments were also *post hoc*, that is, they dealt with problems once arisen, the consequences often of faults in the economy or social conditions. It was this tendency which was to lead, almost inevitably, to the later condemnation of the welfare state as a 'dependency culture', in that it bailed out social casualties without equipping them as productive citizens.

The Beveridge Report

Clement Attlee, for many commentators the most effective peacetime premier of the twentieth century, pragmatically accepted this dosage of 'partial solutions and compromises' as being in line with the public will. If it were a revolution, it was a tidy, gradualist and incremental one. None the less, the speed and energy of the reforms were such that, *in toto*, they do register high on the political Richter Scale of seismic disruption. One reason for this was the Beveridge Report, published to great acclaim in 1943 – the nearest British society has ever come to accepting a social blueprint for its revision.

Sir William Beveridge identified the several possibilities of distress, such as employees, the self-employed, housewives, youngsters, retired people and disabled people. He then postulated a flat-rate benefit in each category, deploying the employer/employee/state formula for flat-rate contributions, and adding a means-tested safety net for miscellaneous or emergency assistance. He presumed that full employment would be guaranteed, if necessary, by state action, alongside the construction of national systems of health and housing.

With wages now improved and voluntary and charitable help not to be discounted, he believed, old-fashioned liberal that he was, that the 'thrift' motif of the contributory concept must prevail. Conversely, he ruled out the alternative, and more far-reaching, notion of providing a national minimum income by way of redistributive taxation. That would have been revolutionary, and would have required much greater control of fiscal and economic levers than has usually been envisaged. In short, there was rather a rounding-up of what existed into a neater entirety.

If there was a revolutionary precept alive and kicking, it was the idea of universalism. Beveridge, and other advocates of the welfare state, believed that all should pay and all might benefit. It was a give and take concept, different in kind to the older dispensation of social provision only for the middling and very poor, in practice the working classes. Out of wartime travail grew some decent recognition of the common bonding of citizenship. So, at the last, and with Labour Chancellors, like Sir Stafford Cripps, ensuring that the income gap, top to bottom, was probably narrower than it had ever been, this was a society in which most people had sufficient money in the pocket for daily requirements, but were heavily, and gratefully, dependent on communal resources for collective services, such as health and education. The balance between self-help and public provision took a decisive dip in favour of the latter over these years.

At the end, however, the process of accretion was still a potent instrument. Although the welfare state offered comprehensive public cover, it never attempted to replace private, that is, mainly commercial, provision. Despite the expansion of state education, the independent schools were left in business, large in prestige if small in number. Despite the creation of the NHS, private medical care was still permitted, and, in fact, it was only the compromise with consultants over their joint engagement to treat both public and private patients that secured professional endorsement of the National Health Service. Despite the more forceful approach to town and country planning and the spread of new towns and municipal housing, owner-occupation was left untouched and began to increase hugely; indeed, many felt that a basic fault of the Labour government was its failure, in spite of heavily cued reports and recommendations, to seize hold of land utilization as a fundamental prerequisite of a planned society. Despite the mushroom growth of state insurance schemes, no effort was made to interfere with private insurance arrangements (although the Labour Party did propose to nationalize the insurance industry at the time of the 1951 general election), and private insurance was, of course, to play a big role in British finance throughout the rest of the century. Despite the efforts made to render the legal system more accessible and less expensive to the ordinary citizen, the law was to stay much more in the prerogative of the well-to-do citizen.

The welfare legislation of the 1940s, large-scale although it undoubtedly was, never threatened the preserves of wealthier people and their scope to buy purportedly superior social and medical services, an obvious recipe for the continuance of a two-tier structure. As in social insurance, so it was across the new millenium. Everyone was assured of national subsistence in all sections of welfare, but no one was guaranteed the more egalitarian option of a national minimum – let alone optimum – common to all in these several social fields.

Approach to poverty

Turning to elaborate in more detail on each of the welfare state's finite components, the attack on poverty was, naturally enough, given much prominence. The Beveridge Report, the official title of which was *Social Insurance and Allied Services*, was something of a best-seller, its author the Chairman of the Committee on the Co-ordination of Social Insurance. It looked back a little to the 1930s, but that reflected the experience of its readers – it has to be said of the Beveridge reforms, and of all the 1940s reforms, that had they been more avant-garde, they might not have been accepted. What rankled was the messiness of the existing legislation, which still left 90,000 people, even in an era of full employment, on outdoor relief. By centralizing relief and making it comprehensive, the new system had the effect of abolishing the poor law.

As token of the consensus character of the times, it was the Churchill coalition government that passed the 1944 National Insurance Act, which established the necessary Ministry of National Insurance (and it was to be amalgamated with the War Pensions department, to become the Ministry of Pensions, in 1953); and it was the Churchill 'caretaker' government (which ran the country in the brief respite between the end of the wartime coalition and the election of the Labour government) which passed the Family Allowance Act in 1945. This break-through owed much to the vigorous campaigning of Eleanor Rathbone, a leading social analyst, against a background of worries about a declining birth rate. One of its effects was to maintain the differential between the wage-earning family and the family on benefit, about which argument continued to rage. Certainly the Conservative Party preferred this solution to anything smelling of a minimum wage. The act gave five shillings (25p) weekly to the second and subsequent child under school-leaving age, and has since become enshrined in the national life-style. Initially some three million families took up the benefit, at an annual cost of £59 million.

The major statute came in 1946, early in the life of the Attlee administration as befitted the priority it was given. It was masterminded by Jim Griffiths, as Minister of National Insurance, a politician whose name has fallen rather unfairly into obscurity. The act allowed for an array of benefits for sickness, unemployment and retirement, together with maternity, funeral – an absolutely new idea – widowhood and dependency grants. All over school age and under pensionable age (since 1940 reduced for women, because of the difficulties of their finding work, to 60, but still 65 for men) 'shall become insured under this Act': such was its universal nature. Jim Griffiths generously insisted on pensions being made available at the full rate immediately, as against Beveridge's more cautionary approach of a twenty-year sliding scale, and a five-year review of all the benefits was included.

In hard cash, 26 shillings (£1.30) was the standard weekly payment for sickness, for unemployment and for the retirement pension – with 42 shillings (£2.10) for a married pensioner couple. Two other acts completed the unifying scheme. The Industrial Injuries Act of 1946 nationalized the existing construct, run by employers and private insurers, and made it the responsibility of the new Ministry. The entire workforce was offered a weekly benefit of 45 shillings (£2.25), a relatively high amount. Then the 1948 National Assistance Act replaced the Assistance Board with the new National Assistance Board, as the means tested safety net for any who somehow fell through this now very coherent pattern of benefits. On 5 July 1948 almost all these proposals took effect: it might well have been called Beveridge Day.

The increases as from hitherto varied. There were only two shillings (10p) on the unemployment and eight shillings (40p) on the sickness payments, whereas, because of kindly Jim Griffiths, the pension leapt by sixteen shillings (80p). However, the chief consequence, it must be emphasized, was the regularity and the commonalty of the new system. Not that it was inexpensive. Including the National Health Service, the initial annual outlay was approaching £540 million, including £300 million from taxation, that is, apart from employee/employer contributions – and this was three times as much as had been found for such programmes in the 1930s. The combination of taxation and benefits did lead to some slight redistribution of income. Over the decade the purchasing power of the top 20 per cent of earners fell, roughly, by a quarter, this fraction being absorbed into the purchasing power of the rest of the population. It was a definite, without being a definitive, move.

Approach to ill-health

Health

The vesting day for the 1946 National Health Service Act was also 5 July 1948, making that date a veritable 'welfare state' day. First conceived of by the renowned social researcher and policy-maker, Beatrice Webb, at the time of the 1909 Poor Law Royal Commission, partially practised and fully theorized about during the Second World War, the National Health Service is famously associated with the Labour Minister of Health, Aneurin Bevan. He certainly ensured that the more willowy, but by no means hapless, proposals of the wartime coalition were subsumed within a more sweeping and dynamic package. It was, quite simply, as the health organization expert Rudolf Klein has indicated, 'the first health system in any Western society to offer free medical care to the entire population . . . it was a unique example of the collectivist provision of health care in a market society.'

First, Aneurin Bevan, perhaps advised by his senior civil servant, John Hawton, quickly determined to nationalize the 3,000 hospitals of England and Wales – and Scotland and Northern Ireland followed suit. This overturned, at a stroke, the then current proposal to leave them in local authority (about 1,700 plus hospitals) and private (about 1,300 plus) hands. Their overlapping and incoherent character made Bevan fearful for any coordinated outcome, short of central ownership. Funding was mixed and sometimes lacking, and few local authorities had fulfilled the intention of the 1929 Local Government Act, which, in ridding the nation of the old poor law administration, had aspired to a complete municipal hospital system. With hindsight, some would come to mock the monolithic rigidity of a central hospital service, but at that time it was probably the best option.

Second, these hospitals were organized under the aegis of Regional Hospital Boards, forerunners of the Regional Health Authorities of today. As some compensation for local authorities, bereft at the loss of the hospitals, what would now be called community medicine was concentrated in their grasp. Immunization and vaccination, ambulance services, health visiting, maternity and school health, including welfare foods, were clustered into the municipalities. Although the much-vaunted health centres for group practice were slow to get off the ground, the ubiquitous clinic more and more became the resort of mothers and young children. Furthermore, the 1948 Children's Act made all child care a municipal responsibility, while the National Assistance Act of the same year permitted councils to build what became known as Part III residential accommodation, principally for older people. Several of the seeds of future social service systems were being nurtured.

Third, the family practitioner service of doctors and dentists was established, including moves to locate medicos in areas of dire need. The British Medical Association fought a bitter struggle against Bevan right until the last minute. Although clinical freedom and independence from the local authorities was granted, Aneurin Bevan insisted that doctors should not be allowed to sell practices willy-nilly and that they should be paid a basic salary plus capitation fees per patient. Lord Moran, President of the Royal Society of Physicians, acted as something of a grey eminence apropos the consultants: Bevan had, in his own trenchant phrase, 'stuffed their throats with gold', securing their support with an agreement both to pay them a salary, something unknown to them, *and* to allow them private beds in NHS hospitals. The wheeler-dealing was successful, helped by the fact that the Lloyd-George 'panel' income, the bread-and-butter for many of Britain's 20,000 general practitioners, would abruptly cease on vesting day. As a result, by that juncture only 10 per cent of doctors had not enrolled for the NHS, and, by the end of 1948, 97 per cent of the population had likewise enlisted.

Fourth, the National Health Service was free. It was this grandiose principle which really set it apart from other schemes in many other countries. Costed at £130–150 million a year, it was destined to escalate its expenditure, as estimates of what people needed, and, as important, what people wanted, seemed woefully wrong. Not without long-lasting political tremors, involving the resignation of Aneurin Bevan, Harold Wilson and John Freeman from the Labour government, and with a massive rearmament programme in the offing, 1951 brought an early end to this free service. Prescription charges and payments for false teeth and spectacles were introduced by the Chancellor of the Exchequer, Hugh Gaitskell. For just three years Bevan's brave precept held, and the enormous take-up of the service was, as he was quick to point out, testimony to enormous need.

Even with these mutations, the National Health Service became accepted as part and parcel of British life. It is difficult now to persuade the younger generation of the change it wrought in everyday life, from a situation in which the onset of ill-health carried as much financial as medical anxiety, to one in which everyone felt reasonably confident in the search for care. Just two contrasting measures: since the coming of the NHS, infant mortality has dropped from 43 to 9 out of a thousand live births; and the percentage of people under thirty with no teeth of their own has fallen from 11 to 3 per cent.

Of course, it is widely recognized that health is dictated by the wholesale nature of one's environment and life-style, and there is no doubt that the national improvements in health owe a considerable amount to changes in social context. It has been said that huge increases, or, for that matter, huge decreases, in NHS expenditure result in only very marginal alterations in overall standards. One must return to the running thread of 'prevention' and 'cure', for the National Health Service has been criticized for being, in day-by-day practice, a national sickness service, the vast proportion of its resources devoted to reactive rather than proactive treatments.

For all that, the symbolism of the National Health Service, especially when its beacon was first lit against the gloom of post-war shortage and dilapidation, is positive and heart-warming. It was much admired in those days as an emblem of a society resolute in its aspiration to make good the peace, whatever the perils and hazards. A. L. Lindsay, the American commentator, has said that the NHS is one of the great achievements of the twentieth century.

Housing

Between the wars there had been much house-building, the majority of it in suburban owner-occupation. By 1939 there were 12.5 million houses in Britain, but nearly three-quarters of a million were destroyed or severely damaged by bombing, and a substantial number were in need of some attention. The authorities had overestimated the number of civilian casualties, but as seriously underestimated the demolition of property – there had been coffins galore, but little by way of resources for housing repair. There was also a rise in population, about to be augmented by the celebrated baby boom: marriages rose by a tenth and births by a third in the first post-war as opposed to the last pre-war years. Finally, there was also a backlog of things undone from the 1930s slum clearance programme, with a million families still in slum properties. Aneurin Bevan had responsibility in this field, such was the continuing perceived relation of health and housing, and there was talk of three-quarters of a million new houses very quickly, and as many as four million in the ten years after the war.

It was not so easy. Essential materials were in short supply, and the economic problems of the government were to affect the high-cost business of building. There was central control and licensing: the 1946 Acquisition of Land Act and the 1947 Town and Country Planning Act streamlined these processes a little, but there was never quite the same coherence of social policy as with welfare benefits or health care. At the top there was confusion among different ministries about these functions, with subsidies, land-use, supplies and so on never drawn into a sensible unity. Aneurin Bevan, although keen to see housing of quality for the working classes, was forced to leave much to the 1,700 or so local authorities of England and Wales, and they were, naturally, varying in size and interest. Suggestions for some kind of 'housing corporation' to organize the programme were not countenanced, strange to behold in a ministry which had insisted on a similar central agency for the delivery of the health programme. Or perhaps they had to accept that enough was enough, and that the local authorities and perhaps the public would stand for no more belabouring.

The upshot was an early reliance on temporary measures, such as the repair of about 125,000 unoccupied houses, the requisition and conversion of empty houses and the refurbishment of occupied houses, to the tune of another million units. Then there was the construction of 125,000 prefabricated houses, which endured, not without affectionate remembrance, for many years. There was even some squatting of, at its height, 50,000 people in about a thousand abandoned military installations.

As for new building, the Exchequer agreed to find three-quarters, not, as before, two-thirds, of the funding subsidy for council houses, the rest falling on the rates, and the approximate formula was urged of five such houses for every private dwelling to be constructed. Slowly, the houses were built, but never in the numbers forecast or required. In total, just over a million houses were built during the period of the Labour government, 970,000 being municipal completions and 180,000 private properties – so, at least, the public/private recipe was more or less observed. It should possibly be noted that the building industry itself remained wholly private, and did well out of all this activity.

Lewis Silkin, Minister of Town and Country Planning, took the initiative in terms of new towns, particularly needed to help solve metropolitan blight. The 1946 New Towns Act decreed a more sophisticated zoning of housing with its announcement of fourteen new towns, to join the existing handful, such as Welwyn Garden City. Eight were sited beyond London's green belt, Hemel Hempstead and Stevenage among them, and six were located regionally, including Cwmbran in Wales and East Kilbride in Scotland. It was, needless to say, in the nature of such ventures that they took many years to come to fruition, but, pre-empting later chapters, it might be added that, over the next generation, thirty-one new towns, including five in Scotland and four in Northern Ireland, and with well over two million inhabitants overall, were built.

This was the most forceful exhibition of direct intervention committed by the Labour government, perhaps, outside of war, by any government. In its very firmness of vision and action (not always popular – Stevenage railway station found itself wittily signposted 'Silkingrad') one may observe both the opportunities for and the barriers against concerted endeavour in the housing field. Without fundamental control of the land and its usage, without an overarching view of what socialized housing should provide, without access to and regulation over the building industry itself and its suppliers, without vigilant and precise power of the financial levers – without these requisites a national plan for housing, set in its fully developed environmental context, is well-nigh impossible.

It was a brave but somehow desperate series of ventures, by no means amounting to a failure, but symptomatic of the dilemma which faced the Labour government. Its predilection and its support called for a valiant righting of the many wrongs arising from a capitalist society, but it never had the will or, to be just, the mandate to reorder that kind of society at its base.

Approach to ignorance

The 1944 Education Act, eternally identified with R. A. Butler, the coalition Minister for Education, stemmed in theory from several pre-war documents, notably the 1926 Hadow Report on adolescent education and the 1938 Spens Report on secondary education, and, more immediately, from the 1943 Norwood Report and the White Paper *Educational Reconstruction* of the same year. This last publication claimed that 'in the youth of our nation we have our greatest national asset. Even on the basis of mere expediency, we cannot afford not to develop this asset to our greatest advantage.'

The 1944 Education Act

Apart from the religious question, which continued to generate heat and to remind of the place of the Churches in social history, there was precious little argument about the 1944 Education Act, and few major statutes have found their way into law with such amicable acceptance. It was perhaps the main purely domestic Bill to be presented by the wartime administration. The cynic might respond that this was, in part, because the Act was a clarifying, not a reforming, edict, putting into national words what had already happened locally.

Organizationally, it made the Board of Education into the Ministry of Education, and it regularized the position of the local education authorities, of which there were now some 150 in England and Wales. Not that the small Part III authorities were to be wholly denied: divisional executives were installed to supervise schools, albeit without any power to levy funds, within each LEA, while sizeable boroughs could act as excepted districts, with many powers, if not financial ones, allowed them. The potency of local pride is strong: many a divisional executive had been a Part III authority, and, prior to that, a school board.

As for the schools, what had been called the council or provided schools were retagged county schools, while the church or non-provided schools were relabelled aided, controlled or special agreement schools, depending on the degree of funding they obtained from the state. The only curricular resolution was that every child should attend daily a collective act of worship and weekly a lesson on religious instruction, with, as ever, an opt-out clause for the conscientiously offended parent. R. A. Butler had managed to tame the angry beast of the religious issue.

The main thrust of the 1944 Act lay in 'secondary education for all'. Fees in maintained secondary schools were abolished, and so was 'elementary' schooling. Henceforth, children would move through a primary school until the age of eleven, and then transfer to a secondary school. The school-leaving age was raised to fifteen as from 1945, but postponed until 1947, and then only accomplished through the insistence of the Labour Education Minister, Ellen Wilkinson. Although she never lit the fires under education that were expected of her, and although oppressed by many difficulties and encroaching death, she did push through this reform, with the aid of an Emergency Training Scheme, which recruited 35,000 teachers from war service, and inventive building and furniture projects. And there was a flurry of primary school construction, with over 900 such schools completed during the time of the Labour government.

Post-war schooling

In practice, the act tidied up a situation where some children were going to grammar schools, either with scholarships or as fee-payers, while the majority stayed at 'all-through' schools or went to 'senior' schools of various types. The act obliged LEAs to organize a two-tier system, and to add, although this remained more in the permissive arena, a further education tier. The Ministry had to approve such plans. What it did not do, and what it is sometimes assumed to have done, was to create the tripartite system of secondary education, whereby what were deemed to be the 'natural aptitudes' of children dictated that they should receive an academic grammar, a technical or a practical 'modern' secondary schooling.

However, the reports which preceded the passage of the 1944 Act all en-thused along these lines, and there was a tacit understanding that the new structure would be of this divisive kind. Thus the notorious eleven-plus examination became the standard practice, with its reliance on the intelli-gence test, then enjoying something of a vogue. Realistically, it is more exact to speak of a bipartite schools system, for, in most cases, the selection was the simple one of sending sheep to the existing grammar school and goats to the redesignated secondary modern. Although there was some urging of the delights of the multilateral school (with differing school types on the same site, the precursor of the more famous comprehensive school), it came to little. The first truly comprehensive school was opened in Windermere in 1945, but by 1951 there were no more than a score of such schools in England and Wales.

The education system thus served the six million children on its registers, about 13.5 per cent of the population. What is most apparent in education, as in all the other social services, is that substantial amounts of money were being expended. At the time of the 1902 Act, something like £14 million (£9 million taxes, £5 million rates) was spent on education, and that amounted to 1 per cent of the nation's gross national product. By 1950 this figure had grown to £272 million (£169 million taxes, £103 million rates), climbing towards 10 per cent of GNP. It followed the trend of increased state inter-vention, further exemplified by the doubling of civil servants during the Second World War to a total of 700,000.

There is no gainsaying that the 1940s, in education as much as in other fields, witnessed a mighty bound upward in respect of the sheer quantity of state control and resources.

Approach to crime

Predictably enough, the police service, like so many others, was subject to more centralized direction in war than in peace, and there were some temporary amalgamation of police forces for emergency purposes. The 60,000 regular police personnel, as of 1939, were expanded, by special, part-time and other means, to 250,000 for the duration of the war, and much of the civil defence of the nation was developed around them. In the provinces, for instance, the Chief Constable usually acted as Chief Warden, controlling the air raid wardens and the rest of the ARP (Air Raid Precautions) services.

The police and crime post-war

The 1946 Police Act, in the prevailing spirit of official tidiness, abolished all non-county borough police forces. A population was used as the rough yard-stick for the viability of an independent force, and, over the next years, there were 45 disbandments and 11 amalgamations. By the end of the decade there were 125 police forces in England and Wales, as against 183 in 1939. The gradual pressure of rationalities of scale was telling, and, here and there, the old local loyalties were being assailed.

As for crime itself, in 1939 there were 300,000 indictable offences in Eng-land and Wales, whereas in the early years of the century the average annual figure had been about 90,000. The figures rose steadily during the war, reach-ing 478,000 in 1945. There was a huge increase in larceny, breaking and entering and receiving, in some part a consequence of rationed goods and shortages and of abandoned or damaged buildings, all tempting the budding black marketeer or looter. Violent crime remained at a low level: there were just 29 convicted murderers in 1945.

The warning note struck was the dramatic wartime rise in offences com-mitted by the 8–17 echelon, up 70 per cent for boys and 120 per cent for girls. Families and communities dislocated by war may have been one expla-nation for this phenomenon. Non-indictable offences dropped by a half, to around a quarter of a million a year, but this was mainly owing to the spiralling drop in traffic offences, given petrol rationing and the absence of domestic cars from the roads. On the other hand, nearly a million people were charged during the war with black-out offences.

Surprisingly, crime then decreased during the late 1940s, by nearly 4 per cent in number of indictable offences, and by nearly 5 per cent when the rise in population is considered. Sadly, they were to bounce above half a million in 1951, and were scarcely to falter again in continuous increase. One may only guess at the reasons for this. One might postulate the resettlement of domestic and social life after the rigours of war; the fact of full employment; the absence of a flood of consumer durables to envy; and possibly the joint sense of discipline and cooperation engendered by the single-minded purpose of fighting a war. The causes of crime hover curiously between need and greed, with both poverty and affluence appearing to be factors. The 1945–51 period was more (to employ Aneurin Bevan's favourite adjective) 'serene' than most eras.

Law and order post-war

There was some movement in the field of law and order. The 1948 Criminal Justice Act abolished flogging as a magisterial punishment, although it was still permitted for offences in prison, and it advanced the idea and practice of probation. A move to suspend the death penalty was checked, and the already nationalized prison system was left largely untouched. There was, however, a rethink of the legal aid system. The age-old 'dock brief', whereby the impoverished prisoner received the aid of a usually not too able barrister for a guinea, had only been inadequately underpinned by statutes in 1903 and 1930 offering discretionary legal aid. Barely hundreds of people had benefited.

As with so many of the 1940s reforms, it was the war – and pressure from, for example, the Haldane Society of left-wing lawyers – which led to action. The 1949 Legal Aid and Legal Advice Act, advertised by the Attorney General, Sir Hartley Shawcross, as 'the charter of the little man' in terms of justice, pressed for Exchequer-funded aid to a wide group of people. Although still discretionary, the presumption now had to be affirmative. Because it was not initially pleasing to all judges and magistrates, and hit, like so many reforms, by fiscal crisis, it was 1955 before the scheme spread from the High Court and the Court of Appeal to the county courts.

A complementary proposal to develop law centres, alongside those sterling creations of wartime Britain, the Citizens Advice Bureaux, never received salient backing, but at least the concept of some degree of fairness in legal matters had been acknowledged. It remains, none the less, a final illustration, in this four-part round-up of the mechanics of the 1940s welfare state, that many of the revisions were, first, backward-looking, in the sense that they did no more than update, tidy and clarify extant propositions and sporadic practice from the 1930s, and, second, incremental, especially in the sense of seldom seeking to disturb the private status quo. The incursion of a moderate portion of legal aid into the judicial system somehow threw into more vivid light that vaster inequity, whereby the law was often subject to the purses and pockets of those required to use it.

In spite of the drab 'utility' culture and the several difficulties of those post-war years, the high days of the welfare state were characterized by a community life of, whatever else, reasonable safety and security. It was certainly a less dangerous milieu than existed throughout the nineteenth century, and than was to exist for much of the rest of the twentieth century. Martin Wiener, the American academic, has concluded, in his analysis of that time, that 'the English way of reconciling respect for individual liberty with a very high degree of public order and cooperation was the envy of the world. Rare was the foreign visitor who failed to remark upon the uncoerced yet pacific and law-abiding character of everyday life.' That is a proud epitaph for any society.

Comparative features

The notion that Britain created the first modern welfare state is, along with many another such judgement, a half-truth, chiefly predicated on the undoubted and shining symbol of the National Health Service. We have seen, in any event, that the welfare state was, at one level, a continuous rather than a novel process, and in Chapter 5 we watched similar machinery being deployed in other industrial states. The social policy analyst Robert Pinker has opined that national survival is the determinant, in war or peace, of state action apropos welfare: 'social policies are functionally necessary at a certain stage of economic growth, especially in urban industrial societies'.

Unsurprisingly, then, other nations were faced with the same problems as Britain, and, in fact, the policies piloted in Sweden and New Zealand had prompted some of the Labour Party's own thinking. Both New Zealand (1938–46) and Australia (1941–9) had elected Labour governments in the aftermath of the slump, and they had experimented with national insurance schemes. Once more it must be pressed that the Second World War acted in many areas, Britain included, as a catalyst engendering economic recovery. Even some more war-torn countries were ready for social reform: the post-1945 Norwegian coalition immediately picked up the pieces of that nation's 1930s Keynesian programme, while Japan enunciated its Living Protection Law, declaring the citizen's right to subsistence, as early as 1946.

Much of the provision was aimed at non-workers, such as old people, widows and children. Family allowances were often used to give some sufficiency to wages, whereas workers were naturally inclined to pursue the advantages of full employment on high wages. The democratic frame of a popular electorate and a trade union movement was obviously playing a part in all this activity, with the same elements as in Britain – a managed financial set-up, some help for essential industries and a reliance on full employment – very much to the fore. Britain led the way in terms of state health care because, elsewhere, the vested interests of the medical profession, the voluntary sector and private insurance companies ordinarily contrived to defeat the onset of universalism.

None the less, the full panoply of welfarism on a worldwide range was not to be paraded until the 1950s and the 1960s, and a larger section in the next chapter is devoted to the building of welfare states across the globe, and to a critical review of the implications of that development.

Specific features

The twentieth century has been called the century of the common man, and the Second World War and its immediate aftermath was perhaps the decade of the common man, at least in Britain. That is said pejoratively. It was not quite as overtly the decade of the common woman. There were swings and roundabouts on the fairground of the welfare state. Housewives were on the Beveridge list of potential social casualties, and the national insurance package, plus the family allowance legislation, was avowedly pro-woman. The health and welfare network was also of enormous comparative benefit, particularly when one recalls that women were the chief carers for both the very young and the very old. In short, they benefited indirectly through the assistance meted out to those for whom they had to take responsibilty.

There's the rub. The 1940s reforms were informed by an old-fashioned liberal conscience, and its progenitors – Attlee, Beveridge and company – were bred in the prim Victorian school of social commitment, precise and incorruptible according to its own lights, but necessarily limited. The welfare state improved the lot of women without changing it. It accepted the place of women in the home; indeed, the very 'cottage' houses and gardens, much loved by Labour housing ministers like Christopher Addison and Aneurin Bevan, are said by some to overemphasize the traditional woman's role. And it endeavoured to protect the wife, mother and home-maker with medical and welfare projects.

Conversely, and despite the vital contribution made by women as part of the war effort, the inequalities in employment remained or, where they had been moderated, were reintroduced. This applied both to access to posts and to the pay on offer. The education service stayed resolutely sexist, with the Norwood Report of 1943 waxing well-nigh lyrical about the different styles of boy and girl education, and in some degree this further closed the employment avenues for women. It was to be another generation before gender equity would force itself radically on to the political agenda, by which time two other groups – disabled people, who had, like women, made some material gains from the welfare state, and ethnic minorities, still insufficient in numbers to concentrate the political mind on their problems – would also begin making their rightful bids for a brighter place in the sun.

Conclusion

It is no accident that, in a study in which eight chapters cover many hundreds of years, one of those chapters reviews but ten years. In the history of British social welfare provision the 1940s are indeed a key decade. And, as the next chapter will describe, the 1940s welfare state, both at home and overseas, witnessed some general acceptance of its precepts and practices over a considerable time.

Advice on further reading

At the end of Chapter 5 a list of key books was promised, valuable for both that chapter and this.

Barker, P. (ed.) (1984) *Founders of the Welfare State*, Heinemann, London.
Birch, R. C. (1974) *The Shaping of the Welfare State*, Longman, London.

Hall, P. (1970) *The Social Services of Modern England*, Routledge, London.
Thane, P. (1982) *The Foundations of the Welfare State*, Longman, London.

These other more specialist books might be also be useful.

Critchley, T. (1967/1978) *A History of Police in England and Wales*, Constable, London.
Gosden, P. (1983) *The Education System since 1944*, Martin Robinson, Oxford.
Jewkes, J. and Jewkes, S. (1962) *The Genesis of the British National Health Service*, Blackwell, Oxford.
Klein, R. (1983) *The Politics of the National Health Service*, Longman, London.
Lawson, J. and Silver, H. (1973) *A Social History of Education in England*, Methuen, London.
Merrett, S. (1979) *State Housing in Britain*, Routledge, London.

It should be readily recognized that several of these studies cover far more than the events covered by the last two chapters. It is recommended that this is the appropriate time to refer to them, for, normally, they place the 1940s in a succinct context.

7 The Butskellite consensus (c.1951–1973/9)

Summary

For about a quarter of a century there was a general support for and further application of the welfare precepts of the post-war settlement. This often involved a massive outlay of funding on public works, while there was the continuing, if occasionally uneasy, partnership of central and local authorities in the implementation of welfare programmes. The upshot was the creation of what has been called 'mercantile collectivism', a coherent option of social democratic tendency, neither statist (that is, with strong central state controls and motivations) after the Eastern European model nor classically free market.

In each of the four fields under review, two features were apparent: first, the insistence on a reactive and specialized response, usually to the symptoms of the problem (e.g. medical treatment as disease presented itself); and, second, the rediscovery of the 'problem' (e.g. a new manifestation of poverty).

By this time, the rest of the developed world, and beyond, had become heavily engaged with welfare projects on the Beveridge/Keynes basis. Moreover, there was a sharpening alertness to the questions raised by disability, gender and ethnicity.

Some modern jargon emerges in this chapter: social democracy – mercantile collectivism – corporate state – giantism – Butskellism – state capitalism – statism – anocracy – bureaucracy and dilettantism – allopathic and naturopathic medicine – selective and comprehensive schooling – consensual and military policing.

Social and economic background

It has always been erroneous, in academic discussion, to divorce welfare from economic policy. It has been urged in these pages that, as a general rule, societies are moved to social amelioration projects under the duress of likely social fracture, the complement to that being the wherewithal so to act. It is, plainly, not enough to have the will, let alone the compulsion; there must also be the material resources available. The twenty-five or so years after the Second World War constituted a period in which there seemed to be more of a plenitude than hitherto of such resources, along with a relatively more conscious attempt to align social and economic practices than had normally been the case.

Corporate state; corporate economy

Although the energy and rail utilities were drawn into public control, no serious effort was made to command the economy in overriding fashion. None the less, principally through financial leverage, there was considerable influence exerted over the British economy of a Keynesian brand. Britain remained a capitalist country, wedded to private enterprise, but with the classical formula of *laissez-faire* (which had never, as we have noted, reigned exclusively supreme) tempered by fiscal management. This certainly led to fits and starts – devaluation of the pound in 1967, reckless expansion of the money supply in the early 1970s, for instance – in the economic journey, sometimes scornfully derided by critics, to right and left, as a stop–go economy.

Even allowing for instances of industrial unrest and allied problems, there was never, when assessed against the longer perspective, outrageous boom or slump. The trade union movement, emerging from the Second World War with wage levels, thanks in the main to Ernest Bevin, at reasonable levels, enjoyed a major share in the general governing process. In this period the trade unions reached their peak of membership – 55 per cent of the working population – and influence. It was a time in which the various interest groups found, by and large, scope for joint and consensual decision-making, with the underlay of welfare benefits and services very much part of the deal.

Industry grew more corporate in nature. In 1900 the top hundred firms had accounted for less than 15 per cent of the nation's output. Such was the transformation into a more concentrated structure that by the 1970s the top hundred companies were responsible for a half of manufacturing output. Such large, sometimes monopolistic, corporations were not unlike the public utilities, such as the National Coal Board or British Rail, in size and style, so that 'giantism' was a looming feature of the economic landscape. In many ways, this 'corporate economy' eased the negotiations for the 'corporate state'.

It was also a time of paradox. Britain had been exhausted, first by the war and next by the pursuit of world status, particularly in terms of defence expenditure, on the back of a second-class economy. During this period, the old Empire was dismantled and liberated, with little bitterness compared with the exploits of other ex-imperial powers, but a sure sign that Britain lacked the capacity (to be just, also, for many people, the desire) to rule over a far-flung set of colonies. Anthony Eden's futile adventure at Suez in 1956 underpinned this combine of inability and unwillingness, and symbolized the termination of Britain's place as a global power. Other economies, notably those of West Germany and Japan, where the mood and creed of corporate state management were dominant, were notably successful, and Britain looked to be a subordinate in every way.

Affluent society

For all that, living standards rose dramatically, and, as Harold Macmillan, the Conservative leader who followed Winston Churchill and Anthony Eden as premier, was quick to observe, ordinary people had 'never had it so good'. Although the distribution of wealth had scarcely altered (the top 20 per cent of the population had a 92 per cent share of the country's wealth in 1938; it had only fallen to 86 per cent in 1972), prosperity was widely enjoyed. A startling and emblematic testimony to that was the increase in house ownership. By the late 1970s, two-thirds of skilled, a half of semi-skilled and a third of unskilled workers owned their own homes, a mammoth change from the private and public rented tenancies of the 1930s and 1940s. By the same juncture, a half of manual workers owned a car, and the refrigerator and the continental holiday had become the norm.

Some of this accumulating affluence was reflected in occupational structure. In the Edwardian period, manual workers numbered about 80 per cent, leaving no more than 20 per cent as non-manual workers, including roughly 10 per cent in the professional and clerical brackets. By the 1970s, there were over 40 per cent non-manual workers, with no less than 25 per cent in the professional and clerical groups, and with manual workers down, in approximate terms, to 60 per cent. Vocationally and culturally, there was thus what has been titled an 'embourgeoisement of the proletariat'. This was to have political effects, some of them in respect of social welfare. In spite of many problems, some element of economic growth, decent wage and salary payments, and a perhaps grudging acceptance of tax and rate bills higher than pre-war levels, cycled to preserve and extend the cash and the kind offered by the welfare state.

It did appear as if Britain, alongside many other developed nations, had discovered some compromise basis for the furtherance of old-style capitalism. An affluent economy, massaged and oiled by governmental financial management, was able to invest in an expensive welfare fabric, largely supported by governmental financial subsidies: the one paid for the other; the other made tolerable the one.

In fact, it was more complicated than that. An aspect of this socio-economic partnership is that the funding of the welfare state needs to be judged as economic as well as social. A crucial component in the equation was the number of people employed in the health, education and welfare businesses during this time. For example, the numbers, full- and part-time, employed in health and education services rose between 1961 and 1974 from 1.7

million to nearly 3 million. Some commentators have said that this relatively cheap investment (in that it did not involve very expensive plant of
an industrial kind) was to the detriment of the British manufacturing base.

Whatever the truth of this, it must be recognized that the expansion of the
welfare workforce was, in due part, an economic measure, which helped in
no insubstantial manner to sustain the principle of full employment – and,
of course, it was on the foundation of full employment that the Beveridge/
Keynes school built their promised land. It is simple enough to spot when,
as in the 1980s, government attempts to cut services for economic reasons:
it should not be forgotten that government may also invest in services for
similar reasons.

All in all, the political administrations of the age, be they Conservative
(with Alec Douglas-Home and later Edward Heath as prime ministers) or
Labour (with Harold Wilson and, briefly, James Callaghan), struggled through
until 1979, as managers of public finance and public welfare. Of course,
there were differences of emphasis in the social fields, perhaps most noticeable
in relation to education, while the Labour Party was also keener than the
Conservative Party to press for personal freedoms in such areas as divorce or
homosexuality. But, by and large, there was a considerable degree of common ground. It was not inexpensive ground. Between 1960 and 1980 public
expenditure rose by 100 per cent, two-thirds of that increase being devoted
to welfare programmes – but both Labour and Conservative were participants
in this bonanza.

Common factors of social provision

This consensus about the welfare state, with the political parties arguing
about its degree rather its kind, was nicknamed Butskellite, after R. A. Butler
and Hugh Gaitskell, high ranking and moderate figures in, respectively, the
Conservative and Labour Parties. Although neither became prime minister,
they came to represent the common view that the welfare state, in its broad-
est sense, was right in concept and practice. It was widely accepted that the
modern industrial state had this obligation to succour its citizens and
provide a sensible range of services.

The growth of welfarism

During this period, there were many initiatives and experiments, but little,
if anything, was added or subtracted from the fundamental nature of
welfarism. A phrase often quoted at this time, most frequently in the educational field, was 'equality of opportunity'. Although most flinched at the
thought or implementation of economic equality, the liberal view was
forcefully expressed that everyone should have the chance to realize his or
her best self and not be inhibited from this by barriers of health, wealth or
other such obstacles. The universalism of services and benefits was amply
justified on these grounds, and the complementary rationalization was the
advantage that accrued to society.

The nursery rhyme desideratum of men and women being 'healthy, wealthy and wise' might be procured, then, through the public nurture of all, so that energies and gifts might be fruitfully used for the greater good of the commonwealth. The metaphor of the garden, and of the cultivation of sturdy seedlings, was much utilized to describe this phenomenon. Less sentimentally, one might claim that the state was buying the support of the electorate and of organized labour through social provisions.

We have seen already that it was an era of large expenditure on resources and personnel – and this remained the dominant feature. Economic growth accounted for about three-quarters of the increase in public expenditure, the other quarter being found from extra taxation, direct and indirect, so much so that by the late 1970s the public sector fraction of the gross national product stood at over a half. The staff of the public sector was correspondingly large. Excluding the personnel of nationalized industries, like coal, railways and the Post Office, and concentrating merely on those employed in health, education and public administration, the total was still a staggering third of the working population in 1981. A hundred years previously it had been less than a tenth.

It is necessary to ponder on the depth and extent of this public momentum, of which the social welfare element was but a part, albeit a major one. It did mean that the population was largely attuned, from birth until death, from dawn until dusk, to living in a society characterized by governmental edict and decree. There is little doubt that 'administrative procreation', the term given to the propensity of bureaucracies to expand, was responsible for some of this, but, in general, it meant that people were very comfortably adjusted to the notion of welfarism among this array of public provision.

The old dichotomies were unmoved, as universalism took root. There were new institutions, among them a series of new universities and the doom-laden experiment in municipal high-rise building. But there were also new domestic and personal services – this was the heyday of the social worker and the local authority home help. There were new benefits in cash – during the 1970s there were over forty means-tested benefits available, ranging from university grants to wigs – and there were new treatments in kind – the establishment of social services departments or the introduction of comprehensive schooling are illustrations of this.

Above all, the balance of central and local direction was maintained. It was sometimes uneasy, especially when local and national politics became entangled, with, for instance, a Labour government trying to persuade Conservative local councils to adopt comprehensive education. None the less, it persevered, the centuries-old agreement that the state would lay down the overall strategy and the municipality fill in the local tactics holding good. That bipartite arrangement was reflected in the financial distinction between grants from taxation for local services and rates locally levied, although, increasingly, the former were assuming a larger proportion of the whole.

The 1972 Local Government Act reorganized local government, so that, from 1974, the English and Welsh system of counties, county boroughs, boroughs and even smaller authorities was made redundant. Instead a pattern of shire counties was scheduled, with some devolution of powers to districts, and with, in the great conurbations, the metropolitan counties, with subordinate metropolitan districts. A year later, Scotland (which had adopted a county council system similar to England's in 1889, revised in 1929) was divided into a small number of regions, and two-tier governance arranged there also.

London underwent its separate reorganization earlier, this taking effect from 1965, with the Greater London Council holding in some sway a group of semi-autonomous London boroughs. This was an attempt to construct local entities according to economies of scale, much criticized for its apparent lack of organic understanding of the historic and cultural sense of identity felt by many people. Nevertheless, the essential central/local partnership for the delivery of public services was not lost.

The welfare state debate

There was much academic cogitation over the precise nature of the welfare state, especially as it spread its effects on a worldwide basis and, equally significantly, as economic activity became ever more enmeshed in international webs. During the post-war boom, international trade grew one and a half times as fast as world output, and the multinationally located company became commonplace. None the less, the nation-state maintained and extended its predominant position as the ambit for political and other activity, and welfare, its size and style, may only be assessed within that context. And the grim definition of the nation-state by the great sociologist Max Weber – 'a human community that (successfully) claims the monopoly of the legitimate use of physical force within a given territory' – is as competent a base for discussion as one may find.

Max Weber believed this dispensation of 'legitimacy' and 'territoriality' to be the prerequisite, not the consequence, of capitalist enterprise, and, in lay terms, as we noted in Chapter 2, the joint emergence of the commercial motif and the autonomous state. Weber also remarks on the essential nature of a central administration and on how, in the sense of rational efficiency, 'bureaucracy' is preferable to 'dilettantism' in private as well as public agencies. Many commentators have dilated on what Theda Skocpol, the political scientist, has called the 'Janus-faced' pluralism, the many-sided nature, of the complex modern state, with many interests vying for a share of the spoils, and with representative democracy having a role in this brokerage of power and resources. The political analyst Michel Foucault has concluded that the state 'consists in the codification of a whole number of power relations which render its functioning possible'.

Another angle on this profound debate is to see the advance of welfarism, within this complicated network of relationships, as adding social to the political (that is, the franchise) and civic (that is, legal and national protection) rights already established. The well-known historian E. H. Carr has described this march of nationhood, from what Lassalle famously called 'the night-watchman state' to a much more heavily socialized involvement, with every citizen, as individual and through collective means, engaged.

What is striking is the sustained hegemony of the state as a piece of political apparatus. The late eighteenth and nineteenth century answers to political questions had been couched in anti-state terms. In the United States Thomas Jefferson had pressed for 'frugal government', based on an 'agrarian democracy' in which, in picturesque mood, no one was sited so close to his neighbour that he could hear his dog bark. In Britain the utilitarians had argued that the state clumsily impeded the fluent intercourse of the human search for happiness, and that its shackles should be sloughed off in favour of *laissez-faire*. The socialistic doctrines, principally the Marxist variant, criticized the state as the weapon of class oppression, arguing that only when, in Fredrich Engels's vivid phrase, it 'withered away' would men and women find perfect release and satisfaction. To both the left and the right of the political spectrum existed this 'anocratic' vision of people freed from the interference of the state.

Nowhere did it truly come to pass, however. Although, in the early aftermath of the 1917 Russian Revolution, Lenin piloted exercises in communalist administration, through the original 'soviets' or local citizen and worker self-management, Russia quickly reverted to a centralized state of unprecedented power. As Nicos Poulantzas, an analyst of these trends, has concluded, 'history has not yet given us a successful experience of the democratic road to socialism'. Before that, as the economic historian Barry Supple has concisely made clear, most states, rather than adopting a *laissez-faire* stance, had reconstructed their institutions for a capitalist and industrial setting. For example, by 1875 Germany had built 28,000 kilometres of railway under state direction, with half of it actually owned by the state. Even the purported non-interference of the British government was 'negative interference', resting on an alert awareness that free trade was, at that time but not later, the most effective mode for the pioneer industrial economy.

The mercantile collectivist state

In summary, all states are interventionist, although some are more interventionist than others. The Russian and East European communist states of the post-war era certainly directed their economies strictly but, in one sense, this was no more than a series of steps down the path already taken by the western democracies: hence the soubriquet of 'state capitalism'. Fascist and pseudo-communist countries might be more rigid in their mechanics than the shifting, bargaining liberal-democratic nation-states, but the corporatist tendency was common to all.

In 1941 James Burnham, in his now strangely neglected *The Managerial Revolution*, observed this phenomenon, and commented on the fashion in which all urbanized, industrialized states converged, whatever their outward show of political colouring and plumage, to the norm. Each deployed a techno-bureaucratic officialdom of experts, diffusing conflicts, securing public compliance, negotiating decisions, in a way which Max Weber would instantly recognize as 'completely indispensable' professionalism.

It is against this general canvas of the corporate or bureaucratic state that the important welfare aspects must be judged. In his 1979 study, *The Idea of Welfare*, Robert Pinker is succinctly able to mount the case for a third and, in the light of the foregoing analysis, dominant precept for welfare politics. He does not see the loosely social democratic version of Beveridge and Keynes as a vague compromise between the classical free market economy and the statist 'oriental despotism', as it has been called, of so-called communism in Eastern Europe. Rather, he views this as an upstanding and integrated model in its own right. With a mixed economy, associated with pluralist values and mitigating social reforms, it offers a happier outcome than the extreme ideologies of rampant capitalism and outright statism, both likely in practice to 'become instruments of oppression and diswelfare'. It is perhaps interesting that the advocates of both those ideals view this model with anxiety, the free marketeer seeing it as an impediment to natural liberties and economic growth, the communist castigating it as a dupe and a snare of the working classes.

Nothing much changes. These were the positions adopted by the appropriate nineteenth-century protagonists. In everyday practice, what Robert Pinker has termed 'mercantilist collectivism' became the mainstream methodology. And the use of the word 'mercantilist' is valuable, for it strikes the memory-chords of early modern history, when the burgeoning nation-states believed firmly in the doctrine of mercantilism, the creed which committed them to the defence and fruitful development of the realm as the end of good government.

The increase in bureaucratic practice

This continued devotion to the sanctity of the nation-state, in its urban and industrial guise, was, as we have noted, typified by the abundant extension of bureaucratic expertise and officialdom. This highly professionalized mode of operation, for all its merit in terms of effective management, had its down-side. It promoted – it may even have originated – the feature of the specialized and, usually, reactive response. This occurred as services became more compartmentalized, centrally and nationally, and as, in pursuance of the normal evolution of their kind, these services became organized by increasingly specialized cadres of professionals.

Some of this trend has been described in previous chapters, observed as 'cure' being preferred to 'prevention', with provision being deployed to dowse flames (to change the metaphor) rather than to prevent fire. But it went further than that. Even within the 'curative' connotation, there was a strong tendency to adopt a single solution, the accepted stock-in-trade of the relevant professional. In medicine, in teaching, in social work, in housing, in crime prevention, this singularity or near-singularity of the received professional wisdom may be discerned. Not only was the symptom not treated until it made itself rudely manifest, not only was the symptom treated rather than the disease, but the treatment itself was often restricted to the one professional certitude.

The worst aspect of this was the non-contextual character of social provision throughout this period. It was rarely assessed and delivered in any universal or environmentally orientated manner. It has been forcefully pressed in this study that the civilized world is heir to social ills, and that these arise, and cannot be divorced, from that world. Sickness, homelessness, poverty, ignorance, crime – they are severally linked together and substantively conjoined with their social context. Their narrow, specific and overly professionalized treatment was, then, the darker side of a social medallion, which, in truth, was otherwise often brighter and more progressive.

For some while this tendency masked the underlying persistence of the problems, the carefully targeted goals of equal opportunity having been separately met. Schools and colleges for all, or free medicine for all, or welfare benefits for all, gave all the chance to fulfil their destiny, or so it was hoped.

By the 1960s, however, it was realized that life was not as mechanistically simple as that, and, one by one, the problems were, in the vogue word of that time, 'rediscovered'. On the one hand, it was demonstrated that with a universalist set of services the well-to-do were strategically placed to glean more advantage than the less well off, and health care was a particular instance of this. On the other hand, because of the interrelated nature of social action and reaction, the social environment continued to dictate outcomes to a compelling degree, with relative poverty reappearing in major part, housing continuing to act as a divider rather than a welder of communities and crime rearing an even larger and uglier head.

The two effects were, of course, closely connected. It was shown, for example, that educational attainment was intimately linked with a middle class ability both to grasp and utilize the system more effectively, and to provide the home background which enabled children to reach high standards. In short, what was exhibited in the round was the truth that, however welfare reforms might modify the harshness of society, they do not change its fundamental structure. Equality of opportunity was shown to be a chimera without something more closely resembling equality of social and economic conditions.

These reflections will be uppermost in mind as each of the main four elements of the welfare state are examined. Within the context of mercantile collectivism, the chief traits of each, during this 1951–73/9 era, will be scrutinized, paying particular attention to the professional specialism in each case and the sense in which the problem was 'rediscovered'.

Approach to poverty

The main changes

Money poured into the welfare system by way of benefits. Using 1980 prices as the calculator, thereby avoiding the distortions of inflation, the real sums involved almost trebled, from about £8 billion in 1960 to over £22 billion in 1980. The pension bill alone catered for half of this growth, increasing from £3.75 billion to £10.75 billion. It is estimated that, overall, the increases were owing in equal part to more people and better benefits. There was a similar growth in personal social services, much of it directed at helping those in social and allied distress. The jump was enormous: £425 million in

1960, £2.25 billion in 1980, over five times as much, again in real terms. Together the bills for social security and social services made up over two-fifths of the growth in public expenditure on social matters over that 20-year period.

During this same era there were a number of alternations in the arrangements for delivering benefits. In 1966 the Ministry of Social Security was established, along with the Supplementary Benefits Commission. These replaced the Ministry of National Insurance and the National Assistance Board, in an attempt to bring more coordination to the system, and to avoid the now sourly viewed word 'assistance'. In 1968 these responsibilities and those of health were drawn together under the aegis of the Department of Health and Social Security.

Locally, welfare provision was in the hands of the new social services departments, known in Scotland as social work departments. The social services departments were formed under the 1970 Local Authorities Social Services Act, which, in chief part, was pursuant to the 1968 Seebohm Report on Local Authority and Allied Personal Social Services. This had expressed a desire to see not only rationally organized departments but also properly qualified social workers, preferably of generic, and not specialized, type. The rather haphazard training of such officers had been improving, and it now gained in impetus with the inauguration of the Central Council of Education and Training in Social Work in 1971, and the launch of nationally accredited professional qualifications. By 1980 there were some 170,000 full-time equivalent staff in personal social services. They included: 25,000 social workers, of whom about three-quarters were qualified; 50,000 residential care workers, of whom 15 per cent were qualified; 8,000 day care and 6,000 probation and after-care officers; not forgetting 13,000 in the ever-striving voluntary and charitable sector.

There were also changes in the fabric of the benefits system. The 1966 National Insurance Act made benefits other than the state pension earnings-related, and in 1973 the contributions, which were no longer flat-rate but income-related, were collected through the more rigorous device of the tax system. In 1970 the Family Income Supplement Act had to be introduced, a statute almost Speenhamland-like in mode, for it offered grants to parents with poorly paid jobs. In 1975 the Child Benefit Act replaced family allowances and the child tax allowance, in an endeavour to target the funding more directly at the mother and child.

The 1975 Social Security Pension Act, passed by Harold Wilson's Labour administration, which came into force in 1978, was a major piece of legislation, the end product of much political bickering and dickering over the thorny topic of pensions. It continued to offer a flat-rate state pension, but with a supplement based on earnings, optimally 25 per cent of final earnings, and an accrual period of 20 working years. This was the state's answer to the growing weight of private occupational pensions, and the anxiety that the income gap in retirement (observed as a class overtone, in that manual workers tended not to enjoy pension rights) was widening. It was made possible for those in private schemes to contract out of the State Earnings Related Pension Scheme (SERPS).

The specialist treatment

Although the social services departments locally provided a modicum of help in kind – around this time 130,000 home helps were making a million annual visits to people's abodes – money remained the principal method of alleviating social casualty. Indeed, the day centres and meals services, for all their infinite variety, were reaching only 4 and 3 per cent of the elderly population respectively, while residential care homes, including the private and voluntary sections, were accommodating about 4 per cent of the older people, much the same percentage as were 'institutionalized' in 1900. Thus the arguments about domestic versus institutional mechanics, or care versus kind, fade rather into the shadows when one is confronted by a figure of £22 billion expended on social security in 1980.

There had been infringements on the purity of Beveridge. Jim Griffiths had dodged the 20-year phasing in of the new old age pension envisaged by the insurance-orientated Beveridge. For all its kindness of spirit, this had effectively destroyed the 'insurance' system. In fact, so much money was immediately needed for pensions that Britain had – and so it has remained – a pay-as-you-go system masquerading as an insurance system. The national insurance contributions became, in effect, a tax used for current expenditure, not saved and invested against personal retirement, unemployment and so on – and, at this time, they had to be supplemented with over a half of what was required from other taxation. There had also been breaches in the Beveridge desire for universality, notably where flat-rate contributions and, as in the case of pensions after 1979, benefits became earnings-related.

However, the abiding characteristic of the Beveridge settlement was, despite the enormous amount of money dished out, its lowness. Couched as temporary props against short-lived interruptions to full employment, they were constructed as subsistence payments. Given the tolerant view that they should be both paid for and received by all, the contributions, and thus the payments, tended to remain on the small side. Over the period the interplay of inflation, wage rises and consumer spending did nothing to help. The vagaries and expensiveness of housing costs added further problems. The upshot was that benefits were usually found to be below subsistence levels, with no chance at all of keeping pace with changing social conditions.

Benefits over this time were, in very rough terms, about 30 per cent of average earnings. To take the example of the old pension, which, as we noted in Chapter 5, had at its installation 'nationalized' but not increased the old-style poor relief, it remained at about a quarter of the annual manual worker's wage. Compare the £36.00 old age pension of 1985, as a fraction of the then average wage of £150.00, against the original pension of five shillings (25p) as a proportion of the average wage in 1908 of 25 or 30 shillings (£1.25/£1.50).

Those in poverty constantly required supplementary benefits to make good their social security payments and bring them up to subsistence levels. Beveridge's hope was that, with full and well-paid employment and reasonable thrift and prudence on the part of British citizens, the need for public assistance would diminish. Like previous devout wishes of social reformers

– compare this with the view of nineteenth-century poor law advocates that they would obliterate the poor rate by forcing idlers on to the labour mart – it was doomed to disappointment. It amounted to a blinkered, over-specialized approach to poverty, unwilling or unable to study it holistically, capable only of providing the drip of money when the extreme case of impoverishment was diagnosed.

The rediscovery of poverty

All these eventualities led naturally to the conclusion that poverty was not a slain giant. Social scientists like Peter Townsend and agencies like the Child Poverty Action Group were active in emphasizing that the welfare state, for all its excellent aims and practice, had assuaged and not destroyed poverty. William Beveridge had, to be fair, never believed that unemployment would vanish entirely, for the matching of people and jobs is rarely an exact science even at the best of times. However, from 1940 onwards, employment had been as near full as might realistically have been expected. A main cause of continuing poverty was that age-old bugbear, the long-standing condition of low pay. Women remained particular sufferers, while they were also the chief victims of marital disruption, whether caused by widowhood or separation and divorce. Disabled and elderly people were others finding economic life hard and difficult.

In summary, where in 1948 there had been 1.5 million claimants for what was then the topping-up of national assistance, there were as many as five million in the late 1970s. Of course, these included the recipients of new benefits, such as the million people in receipt of rate rebates by the end of the 1960s – it was, as we have observed, a period when benefits were widened and improved. None the less, Peter Townsend estimated that, in the late 1960s and beyond, 6–9 per cent of the population were in poverty, and as many as 22–28 per cent were close to the quasi-official poverty line, measured in terms of the need of supplementary income.

The definitions of poverty remain nebulous, ranging from the absolute yardstick of very basic subsistence to the more relative criterion of an ability to maintain something akin to a normal life-style. Even allowing for these technical and philosophic posers, it may still be concluded that, while social welfare schemes had certainly helped many, they had not permanently arrested the curse of poverty or made inroads into the general circumstance of inequality.

The gap between rich and poor remained as wide as, if, possibly at this stage, no wider than, at the end of the Second World War, but any attempts to redistribute income in any basic fashion – such as a realistic minimum wage, a definitive wealth tax or even the ambitious, but failed, essay in major pension reform advanced by Labour's Richard Crossman in 1957 – came to nothing. The improvements in the labour market did mean that what is sometimes called primary poverty had diminished: unlike in the past, the majority of those in full-time, tenured work were in receipt of reasonable and, just as meaningful, regular income. But this still left a sizeable proportion of the population in a condition of poverty.

Approach to ill-health

The main changes

The health service proved to be a voracious maw – as, indeed, did public housing, a topic which will be addressed as a separate issue at the end of this section. Again using 1980 valuations to give real comparisons, spending on health nearly trebled in the 20 years from 1960 to 1980, that is, from £4.5 billion to £11.5 billion, equal to a fifth of the total growth in public expenditure over that phase of soaring finance. Everything burgeoned: patients' expectations; techniques and drugs, the real cost of which rose by 50 per cent in this period; professional employment, including 15 per cent more general practitioners and 25 per cent more dentists, but also including a huge number of ancillary workers. The National Health Service became one of the world's biggest employers – in the mid-1970s it had a million employees.

So mammoth an organization, expending possibly 5 per cent of national wealth annually, naturally attracted considerable research and criticism, including a Royal Commission (1974–9) and, through the 1973 National Health Service Act, an administrative shake-up in 1974. This tried to meet the fragmented character of the NHS by creating a three-tier managerial structure of 14 Regions, 98 Area and 201 District Health Authorities in England and Wales, alongside which 98 Family Practitioner Committees and 201 Community Health Councils, with a consumer orientation, operated. The District Authority, based on an average population of 200,000, employed a community physician as its overall adviser, and was usually grouped around the district general hospital.

In effect, the National Health Service, true to its late Victorian antecedents, was firmly welded to the hospital – there were now about 2,500 NHS hospitals – as the centrepiece of the whole enterprise. But, to its great credit, the NHS won and sustained a high level of satisfaction among its users over this extended period, and became a valued part of the social fabric. Between 1974 and 1981 there were, in rough terms, a 5 per cent increase in outpatient attendances, a 10 per cent increase in prescriptions, hospitalization and dental courses, and a 20 per cent increase in eye tests.

The specialist treatment

There is little doubt that in the post-war era the standards of health improved. Although these were not quite as good as in some comparable countries, the 1960–80 period showed a decline in infant mortality from 22 to 12 deaths per thousand live births, while the same period witnessed a decrease in many diseases which had ravaged social life in the nineteenth and early twentieth centuries: tuberculosis, diphtheria, polio and a variety of infectious complaints are examples of this. Yet it is difficult to judge how much this is owing to the instrumentality of the health services and how much to the general improvements in social life.

This leads to some commentary on the abiding 'biological' character of medicine, and its classic approach to the treatment of the sick individual, rather than, to pose the other extreme, the furtherance of a healthy society. It is claimed that 90 per cent of NHS resources are spent on cure rather than prevention, and for some commentators the criticism goes deeper than that. It is argued that medical practice is hazardously restricted to 'allopathic' treatment, that is, a method 'which treats disease by inducing an opposite or contrary condition', through drugs or surgical practice.

It is suggested that its merits have been exaggerated (for instance, tuberculosis had fallen to a tenth of its Victorian incidence before the use of the much-vaunted streptomycin drug); that it sidelines the use of alternative 'naturopathic' medicine, which works holistically with the body, rather than specifically against it; and that it introduces iatrogenic or 'doctor-induced' illness. It is certainly true that the NHS had the effect of bringing free allopathic medicine to the entire population, and that, apart from a medical profession wedded inexorably to its use, we inhabit a 'medicalized' society, with patent medicines and other such accessories rampant.

It is equally evident that, whereas the nineteenth-century public health movement fought vigorously to rid the nation of communicable diseases through an adherence to hygienic codes, there was a similar need for an environmental approach in the mid-twentieth century. Radical epidemiologists began to take the view that the new killers – cancer, heart disease, hypertension, stroke, mental illness, drug addiction – were the consequence of social conditions in exactly the same way. By the late 1970s three-quarters of Britain's average annual death rate of about 660,000 was caused by circulatory or cancerous disorders, many of them the result of smoking, industrial conditions, pollution, diet, chronic stress and so forth.

In 1990, 170,000 people died of heart disease, and approaching 300,000 people per year suffer a heart attack. Heart disease is now the biggest cause of premature death, accounting for a third of male deaths and a sixth of female deaths before the age of 65. Yet, in Victorian times, doctors would send for colleagues to come and witness a patient with a heart complaint, such was its rarity. Although the victims of modern diseases were and are not so concentrated physically as with the old infections, these are equally 'epidemics', arising from a mesh of dysfunctional social factors. The medical sociologist E. Stark went so far, in 1977, as to claim that 'death is now socially constructed . . . it is endopolic, not endemic, the outcome of politics, not biology.'

The rediscovery of ill-health

It is in this divorcement of health and clinical medicine that the readiest explanation may be found for the continuing inequality in the incidence of ill-health. As with poverty, the post-war optimism about ill-health suffered a rude awakening during this period, when it was revealed that, for all the free (albeit modified by a range of prescription, dental, optical and allied charges) health service, inequities remained. By 1982, analysts such as Jules le Grand were able to demonstrate that public expenditure 'systematically favours the better-off', and that, for instance, in the mid-1970s, for every £124.00 spent on the health care of a professional person, only £88.00 was expended on that of a semi-skilled or unskilled worker. Regional differences were also telling, with poorer areas often not having access to the same facilities as, let alone better facilities than, more well-to-do districts.

The 1980 Black Report on Inequalities in Health, which the government of the day seemed not keen to encourage, became the focus of this exposition. To quote a couple of illustrations, the report showed that infant mortality in unskilled workers' families was twice as high as in professional families; and that the death rate for working-class men was really no better in 1972 than it had been in 1949. It urged that the gap in health had actually widened between the top and bottom echelons of society. Apart from any failings of the NHS, especially in terms of ease of access and approachability, the report pointed the finger at glaring inequalities of social circumstance. As with poverty, and despite the creditable aspects of the NHS and allied features, ill-health needed to be treated comprehensively as an integrated aspect of the social environment.

Housing

It is symptomatic of this analysis of the health scene that, in the post-war years, housing, for so long the proper protégé of public health, became cast off from health, and ended up as an adjunct of the Department of the Environment, as central custodian of local government responsibilities.

There was to be some shifting of emphasis according to the government in power. The Conservative Rent Act of 1957, which decontrolled rentals of privately let tenancies, was, for example, countered by the Labour Rent Act of 1965, which reintroduced controls and a 'fair rent' assessment. But, by and large, housing policy remained *ad hoc* and nebulous. Although the Housing Corporation was formed in 1964, to stimulate the growth of housing associations, and there were various other White Papers and Acts, the state's role grew more and more 'residualist'.

In effect, owner-occupation was glorified and became the norm, with the state providing a long-stop for those who could not make the grade. The aspirations, indeed the successes, of the new town movement in creating socially coordinated communities were not sufficiently regarded, and state housing became the accommodation of the working classes. This somewhat divisive outcome obviously then played its part in the environmental causes and effects of poverty, ill-health and, as we shall later see, ignorance and crime. In caricature, the salaried middle classes lived on owner-occupied sub-urban estates and the waged working classes lived on municipally rented urban estates.

Housing did have a substantial amount of public money spent upon it, none the less. Expenditure rose, once more at 1980 values, from £2.7 billion in 1960 to £7.3 billion in 1980, climbing towards three times as much. It was a busy time for house-builders, and, again, one should recognize the positive impact on the employment situation that this brought. Successive governments were quick to assist private purchasers, so that they, as well as municipal tenants, were subsidized. By the 1980s, well over £6 billion went annually on mortgage tax relief, an enormous bounty of something over £700 to every mortgaged household. This further widened the distribution of income, and strikingly so in this crucial area of accommodation.

The split of public and private building gradually altered. In the first six years after the Second World War, it may be remembered, the former out-built the latter in the ratio of five to one. From then until 1976, 3.75 million council units were built, while 4.5 million private dwellings were completed. The picture in 1980 was of a nation of 22 million houses, 10 million of them built since the war, with a half of those in the public sector. It should be noted that a million slum properties had been cleared. At this stage 55 per cent of those 22 million homes were owner-occupied, 32 per cent were council houses and flats, 10.5 per cent were privately rented and 2.5 per cent were housing association units.

In terms of any specialist treatment, there was, after 1954, a definite swing to resettlement and redevelopment, much of it of a high-rise nature, some of it at a distance from the original, often inner city, base. Suffice it to say that, by the 1980s, this policy had fallen into sad disrepute, and efforts to demolish or refurbish such properties were in hand. Many of these overspill or redevelopment sites were to remain as the location for inner-city and outer-city social problems.

In the main, and because of the impetus of the private market and the presumed wish of all to be house-owners, housing was never made the subject of a disciplined and socially cohesive programme. Labour's Land Commission, set up in the late 1960s, was a puny and stillborn attempt to tackle the broad issue of land usage and planning, its rank failure a token of government's underlying incapacity to do more than tamper with these great matters. Obviously, of all the welfare areas, housing is the one where the imbalance very much favours the private sector in quantitative as well as qualitative terms.

One can still spot a similar trend as with income maintenance and health care: there was the expansion of public investment; there was a specialized treatment, that is, the high-rise overspill solution; and there was a resultant lack of parity in housing, not so much, perhaps, a rediscovery of poor housing, but a grudging recognition that it continued to force itself on to the political agenda as a pressing problem.

Approach to ignorance

The main changes

Education gained enormously from the bonanza of spending in the post-war decades. Between 1960 and 1980 public expenditure on education rose, at same values, from £5.5 billion to £12.5 billion, two and a half times as much, and accounting for a fifth of the growth in public expenditure in these social areas over that period. Local education authorities became the employers of many people. By 1980 something approaching two million people were employed, full- or part-time, in education, although critics were quick to point out that perhaps only a half of them were directly involved in teaching. Inclusive of higher, further and adult education, the system had ten million customers, and there were some 35,000 schools and colleges. The state education service was a massive business.

The LEAs, with responsibility from 1974 at shire and metropolitan district level, continued to control affairs under the aegis of the Department of Education and Science. New schools were built (for instance, 729 schools were completed in 1967, as opposed to ten in 1947); the school-leaving age, after some dithering, was raised to sixteen in 1973; and, by the late 1970s, there was a much bigger range of higher education institutes, with 44 universities and 30 polytechnics.

Where there had been fewer than 200,000 full-time teachers in 1947, there were nearly half a million in 1977; where 134,000 pupils had taken public examinations in 1947, the figure was 1.5 million in 1977, all of them doing CSE and GCE exams, the predecessor of the GCSE qualifications of today. With the post-war baby boom coming into fruition, the school population reached its highest ever peak of almost nine million in the late 1970s. Some 288,000 students were attending university in 1979 – there had been 50,000 in 1939. There were now another 200,000 in the polytechnics, and another concourse of chiefly part-time students, nearly two million of them, in further and adult education classes. On the welfare side, in 1969, 70 per cent of pupils were eating school dinners, of which 5.2 million were annually served, against 53 per cent of pupils eating 2.7 million meals in 1947.

Amid this welter of activity, the main structural alteration lay in a pronounced shift, under the pressure of Labour governments and local authorities, from the selective or bipartite to the comprehensive system of secondary education. This tendency to make secondary as well as primary education a matter of common schooling was driven by practical as well as ethical motives. The eleven-plus examination, which was employed to sort the 'grammar' sheep from the 'modern' goats, was shown to be fallible as well as too conclusive, with probably a 10 per cent error of children wrongly placed. By the late 1970s, 80 per cent of secondary age children, over three million of them, were in comprehensive schools, leaving just 200,000 in 400 secondary modern and 100,000 in 150 grammar schools – in 1965 there had been 1,180 grammar schools. It was a remarkable achievement.

The specialist treatment

For all the increase in resources for education, there were not many basic changes in the type of provision. It is true that many of the primary schools adopted more child-centred methods and, on the whole, were sane and civilized places to be, but the content of the curriculum and the very institutional format of the school showed hardly any change. The architectural determinism of schools continued to enforce a mould of class teaching by subject, by age and, often, by aptitude, while the lessons themselves, driven by the public examination systems and the purported needs of higher education, stayed loyal to ancient academic values.

In content and methodology, therefore, teaching remained as limited and narrow as had medical practice. For example, the huge extension of secondary education, and its widespread change to comprehensive modes, brought relatively little alteration to the actual teaching input. Britain never created a novel, modernized secondary system, aligned to the needs of the late twentieth century: what it did was to make the old system available to all, just as the NHS had made available to everyone the standard processes of medicine.

The brightest omen was perhaps the invention of the Open University, 'the lasting monument' of Harold Wilson's Labour administrations. Started in 1968, it soon established a norm of 6,000 graduates a year, although it was tardy in developing non-graduate courses. But, apart from its fine work in offering many a second chance to sustain their education, it was the use of modern techniques which was significant. As well as broadcasting, a range of sophisticated 'distance learning' methods were introduced, all of which made the rather static mainstream system look a trifle hidebound.

The rediscovery of ignorance

It was this rather old-fashioned approach to education which was at the heart of the realization that equality of opportunity in education was not enough. It is true that, as with health, there were deficiencies in the distribution of resources. It was calculated that, in 1973, where £90 was annually spent, on average, on a child of the professional classes, it was only £60 for the child of a semi-skilled or unskilled worker. That was the outcome of the estimate made that, during the 1960s, while educational expenditure rose swiftly everywhere, the increase was of 136 per cent for the children of professional families, and only 80 per cent for those of working-class families.

However, it is likely that the relation of home and background to school, in respect of language, values and content, proved even more of a barrier. It was not necessarily a matter of parental interest or affection; it was more to do with the cultural continuum of home and school, in middle-class districts, in terms of what happened and what was taught. Whatever the case, it was made abundantly explicit in the research of sociologists, such as A. H. Halsey, and in government publications, such as the Plowden, Robbins, Crowther and Newsom Reports, that social disadvantage remained a permanent factor in the resolution of educational outcome. Michael Rutter and other educational researchers were able to demonstrate that schools did, for good or ill, make a difference, but they did not close social gaps; in other words, they did equally well or badly by all pupils, irrespective of background.

The upshot was a continuation in the age-old hurdles of social class. To cite one from a plethora of instances, the 1960s witnessed a doubling, from 4 per cent, of the actual number of young people going on to university. However, as many as 70 per cent of these students still came from the 30 per cent of the population deemed 'non-manual' (as opposed to 73 per cent in 1960) and only 30 per cent from the 70 per cent 'manual' proportion (27 per cent in 1960). The gap was dug early. At age seven, there was a crucial difference in reading ages of 17 months between children from the opposite poles of class composition.

Nor could the genetic factor be claimed in evidence: the Robbins Report calculated that, of the top third of grammar school entrants, as graded in 1960–1, 91 per cent of those from professional families went on to obtain five or more GCE O levels, but only 49 per cent of those from semi-skilled and unskilled backgrounds managed this. The research done for the Plowden Report on primary children suggested that, if 100 points were allocated to represent the determinants of a child's schooling prowess, 82 would be awarded to the home and the neighbourhood, and only 18 to the school.

It was at about this time that Brian Simon, the education historian of Marxist orientation, claimed – for regional and gender discrepancies were also present – that the son of a Carmarthenshire solicitor had 180 times the chance of moving on to higher education than the daughter of a West Ham docker. Although the numbers involved were, of course, much higher, the proportion of working-class children at university in 1966 was the same as in 1926.

Of all the social policy fields, the educational one pointed up the 'redis-covery' of the relevant problem with the most lucid clarity. The optimism of the late 1944s was now out of countenance, as it was realized that the school, like the hospital or any other man-made institution, cannot operate in a social vacuum. As with health and crime, the social environment remains the governor of the situation. The liberal credo of 'equality of opportunity', despite its fine intentions and occasional triumphs, could not contend with inequalities of social circumstances.

Conversely, the kind of society which might procure such a degree of social equity could only do so with a loss of cherished liberties: the tension between freedom and equality was very much underlined by the social re-forms of this period and their not always heartening outcome. Put briefly, the social reformers of the post-war years found that one cannot for long run a comprehensive school in a selective society.

Approach to crime

The main changes

The increase on expenditure on law enforcement was substantial, if less dramatic than that in health, benefits and education. The number of police rose from about 70,000 in the early 1950s to 107,000 in 1975, by which point there were also over 14,000 staff employed by the prison service, with some 135 prison units to control, containing approaching 50,000 prisoners.

The 1962 Royal Commission on the police, appointed because police-work seemed not to be sufficiently challenging the onrush of crime, led to the 1964 Police Act. This rationalized the system somewhat. The duties of the Home Secretary and the Chief Constables were clarified and, at the same time, strengthened; the scope of the Inspectorate of Constabulary, the Police Advisory Board and the Police Council of Great Britain were all extended; and the responsibilities of the police authorities, two parts councillors to one part magistrates, were made clearer.

Moreover, the long-term trend of larger policing areas was sustained. The number of actual police forces in England and Wales was drastically reduced from 117 to 49, and the effect of local government reorganization was to abolish the few remaining borough forces, so that by 1974 there were just 41 forces remaining. This all amounted to a definite step towards a more centralized form of policing.

Attempts were made to rationalize the legal system, but it remained largely impervious to such efforts, and, for instance, the Law Commission, established by the Labour government in the late 1960s, proved as abortive as that administration's Land Commission. There was some movement. The Court of Appeal was bisected into civil and criminal divisions in 1966, and in 1971 the plethora of quarter sessions and assizes yielded to a neater scheme of crown courts, operating at ninety centres over six circuits. There were now some fifty stipendiary (that is, salaried) magistrates, and over 22,000 JPs, and it should be remembered that they dealt with 98 per cent of the crimes brought to book.

Finally, there is little doubt that, symbolically, the *coup de théâtre* of criminal justice in this era was the abolition of the death penalty, temporarily in 1965, permanently in 1969.

The specialized treatment

Of all social problems crime is the least susceptible to single, sharp solutions. It is variously caused by a complex of social and cultural factors, difficult to explain, even more difficult to change. The uncertainty and instability of modern life; the temptations of life in an acquisitive ethos; some collapse of respect for organized, communal and domestic authority – these, and a dozen other elements, may be quoted in evidence. The social historian, Arthur Marwick, has suggested that the criminal tendency probably always exists, 'but certainly the special conditions of the late fifties onwards gave deviants full rein'.

The 1962 Royal Commission on the police echoed its forebears in stressing the civil role of the police, with the constable 'a person paid to perform, as a matter of duty, acts which if he were so minded, he might have done voluntarily'. As well as emphasizing that ancient tradition of civic process, the Commission appealed for a continuance of a local/central partnership. Against the fear that an 'ill-disposed government' might abuse its control of a national police force, evidence was cited that some fascist regimes had taken advantage of weak local police forces. The Commission sought harmony and safety in a centrally controlled force, regionally administered.

Given the whirlpool of conditions which throws up crime, the idea that a police force, of any description, is a complete answer was obviously doomed. However, during this period, British policing became even more restricted than hitherto in its format and approach. The Royal Commission's placid faith in a civil police, rooted in friendly soil, tilled in amiable local and central partnership, never quite materialized. Faced with a bewildering increase in crime, prevention was scarcely on the agenda, and even detection suffered, leaving something close to containment as the key.

First, the move to create a more 'professional' police, especially during the 1970s, involved a breakaway from local authority shackles, on the grounds that the police should eschew political bias, and, in the words of Sir Robert Mark, Commissioner of the Metropolitan Police at this stage, 'act on behalf of the people as a whole'. In practice, this meant that the Chief Constables and their junior colleagues operated in a managerial fashion which excluded much public consultation. It would be foolish to exaggerate the past repose of police and local authority, but there is little doubt that the large-scale nature of the new police forces, and the technology available to expert managers, did make local political oversight more difficult.

Second, some commentators have divined in modern policing a shift from 'consensus' to (the rather pejorative word of the sociologists J. Lea and J. Young) 'military' policing, the one dependent on communal consent and a helpful flow of information, the other working in a suspicious and sullen climate. These are, self-evidently, the opposite poles of a policing gamut, and, it needs no reminder, some areas have been difficult to police in all ages. Nevertheless, the combine of a more autonomous professionalism with a rather more *gens d'armerie* style does represent a restricted view of policing, over against the complexity of the problem.

The rediscovery of crime

Not so much rediscovered, some might sigh, as never lost . . . However, there is a sense in which, on the longer perspective, the tidal wave of crime after 1950 might be interpreted as a reversion to the high incidence of crime in early industrial society. Although there were always particular instances of heavy crime, notably in the large cities, law and order had been relatively tidy for up to seventy or eighty years, with communal disciplines at especially effective levels. To the horror of the optimists, the onset of a society flushed with prosperity and protected by social welfare buttresses gave rise to a disappointingly high incidence of crime.

Even allowing for the vagaries – for example, the crop of unreported crimes – in criminal statistics, the hideous jump in yearly criminal offences from under half a million in the 1940s to over two million in the late 1970s tells its own sombre story. Young offenders, drug-related crime and other elements typified this swirling mass of criminality, and, with it, grew almost as perfidious a menace: that malaise which hung over so many areas and gave rise to a fear of crime more widespread than for over a century. Violent crime was of particular concern. Violent crime had risen by 5 or 6 per cent during the 1930s and 1940s, but after 1955 it grew at an average of 11 per cent annually: there were just under 6,000 reported crimes of violence in 1955, and there were over 21,000 in 1968. Little wonder that, in 1966, 'law and order' for the first time became a major general election issue.

Comparative features

Worldwide welfare

Because Britain made an early and valiant post-war endeavour to improve welfare arrangements, most dramatically in respect of the National Health

Service, it is sometimes forgotten that almost all developed nations, as well as some developing nations, made massive investment in such procedures during the 1950s and 1960s. The two controlling influences were industrialism and boom.

On the one side, it did appear that urbanized, industrialized societies required some form of welfare net to ensure their internal security. For some commentators, this was not so much a sentimental surge in the milk of human kindness – it was more that whatever natural altruism existed, probably neither more nor less over the years, was now channelled through state, and not so much individual or family, conduits. On the other side, the traffic of world trade bustled energetically and there was high employment in the post-war decades, and this meant that, in general terms, there was more of a dividend to spend on welfare policies.

These explanations very much illustrate some of the underlying elements of the welfare story. One is reminded that, worldwide, the switch from a more informal and domestic to a more formal and institutional delivery of welfare was not guided by politics and ideas as much as by economic organization. Robert Pinker has rightly concluded that, for national survival in the world economy, some form of social welfare is essential: 'social policies are functionally necessary at a certain stage of economic growth, especially in urban industrial societies'. The optimistic view, looking at the issue more from the individual's viewpoint, had already been expressed by T. H. Marshall in his 1949 classic, *Citizenship and Social Class*, in which he had prophesied that the acquisition of social rights to, for instance, education and welfare provision would moderate the worst aspects of capitalist inequality and selfishness.

Individual nation-states

Sweden became something of a market leader in these concerns, doubling its gross national product over this period, yet increasing its public expenditure by four times. Over half of this expenditure was on social welfare, with, interestingly, almost a fifth on public transport – a reminder to those who forget that the opportunity to travel is a significant element in social citizenship. Defence spending dropped from 15 to 5 per cent of the budget, while employment in the public sector sprang to 1.5 million workers, more than a third of the labour force. The social wage state, with its universal programmes of cheap (not free) access to health, integrated school and post-school systems, grand outlay on benefits and government-led housing schemes, was a mammoth creation, especially resonant in the 1960s. Sensibly, a parallel manpower policy, run through the National Labour Board, was attempted – Beveridge-type programmes were, of course, predicated on the assumption of full employment.

The United States, rarely seen as the home of state provision, witnessed, if not the arrival of a welfare state, at least a major investment in 'state welfare'. The John Kennedy and Lyndon Johnson presidencies, with their 'War on Poverty' and 'Great Society' slogans, encouraged the use of federal funds, particularly targeted on older age and health care. Between 1960 and 1980, the total social expenditure rose from $68 billion to $314 billion yearly, and the welfare share of the gross national product approached a fifth. For a nation besotted with the individualist tradition of 'frontier' self-help, it was an amazing change, bringing taxation to an all-time high of 30 per cent of average income.

Canada, in the shadow of the United States, likewise developed several welfare policies in the 1960s. These included the Canadian and Quebec Pension Plans of 1965, with employee levies or contributions backed by state supplements; the Medical Care Act of 1968, amended in 1971, which offered health treatment on a provincial base; and unemployment insurance and family allowances. Perhaps because of greater European influence, or simply because there was not the same breadth of economic conditions and wide spread of population, the schemes were somewhat more compact and unified than in the United States.

Italy made spectacular progress towards welfare statehood. Over the thirty-year period to 1980 Italy almost doubled – to 45 per cent – the proportion of the gross disposable income spent on public matters, the greater part of them of a social kind. An export-led trading expansion, based on the industry of Northern Italy, financed what, in the main, was a cash- rather than a service-orientated programme. In this, Italy was akin to France and the Benelux countries, whereas Britain and the Scandinavian nations opted more for services. Spending on health and education in Italy quadrupled between 1965 and 1975, and the 1978 National Health Systems Act tried to offer some comprehensive medical care. Nevertheless, it was the benefits system which really caught the eye. This grew incrementally out of the social insurance funds organized around vocational groups (*clientelismo*) until, in 1969, pensions were universalized and other benefits were agreed.

Austria, Italy's neighbour, enjoyed some post-war stability from its coalition governments, and advanced steadily as an industrial power, its gross domestic product trebling between 1955 and the early 1980s. Of this augmented sum, over a half was eventually devoted to public expenditure, and within these totals social welfare had risen from 16 to 27 per cent. It might be mentioned that, as in Italy, the previous fascist regimes had eroded the voluntary effort substantially, so that resort to public sector care was that much more necessary. The 'social partnership' of government, employers and employees made for a relatively trouble-free consensus on comprehensive programmes of social insurance, with family allowances being especially generous. Social aid – for instance, the 'contact visiting service' – was also sound and competent, although health care, while modern in treatments, tended to be fragmented, in part for geographical reasons, in part because insurance-based schemes tend to be more haphazard than universalist schemes.

Yugoslavia is an example of a purportedly communist country undertaking welfare schemes in an area considerably wracked by war. As elsewhere, political legitimacy rested on the consent of the governed – it has been said that it is usually less stressful and less expensive to procure the acceptance of the citizenry by welfare than by martial domination. The 1963 Constitution gave legal status to social protection, and by the late 1970s beneficiaries had doubled to 16 per cent of the population and there were three times as many old age pensioners. The number of doctors had trebled, the numbers in secondary and post-secondary education had trebled, spending on health had risen by five times and the number of welfare centres had jumped from 95 to 238. Overall, the amount of gross national product expended on social welfare had doubled from 10 to 20 per cent.

Israel, established as an autonomous state in 1948, realized, like the United States beforehand, that education may act as the unifier of a new and polyglot nation, so that more money was spent in that direction rather than on, say, health care. None the less, yearly programmes of social welfare became the norm, with something of a priority given, in the Hebrew tradition, to in-kind services. At the same values, the expenditure for social security payments, as well as such direct services, leapt from 7 billion Israeli shekels in 1970 to 53 billion in 1980, an enormous increase by any standards.

Japan, noted for the high-speed growth of its economy (usually 10 per cent per annum through the 1950s and 1960s) and faced with no defence commitments at all, moved swiftly to complement this success with high levels of social protection. As early as 1946, a Living Protection Law was enunciated, obliging the state to secure the right to subsistence, and by 1961 Japan was covered by often work-based health and pension insurance programmes. Child allowances, health care for old people and other free social services followed. The Japanese gross national product shot up by six times from the beginning of growth in about 1954 to 1980, but spending on social security increased by the colossal rate of 56 times. By 1981, 6 per cent of gross national income was expended on health and as much on pensions. There was a continuing strand of paternalism in Japan's welfare arrangements, but no one could claim that these had been neglected. One might make fairly obvious comparisons with *West Germany*, a defeated power: helped to recovery by American assistance, not least for political reasons, unburdened from defence commitments, the beneficiary of an 'economic miracle' and the organizer of the very impressive 1957 state pension scheme, as well as other pieces of top-rated social welfare machinery.

Such a series of snapshot illustrations, drawn from a variety of geographic and political typologies, may serve to demonstrate that, for all the colourful wealth of detail, the main contentions about modern welfare statehood hold good. This section pays due tribute to R. A. Friedmann, N. Gilbert and M. Sherer, authors of *Modern Welfare States: a Comparative View of Trends and Prospects*.

General résumé

Any descriptions of welfare on a nationwide scale very properly point up the relation between welfare and the economy, and demonstrate how some states, such as Sweden and Austria, endeavoured to influence employment policy accordingly for welfare reasons. It is also possible to note how other findings and conclusions about the British scene had a worldwide character, particularly in regard of winners and losers.

Swedish and other evidence from overseas confirms the British testimony that, in education, middle-class children maintained their advantage over working-class children, despite seemingly equal opportunities. This was because of the in-built weight of social circumstance, and a similar tale could be told about health care outcomes. In the United States and Canada the same phenomenon was witnessed apropos social security payments – in Canada, for example, the gap between the richest and poorest fifths of the population widened two and a half times during this period. One was seeing, in Britain and elsewhere, a distributive, but not a redistributive, mechanism at work. Across the world, welfare states were certainly distributing money and services to people, but they were making little or no impact on the fundamental balance of which groups had plenty of income and which had much less.

It is likewise apparent that the existence of the welfare state on this world scene was, in practice, free of party political or ideological rationale, however much the texts and mottoes used to justify such proceedings indicated otherwise. The pressure to develop welfare policies was a global phenomenon. It followed on from economic organization on an industrial basis, and the corresponding social organization of people's lives on an urban basis. In these circumstances state bureaucracies, whatever the political banners at their masthead, were forced to act to guarantee the reasonable stability of the nations for which they held responsibility. This they did, in part, by enacting largely similar welfare schemes.

Special features

In the post-war period in Britain there was a major advance in the campaigns to obtain equal civil and other rights for oppressed and disadvantaged groups. Widespread publicity, as the whole business of communications became transformed by modern technology; a greater degree of social awareness and tolerance in consequence; a social condition of generally rising living standards and availability of funds – these were some of the relevant factors.

Mental and physical disability

In 1957, for example, there was a Royal Commission on Mental Health and Mental Deficiency, followed by the 1959 Mental Health Act, which attempted further to define with more care and sophistication the range of mental suffering, and to deal accordingly with the sufferers. At this point there were some 250,000 outpatients and 100,000 inpatients in these categories and, compared with the bad old days, relatively few, just 5 per cent of those hospitalized, were detained by compulsion or force.

The 1970 Chronically Sick and Disabled Persons Act laid down a menu of provisions for local authorities to undertake in this connection, and there was a further act of this kind in 1981. These perhaps lacked sufficient clout to alter the basic environment for disabled people, but there was welcome evidence of good practice in several local authorities. One might judge that the chief creators of any new climate in relation to physical or to mental disability were handicapped and disabled people themselves, as well as the largely voluntary agencies which represented them. Although the situation, round about 1980, was far from ideal, there had been a decided shift in public attitudes and public practice (in relation to access to employment, or to buildings and the like) over this time.

Women's rights

The same is true of moves towards gender equality, which were very much guided by women themselves in the more open kind of society that emerged after the immediate post-war years. As with disabled groups and ethnic minorities, the issues are far wider than welfare ones solely, entering naturally into every aspect of national life and values. Nevertheless, not least because, given the construct of British society, children's rights are inextricably entwined with those of their mothers, welfare is of great import.

In the workplace, the 1973 Equal Pay Act, the 1975 Sex Discrimination Act and the 1975 Employment Protection Act, especially as it related to jobs protected during pregnancy, were of the essence, together with the responsibilities of the Equal Opportunities Commission. Family planning services were by now well-established, although, in the 1980s, it was still claimed that two million women were not using reliable birth control devices.

Child care for working women remained a problem. By this stage, more than half the country's mothers were employed, a return to the older tradition of agricultural and early industrial Britain, after a period when many mothers had, for social and economic reasons, stayed at home with the infants. This wave of female workers included 30 per cent of those with children under five, but there was now the growing phenomenon of the single-parent family. Only two out of five mothers living alone were able to work, chiefly because of inadequate nursery provision. On the face of it, such amenities had increased: there were 300,000 state nursery school places and twice as many voluntary and private ones, with close on 80,000 registered child-minders, plus an unofficial figure of 300,000. But there were only 80,000 day nursery places with perhaps another 25,000 places in company and other creches. It was this fuller cover which remained insufficient, and denied many women the chance of employment. It might be added that this extremely poor day nursery provision compared very disfavourably with most continental countries.

Marriage continued to discriminate against women when it came to welfare rights. With regard to pensions, the Victorian curio of the married couple's state pension being less than twice the single state pension has been permitted to persist. As for the 1976 Invalid Care Allowance, for those having to give up work to look after a dependant, married women were ineligible, it being assumed that they might not have employment to forfeit. Then there were the general questions arising from cohabitation, which, in the late 1970s, led to the annual refusal of around 8,000 benefits.

Overall, by 1980, only 20 per cent of married men supported a family without additional income from the spouse, contributions that, on average, amounted to nearly a third of the household income. Yet women remained disadvantaged on the labour market, with low pay for part-time jobs a main element, with difficulties over work-related benefits such as insurance payments and occupational pensions, and with their benefits, such as family allowance, directing them towards home rather than work. On the credit side, the 1980 Housing Act made joint tenancies mandatory for married couples, a significant shift in the ancient arguments about the property of married women.

In education there had been many improvements, and the 1975 Sex Discrimination Act legislated for a similar curriculum for boys and girls. What has been called the 'past powerlessness' of women continued to cast a sombre shade, with families making decisions on gender grounds about schooling, and, as late as 1963, the Newsom Report had presumed differences of curriculum, for instance, in the sciences, for girls and boys. Perhaps luckily, the primary school, with its more familial culture, itself aided by the profusion of women teachers, matched the domestic convention, wherein girls remained indoors more than boys and were pointed towards sedentary habits like reading. This helped girls to do well, until, aged eleven, they were faced with, on balance, fewer available grammar school places, a less amenable climate where they existed, and all manner of pressures to leave at sixteen. This meant that, ultimately, girls in sixth forms and thus in higher education were in shorter supply than boys.

As far as health and social services were concerned, women tended to remain at some disadvantage, with the upper echelons of these services male preserves. In the mid-1970s, where 70 per cent of NHS staff at the lower grades were women, 75 per cent of the doctors were men; and, where 83 per cent of social work assistants and 64 per cent of social workers were women, 91 per cent of social services directors were men. Below this professional imbalance, it was well-rehearsed that women were much more likely than men to be the domestic carers of sick, disabled or aged people, frequently with the minimum of support.

Some commentators urged that, alongside the marital control exerted by men over women, on legal and cultural grounds, there also existed a corresponding patriarchal domination in the crucial areas of medical and social care and treatment. It might even be persuasively argued that, as was hinted in Chapter 3, the establishment of medical and welfare professionalism had completed a transfer of these issues from domestic and female to official and male authority. Despite, therefore, the compensation of very much higher standards of life, women were still, proportionately, the losers in the gender battle for dominion over these social affairs.

Ethnic minorities

There were about 20,000 black people in Britain in the eighteenth century, and they were joined, first, by the great migratory sweeps of Irish people in the nineteenth century, and by several groups of continental Europeans in the first half of the twentieth century. It was, however, the arrival of the so-called New Commonwealth immigrants, mainly from the Caribbean and the

Indian sub-continent, which has focused present attentions, and this occurred crucially in the 1950–80 period.

In the first part of that period, labour demands encouraged immigration,
only to lead to limitations on such incoming as circumstances altered. By
the late 1970s, approaching three million of the UK's population of 55
million were of non-Caucasian origin, although over 40 per cent of this
three million were, in fact, born in the new homeland. Their age profile is
'younger' than that of the white host population, which means, for instance,
that, *pro rata*, they will for some time make more use of the education service
and less of the health service, the one the province overwhelmingly of the
young, the other largely of the old.

The ethnic minorities have tended to concentrate in particular areas, and
to find employment in particular, often poorly paid and unprepossessing,
occupations. There is evidence that they are discriminated against because of
this initial social disadvantage, in terms, for instance, of employment,
education and housing, and that, next, there is the extra jeopardy of racial
discrimination. In the late 1970s, whereas 5 per cent of white children in
London were enjoying university education, the figure for Asians was 3 per
cent, and it was only 1 per cent for West Indians.

At the same time, the proportion of the white population who were owner-
occupiers was 55 per cent (30 per cent were council tenants), while the
related figures were 36 per cent for West Indians (45 per cent council tenants) and 23 per cent for Africans (29 per cent council tenants, leaving a
high total in rented properties). It should be noted that the figure was 70 per
cent for Indians (10 per cent council house tenants). That warns us not to
scrutinize the question as if we were faced with a heterogeneous cohort:
there are some other distinctions, for instance, in type and pattern of employment.

In 1981 a Home Office report assessed the rates of racially motivated
incidents, per 100,000 of the population over a three-month phase, at 1.4 for
whites, 51.2 for West Indians and Africans, and 69.7 for Asians. This disturbing
finding was but the criminal tip of a mountain of racial abuse, tension and
active and passive enmity. In respect of social welfare policies, it is not, of
course, possible to point out statutory discrepancies, as one might reveal, for
instance, in the differences between men and women. All are equal in the eyes
of the law, including those statutes that establish civic rights in education,
health, the social services, social security, and law and order. Yet, in practice, it
is well-known that inequalities existed on an extensive scale, so much so that,
by the end of the self-styled Butskellite period, there were those who spoke
of the large parts of the ethnic minority population as part of an 'underclass'.

Conclusion

The crucial feature of this (roughly) 1950–75 phase was, therefore, the
common progress of welfare in relatively affluent times across the industrialized world, underlining the need always to scrutinize social alongside economic considerations. Another feature was the recognition that welfare policies

only moderated the superstructure of society, but did not change its basic structure, in part because somewhat narrow, over-professionalized systems were usually employed. As for the balance of economic and social factors, and as the final chapter will show, it was to be a decided lurch in economic development which led to a serious questioning of the make-up of the welfare state.

Advice on further reading

Several of the books listed at the end of Chapter 6 will continue to be of assistance for this chapter. Two other books might be consulted in terms of this period of settlement and consolidation for welfarism.

George, V. and Wilding, P. (1984) *The Impact of Social Policy*, Routledge, London.
Halsey, A. H. (1978/1986) *Change in British Society*, Oxford University Press, Oxford.

Beyond that, Chapter 7 has majored on the extent of welfare politics across the world, and on the place of special groups – disabled people, women, people in ethnic minorities – in the welfare frame of reference. It was during this period that proper consideration began to be given to both these features.

Ashford, D. E. (1986) *The Emergence of Welfare States*, Blackwell, Oxford.
Friedmann, R. A., Gilbert, N. and Sherer, M. (1987) *Modern Welfare States: a Comparative View of Trends and Prospects*, Harvester Wheatsheaf, Hemel Hempstead.
Held, D. *et al.* (1983) *States and Societies*, Oxford University Press, Oxford.

Those three are invaluable for discussion of the international context of welfare provision. The following are useful for family, gender and ethnic themes.

Allan, G. (1985) *Family Life*, Blackwell, Oxford.
Beechey, V. and Whitelegg, E. (ed.) (1986) *Women in Britain Today*, Oxford University Press, Oxford.
Brown, C. (1984) *Black and White Britain*, Heinemann, London.

8 | The questioning of the welfare state

Summary

This concluding chapter has two purposes. First, it attempts to offer a straight-forward factual account of the position of social provision in Britain in the early 1990s, the end product, so to speak, of the previous seven chapters of social history and analysis. Second, it attempts to place that description in the economic and political setting of welfare principles and practice under attack.

This amounted, during the late 1970s and 1980s, to a global mood-swing away from post-war collectivism and social democracy. This may be attributed to the end of the post-war boom, occasioned by the oil price crisis of the 1970s, together with a reaction against the bureaucratic stolidity of much governmental process. In Britain this tendency was formalized in the critique of the 'nannying' state, associated with Margaret Thatcher and the right-wing Conservatism of the 1980s. Its thrust was to reduce governmental intervention in both the economy and the social welfare services, with something of a return to a reliance on private supports. As important was the classic sense whereby, in aiming at a free and 'privatized' market economy, Conservative governments were impelled to strengthen central controls. There was, then, a centripetal flow of authority back to the central state, to the grave detriment of the sharing of power between local and central government, so characteristic of Victorian administration.

As a final contribution to the glossary of jargon and specialist terms, there are: integrated/differentiated welfare state – privatism – quango.

Social and economic background

Thus we move to the past score or so years, which, against the canvas of the thousand years covered by this study, are like the flick of an eyelid. Their proximity makes them difficult to judge dispassionately, and their problems especially assume magnified proportions.

The more we change . . .

There is talk of economic crisis, yet with a substantial number of people enjoying life-styles which would have been the envy of men and women forty, let alone a thousand, years ago. There is talk of a crisis in the welfare state when, for all the huff and puff, the provision of public services remains prominent. To be sure, there have been critical questioning and even savage cutbacks, but a mesh of pension and other benefits, health care and educational provision is still available. By the standards of the 1960s and early 1970s, there has certainly been a quantitative deterioration in the supply of social provision, bringing, alternately, gloom to welfare adherents and delight to welfare sceptics. But welfarism has not been stopped dead in its tracks and removed without trace.

Here we see demonstrated the advantages of historical perspective, permitting the calmer and the truer view. Over the past ten or more years of political argument, one would have been forgiven for believing that the welfare state was primarily and exclusively the product of the late 1940s. In the event, the 1945–51 social settlement, as we observed, was the culmination and the coordination of a hundred years of reforms, responding to the problems of industrialism. The curbs and dismantlings of the 1980s were no more than a lurch, noticeable enough, but still a lurch, away from that position.

The truth remains that all societies must come to terms with the perils of social ills, and, for instance, the arguments voiced in the 1980s, about the pros and cons of providing welfare, would have been entirely familiar to Tudor politicians. As a rider to that, it appears that all urbanized, industrialized societies find it necessary to provide welfare in some public form, however minimal, for the upkeep of the state, and the United Kingdom emerging into the 1990s was and is no exception. In 1890 less than a tenth of the nation's wealth was devoted to public expenditure, and only a fifth of that (perhaps 2 per cent of the total wealth) went on social services; a hundred years later, despite criticisms and cuts, nearly a half of the nation's wealth was used in public expenditure, and a half of that went on social services.

The end of the post-war boom

The right-wing Conservatism of Margaret Thatcher gave political vent to the critique of the welfare state in Britain, and during her premierships from 1979 to 1991 scope was found to attack Butskellism in a well-defined and forceful way. However, the high profile of that political initiative should not too much distract from the basically economic milieu in which it was taken. The crucial factor was the end of the post-war boom in the mid-1970s.

Despite the so-called stop–go nature of economic activity over the previous quarter century, with its recurring mini-booms and mini-slumps, private affluence had been relatively assured and, in consequence, public spending had not been unduly threatened. Growth became taken for granted and, with that, an impression developed that welfare expenditure was inviolate.

The oil crisis of 1973–4, when oil prices quadrupled, threw the world economy into turmoil and triggered a global recession of long standing. In Britain, apart from a somewhat synthetic and debt-led rally in the early 1980s, it continued deep into the 1990s. Some economists spoke of 'the new reality', suggesting that developed societies had found a lower plateau of economic achievement, but one of some permanence.

Between 1955 and 1967 the British economy grew at an annual rate of close on 3 per cent; the most optimistic estimate for the last decade of the century is not much more than 1 per cent. There was a gradual disappearance of much of the industrial resource of the nation. The proportion of the workforce engaged in the manufacturing trades, which had held good throughout the century at about 48 per cent, had dropped to 30 per cent by 1987, and continued to fall.

Andrew Tylecote, echoing the earlier thoughts of the Russian economist Nikolai Kondratiev, has argued, in his *The Long Wave in the World Economy* (1993), that this periodic slump is caused by the mismatch of fresh technologies – principally electronic – with outdated business and financial institutions. One is reminded that the transition from one 'techno-system' to another is usually marked by disruption and depression; the 1930s slump, for instance, had much to do with the switch from coal and steam to oil-based technologies.

Others – for instance, P. J. Cain and A. G. Hopkins in their 1993 study *British Imperialism* – blame the dominion of finance over manufacture for many of the troubles. This thesis urges that British financial interests have for many years been paramount, and that industry flourished almost as no more than an adjunct to this between about 1780 and 1950. During the 1980s, many countries, including Britain, went so far as to abolish controls over the movement of capital. With international finance operating in a free market, this meant that individual states found it difficult, perhaps impossible, to control both their interest rate and the exchange rate of their currency – one of them constantly had to yield to the movement of short-term capital in search of the best bargain. This had a most destabilizing effect on economies such as Britain's.

At a more humdrum level, inflation was an overt signal of the dislocation of economic life. In Britain, and taking the base of 100 for the Retail Price Index as of 1962, with world prosperity in full spate, one finds that by 1981 it had passed the 500 mark, and by 1992 the 1,000 mark. The days of what appeared to be 'costless' public policy were numbered.

The turn to market solutions

Confidence in the theory and machinery of public authority lapsed. The legitimacy of the welfare state rested on the harmony of its Keynesian and Beveridge components, a moderate concept uniting a public vigilance over the economy with a public responsibility for social matters. Market-orientated economists, such as M. Friedmann and F. A. Hayek, exulted in what appeared to be a failure of the former of these elements. There had been, it was claimed, a temptation to practise 'irresponsible' Keynesianism. Politicians naturally had found it easier to let deficits run in the bad times than to extract surpluses prudently in the good times. Expanding credit and increasing money supply had perhaps become easy options, and, in continental Europe and North America as well as in Britain, the call for balanced budgets, tighter money supplies and market 'law' grew loudly.

An attractive aspect of this assault on what is sometimes termed 'supply-side economics' was the old cry of lower taxation, for, again, high taxation was seen as another flaw (although, truth to tell, research suggests that the disincentive of high taxation as a bar on productivity is hard to identify). The highly corporatist models of Eastern Europe offered few glimmers of hope, and were to collapse politically by the end of the 1980s. Increasingly, they were to turn for succour, both material and philosophic, to the west.

As for Marxist critics, they continued to claim, with some precision, that the welfare state had shored up, not changed, the capitalist system. Balm may have been applied to the social sores, but they had not been healed – in 1990 one in five people in the United States was estimated to be living in abject poverty. But that same argument could be turned by the free marketeers – the rediscovery of poverty in Britain and elsewhere proved to their satisfaction that social engineering was a failure. They felt that people had been forced into a modern form of 'serfdom', existing in the welfare 'treacle-well', not the 'trickle-down', state, with free enterprise bringing rewards to the top, which eventually flowed down to the bottom of society. All was ripe for a swing back towards an economy free from as much state tinkering as was deemed feasible.

The effects on welfare policies

This is very relevant to the discussion of welfare, for the economic stagflation of the later 1970s and onwards succeeded in cutting loose the economic from the social component of modern statehood. It is true that the adhesive had not always been secure. R. Mishra, in a valuable analysis of these issues published in 1984, helpfully distinguishes between the integrated and differentiated welfare states. In the 'integrated' model, the economy is rigorously regulated on both the demand and the supply sides, enabling social policy to be joined with economic policy in well-developed 'social partnership'. In the 'differentiated' model, the economy is regulated only from the demand side, the social element hangs free from it and sectional interests clash. Austria and Sweden are cited as examples of the former, and France and Italy of the latter.

Naturally, the more integrated the welfare state, the more deeply embedded its methods and supports, but, in more or less degree, all states were faced with institutional challenge in the 1980s. It was urged that the welfare bureaucracies had become overloaded and extravagant – it was said, not without some truth, that, where businessmen seek to maximize business, bureaucrats seek to maximize bureaucracy.

This, in turn, had a debilitating effect on the economy, not only because the welfare industry tended to create its own constituency of dependent clients, but also because it created its own vast workforce. We saw in Chapter 7 how some commentators argued that the economy was 'deindustrialized' at the expense of the service trades, usually of a public kind. Although public expenditure helped to succour children and others in need of care, and to release people, especially women, to the labour market, the overall outcome, in this form of analysis, witnessed a loss of two million workers from productive manufacture in Britain between 1966 and 1977, and a gain of one and a half million workers by the public sector. By the end of the 1970s, there were five million central and local government employees in Britain.

Particularly as a more positive mood of consumerism grew in the 1960s and 1970s, aspirations burgeoned and some of the austere and anonymous practices of the welfare state, associated with its 1940s utility-bound image, looked now to be abrasive and officious. Disillusion set in, and the welfare agencies became the butt of fault-finding about their incompetence and insensitivity. It was all of a piece with the kind of criticism levelled at large offices and state officers – witness the Russian playwright Gogol's *The Government Inspector* or Dickens's parody of the Circumlocution Office in *Little Dorrit* – throughout the ages.

Worst of all, the synthesis of economic life and social action was disturbed at its most vital conjunction, that of full employment. It is a moot point as to how far the ravages of the world recession are responsible for unemployment and where the blame rests with governmental ineptitude, except to say that the switch from Keynesian monetary policies, while fast-forwarded by the Thatcher ministries, had already begun under the banner of her Labour predecessors. What is not in dispute is the emergence of unemployment as a major hazard in British life – and in almost every other industrialized nation – in the aftermath of the oil crisis.

Apart from the false blip of the early 1980s, unemployment in Britain has hovered up to and above three million, with, in the early 1990s, a million of these out of work for more than a year. With premature retirements, youth training schemes of doubtful virtue and people, often women, not presenting themselves for work, it was widely felt that this figure was, in practice, much higher. Prophecies of six million unemployed were heard in the land.

Massive unemployment of this sort is a double-bind for the welfare state. On the one hand, the welfare state, in the thoughts of Beveridge and his confrères, was founded on full employment, the welfare being available for those not able to, as opposed to not wanted for, work. On the other hand, the incidence of great unemployment levied a financial burden on the welfare state which knocked askew its reckoning. Unemployment benefits had to be poured out to millions, who, in turn, were not replenishing the treasury with the necessary tax revenue. There were parallels with the scenes in the 1860s, when, with trade at a low ebb, the workhouses in many towns were simply not big enough to accept the teeming unemployed; workhouses, that is, which had been constructed to deter the indolent and force them on to the labour mart.

As well as unemployment, there was also the emergence of a low-paid, casual component in the workforce, especially as the old manufacturing crafts vanished, giving way to 'service' businesses, often with sporadic calls on unskilled labour. For the first time for many years, Britain was faced with a long-gone problem: that of underemployment and underpaid employment. Many thousands of these people were social security claimants, and, of course, they were not paying taxes. This accounted for another mighty increase – one estimate put it as high as a yearly £12.5 billion – in public spending. It was back to the bad old days with a vengeance.

The contented majority

At the same time, however, there was something of a paradox, for despite the wholesale poverty and indigence of a large minority, the majority, in employment, had decent life-styles and living standards had continued to improve for many of them. Memories of the 1939–45 war, which had fuelled feelings of solidarity and the need for a collective effort to succour all, had faded, affluence rather feeding the view that perhaps welfarism was a dated concept.

The values of liberty, and the rights of the individual to pursue his or her own ventures and paths, are always in some tension with the values of community, and the necessity to provide collective social defences for the benefit of all citizens. At this stage, there came a definite veering to the former side, reflected in the popular support for Conservative governments which, more than any since the Second World War, turned away from Tory paternalism in favour of individualism.

In his 1979 study *The Politics of Economic Decline*, J. Alt has written of 'a politics of quiet disillusion', with the welfare state no longer regarded as the sole or the permanent answer to social distress. That sagacious and reputable American economist-cum-philosopher, John Galbraith, wrote astutely in 1992 of 'the politics of contentment', with the majority, reasonably comfortable and well-placed, strangely unmoved by the afflictions of their fellows. One element in this was the slippage of the manual working class from three-quarters of the population in 1900 to a third in 1990. It meant that an *arriviste* middle class was in existence. Irregular and under-waged involvement in the economy had left the working class relatively poor practically until the Second World War. In the 1930s low-price/low-wage recession, for example, the difference between being in work and being on the dole was not all that substantial.

By the 1980s and 1990s this gap was considerable, so much so that commentators spoke of an 'underclass' or a 'sub-class', words fairly new to the sociological lexicon. Certainly, by the early 1990s, and in spite of some opinions to the contrary, it was argued that Britain, and other countries for that matter, found themselves divided into 'two-thirds/one-third' societies, with a 'contented' majority and, by default, a discontented minority. Although most opinion polls still showed a definite leaning towards retaining the welfare state, there appeared to be no escape from the remorseless dilemma. In a period of long-term slump, the well-to-do majority found it difficult to translate their affection for state-supported services into an equal delight in stumping up the necessary taxes to sustain and improve them.

Common factors of social provision

The opinion has been pressed throughout this study that the motif of social action has ever been the preservation of stability. Time and again politicians have been noted moving on social reform under the pressure of social threat or stress. This was openly acknowledged by the founders of modern welfare policies. Jose Harris, Beveridge's biographer, has confirmed that Sir William thought it 'desirable to foster social solidarity and feelings of identification'. Talcott Parsons, in his famous work *The System of Modern Societies*, published in 1971, explained his theory of 'functionalism', the fashion in which 'social institutions evolved out of functional necessity', rather than, for example, ideological purity and faith. It was as if, out of the hard-fought battles of capital and labour, there had emerged the compound of a managed economy, underlain with a managed series of social agencies and amenities. How may these concepts of social provision be interpreted in the changed environment of what has been nicknamed Reaganomics or labelled Thatcherism?

Welfare and capitalist economics

First, one must repeat and emphasize the point that the western welfare state meant no real harm to capitalist economics and inflicted no basic damage upon it. In practice, the welfare state narrowed the problem to the individual, even, and perhaps increasingly, heaping the blame on that individual rather than finding fault with the system. Problematic or flawed individuals are susceptible to minor change, where problematic or flawed societies require structural remedy, and that was never on the political agenda. Indeed, that treatment of the individual, and not collective or communal problems, led to the tendency to see posers separately, as riddles of health, or education, or law and order, when in fact they were symptoms of a profounder composite question.

Moreover, there is evidence that the social and public services are deployed not only to stabilize society, but actually to construct, in the tradition of Bismarck, its defences. As Pat Thane said of the German leader's social reforms, they were 'a means of winning working class allegiance and destroying Socialism'. Robert Pinker, in his well-known book *Social Theory and Social Policy* (1971), has claimed with much justification that 'social services are used to impose sanctions as well as to confer benefits'. Schools have also, like social work services, been castigated for stigmatizing failure and inflicting social disciplines, and generally trying to create 'an allegiant, compliant, subordinate working class'.

So the doctrines of Margaret Thatcher did not need to be nor were they revolutionary. Welfarism had existed alongside, and not supplanted, the capitalist economy, so that, in a new situation, adjustment was all that was required. The new situation, as the previous section outlined, was about economic anxieties, high taxation, a backlash against officialdom and a well-heeled majority. Property, money and possessions obviously play a leading role in the drama of social stability. Mishra, writing in 1984, proposed that 'welfare is only tolerable so long as it does not interfere with the logic of capitalist production'. In other words, the boot was on the other foot, kicking, so to say, at the other leg of social stability, with too much welfare now menacing, as they perceived it, the commonwealth of owner-occupiers and car-owners.

The matter may be simply summarized. Throughout the history of social welfare, certainly in its modern dispensation, there have been few with political influence who have sought either a structural change via state welfare or, alternatively, no state welfare at all. But there have always been both eager and reluctant exponents of the science. The former, in the ascendant in the years after the Second World War, were happy to get away with as much as they could, short of upsetting the apple-cart of the capitalist state; the latter, in office over the past twenty years, were happy to get away with as little as they could. There were frictions – inner-city disorders, struggles with organized labour, poll tax riots – but these only had the effect of causing the government of the day to tack rather than change course.

The techniques of Thatcherism – financial

Second, this search for a novel kind of stability followed the path of restructuring rather than dismantling. Taxation was a main weapon. In the first ten years of Margaret Thatcher's premiership, tax cuts reduced the take by £27 billion, at the expense, in part, of social security and allied payments. By breaking, for instance, the earnings link for the indexing of old age pensions, cuts were indirectly achieved, while there were significant decreases of spending in the state housing field, and decreases or decelerations in the growth of spending in health and education.

As for the spread of taxation, whereas in the late 1950s the bottom half of tax-payers contributed only 5 per cent to the income tax fund, by the late 1970s they were contributing 20 per cent, while increases in indirect taxation, such as VAT, of course hit the lower paid proportionately more than the higher paid. VAT was increased in rate, and then extended to essential items, such as domestic fuel.

The privatization of the public utilities, such as gas, electricity, telephones and water, whatever the intrinsic virtues or vices of such a process, helped the Exchequer substantially, while the 1980s was also the decade when North Sea oil produced its fruitful dividend for the public purse. This allowed what, to many, was a welcome decrease in personal taxation, although, of course, as unemployment remained high, the outlay in unemployment benefit stayed well above the hoped for norm.

The upshot was that, between 1979 and 1991, the income of the average household rose by 36 per cent, but the income of the bottom tenth of those households actually fell by 14 per cent. The number of officially poor people – those living on less than half the average income – rose over the same period from five million (including 1.4 million children) to 13.5 million (3.9 million children, a third of all under-16s). This amounts to a quarter of the whole population, and it gets close to making numerical sense of the 'two-thirds/one-third' society. One sees the political astuteness of ensuring that the prosperity of a 'contented majority' is maintained.

Few doubt that these actions have brought grave relative poverty to many members of the community, and have created an enormous amount of distress – even if the welfare state has not been, as some colourfully claim, dismantled. The gap between rich and poor has widened considerably; but, at the risk of tedium, it has to be said again that the welfare state, British style, never aimed at equality, only at the relief of distress. This agreement about the 'primacy of minimum standards in social policy' ranged from Anthony Crosland, the Labour Party politician and writer, who saw the purpose of welfare as 'the relief of distress and hardship', not 'social equality', to F. A. Hayek, doyen of the New Right, who felt that welfare should offer 'security against severe physical privation'.

The techniques of Thatcherism – organizational

Alongside these financial measures, the Conservative administrations after 1979 were keen to apply the disciplines of the market to the public sector. These have been very varied. They have included the privatization of, the competitive tendering for and the contracting out of services, the introduction or the augmentation of charges for services, and the subjection of services to more exacting budgetary controls.

While some of the public utilities, such as gas and electricity, have been completely privatized, and while private provision has been encouraged in the 'welfare' areas, none of the four elements of social provision scrutinized in this study has been denationalized. There is still, that is, a National Health Service, a state educational system, a state-run police and prison facility, state benefits and welfare agencies, and even the rump of state housing. These practices, as well as the effects of the fiscal measures alluded to in the previous section, will be discussed in the sections devoted to each of the four given fields.

Centralization

Against the historical perspective, the greatest change initiated by the Conservative ministries of the 1980s and early 1990s was possibly that of massive centralization. A significant theme of any study of the relation of public and private provision of social care is the place of public bodies intermediary to the central state. In Britain this has normally meant local government (in other nations it might be regional or provincial governance), and throughout British constitutional history that relationship, central and local, has veered and altered in its strengths and sympathies. First one and then the other has been in the ascendant, but, crucially, in the industrial age a working partnership of elected local and central authority became the norm.

It might be said, by way of simple summary, that the Victorian age added the convention of elective municipal administration to the eighteenth-century Hanoverian settlement of the parliamentary system. There were experiments with both single- and multi-purpose authorities, with, on balance – the NHS being a patent exception – the latter winning the day. We have watched, in the course of this study, the emergence of local department in harness with the appropriate national ministry; housing department centrally, for instance, overseeing housing department locally. It was not necessarily a harmonious tandem, particularly where there was political dissonance between the two components, although some felt that was an essential bulwark against central aggrandisement and were prepared to tolerate some such confusion.

The actions of the Conservative administrations of the Thatcher period and beyond have undermined that duality from above and below. The usually Labour-controlled metropolitan counties, the Greater London Council and the Inner London Education Authority were all abolished, so that no large-scale anti-Tory bastions existed with an interest in what the Conservatives regarded as overmighty government. National powers were very much increased in some matters; for instance, through the insistence on a national curriculum and other educational diktats, or the erection of bodies like the London Docklands Development Corporation, which has no democratic oversight. Policing also grew more centralized in scope and organization.

Inroads were made from beneath, in the sense of encouraging the private sale of the municipal housing stock or the opting-out of schools from local authority control. The establishment of trust status in the NHS also reduced the input of localized influence. Together with other actions – such as a more central interventionist approach to county structure plans for land-use – the power of local government dwindled to a low ebb, with a corresponding flow towards the centre.

A characteristic of this approach has been the continued use of the so-called quango, the quasi-autonomous non-governmental organization. These are bodies set up to conduct public business with memberships appointed by the government and without accountability to any electorate. Such 'non-departmental public bodies', to give them their official title, have long existed, and initially there were objections to them from Thatcherite critics of the public sector. None the less, they have grown in significance. There were over 1,400 of them in 1993, served by some 40,000 government appointees, many of them businessmen and women, as Conservative administrations sought to bring commercial efficiencies into public life. Increasingly, these have replaced local government functions, and critical terms, such as 'the quangocracy', the 'unelected state' and the 'new magistracy', were used to underline what some believed to be a characteristic of new-found patronage.

Most significant of all in this revision of the public sector was the stringent control of central over local taxation and expenditure. This was most vividly exemplified by the rows in the late 1980s over the community charge or poll tax, the per capita tax which replaced the long-standing household rating scheme. The poll tax was replaced in 1993 by the council tax, something of a hybrid of the two. This retained the essential feature of central interference, which amounted to the reduction of funding to local government and the exercise of rate-capping, whereby the central state stepped in to stop the municipality from levying the taxes it wished to.

There were various cuts in local services, although it must be said that between 1979 and 1987 the number of local government employees, about 2.3 million in number, fell only marginally. What was possibly more critical was the falling proportion of the money spent locally which was raised locally. From a point years ago when many of the monies expended by local authorities, single- or multi-purpose, were raised by themselves, albeit at the behest of the state, by the early 1990s it was estimated that only 15 per cent was the product of local taxing and charging. It was very much a case of the piper calling the tune.

Free markets and central controls

How is one to explain the apparent paradox of a government, hellbent on freeing the people from public shackles and relying on enterprise and market forces, actually swelling the potency of central government? The answer lies in the duality of the money-economy and the nation-state. Were the freedom of the market to be completely untrammelled, then political boundaries would mean little, and private enterprise would let rip without constraint.

But the commercialism of the modern world, as we have seen in Tudor times and since, has evolved in concert with the concept and practice of the omnicompetent state, the one the prop and benefactor of the other, and vice versa. Although multinational companies and international trade abound and are mightily influential, this rule still applied. It was noticeable that when external links, such as engagement with the European Community, were discussed, the yardstick used was always 'the British interest', not some overarching concern.

Thus the 1980s presented us with the classic case study of a right-wing government, anxious and eager to establish credentials as the protagonist of free markets and individualism, finding it necessary to protect the arena in which that happened by an excessive deployment of centralized control. In order to ensure that economic liberty prevailed, it was necessary – not for the first time in history – to erect centralized political control of a relatively authoritarian kind.

Approach to poverty

In the early years of Margaret Thatcher's governments, steps were taken to reduce expenditure and increase efficiency, such as the abandonment in 1981 of the Supplementary Benefits Commission, which had had 40,000 staff. There were also attempts to standardize and limit payments – for example, in 1981 earnings-related unemployment payments reverted to flat-rate benefits. However, the centrepiece of the strategy was the 1986 Social Security Act, implemented in 1988. Adopting the notion of the 'twin pillars' of state and individual, this tried to focus and 'target' (a buzz-word of the time) monies more effectively.

The 1986 Social Security Act

Alarmed at the astronomic costs looming for SERPs in the twenty-first century, but unable to dismantle the system basically, the 1986 Act made reductions in the provisions of this earnings-related scheme. The life-spread average, rather than the best years, was used as the key, making the full pension a fifth not a quarter, as originally planned, and the widow's full benefit was halved. It was hoped this would reduce the mid-twenty-first century bill by a half, from £35 billion to £16 billion.

Let us digress slightly to follow the story of old age and income mainte-nance. The old age pension had been linked from 1979 to prices rather than earnings, a not too discrete way of reducing its growth. Certainly, by 1987, against an average household income of 1.0, the average for the household headed by a 65–74 year old was 0.55, and for the average 45–54 year old's household it was 1.3. By 1993 it was calculated that a retired couple had lost £25.00 a week as a consequence of the change. The age-old gap between worker and ex-worker, despite great differentials in the income of older people, remained. An aspect of those differentials was the government's encouragement of occupational or private pensions by legislation, which allowed for portability of pensions from one job to another and proffered more choice to employees. A further encouragement lay in generous tax relief, worth over £13 billion annually by the mid-1980s.

After a wide plateau of years during which the number of workers with such pensions had been static at 50 per cent, the fraction sprang to 65 per cent and rising in and after the Thatcher years. Over 11 million were on such schemes by the mid-1980s, and an estimated four million plus were already in receipt of occupational pensions, although some of these were quite tiny. It should be noted that three-quarters of salaried workers were in private pension schemes against a third who were waged, and three-quarters of owner-occupiers against a quarter of council or private-rent tenants.

Returning to the 1986 Act, its proposals included the replacement of sup-plementary benefits by income support, a system of 'personal allowances', with 'premiums' for different circumstances, such as responsibility for de-pendants. In addition, the 'social fund' offered loans on a restricted basis for emergency purposes, replacing the supplementary benefit's previous and more open-ended programme of 'exceptional' payments. A more unified family credit mode replaced the family income supplement, in being since 1971, for low-income families, while housing benefit remained available. Child benefit took the place of family allowance, but it stayed as a universal payment, despite some argument.

Welfare in the 1990s

Much of this was by way of cautious tidying of the system, but the old criticisms from left and right remained: benefits were not high enough; there was stigma attached to their receipt; they were complex to obtain; there was insufficient take-up; a poverty trap existed, with people caught between low-paid jobs and social security; many people were receiving social security who had sufficient income or who were (a trait apparently traceable to Elizabethan times) 'scroungers'. In practice, British social security was still over-complicated. It was comprised of every strand: the contributory insurance items, such as unemployment or retirement benefit; the universal, non-contributory items, such as child benefit or the small subvention made to those over 80; means-tested items, such as income support, the social fund and family credit.

It was an elaborate mix which meant that, by the end of the decade, and with twelve million on child benefit, nearly ten million on the state pension, over a million on invalidity pensions, rising towards three million on unemployment doles, as well as others on a motley of temporary and permanent payments, in any one year over half the nation was on some form of social security.

The SERPS controversy betokened growing anxiety about the demographic switch which had produced a group of over 14 million who were over 55, a quarter of the total population, of whom over 11 million had completed full-time work. This trebling of the fraction in older age, in part explained by the fall in the proportion of those of younger age, in part by the unprecedented survival of most citizens to enjoy a normal life-span, led to much financial head-scratching. The universality of the old age pension, particularly with occupational pensions growing in numbers and with many older people well-to-do, was several times questioned during this period.

In the shorter term, it was unemployment which caused most embarrassment and fuss, not least because the whole welfare structure assumed full or near-full employment as its premise. In 1993 there were, officially, three million out of work, although what some felt to be a polite massaging of the figures perhaps hid another million who were in training programmes or not actively presenting themselves for work, and so forth. Most worrying of all, some two-fifths of these had been unemployed for over a year, compared with only 6 per cent, for example, in the United States. These were four times less likely to obtain work than the others, and medical opinion was trenchant in its accusation that long-term unemployment was a killer disease.

The Beveridge-orientated harmony of employment and subsistence welfare had collapsed. The irony was that, with three million and more out of work, the state, keen to reduce public expenditure and looking in 1993 at a public spending deficit of an unheard of £50 billion, was paying out an average £9,000 a year on each unemployed person. Equally, the Beveridge proposition no longer applied to the 'contingency' of retirement, not with some ten million retired, many of them for extensive periods.

The original and rather austere flat-rate subsistence hand-outs were now looking miserable, especially as they amounted to many people's income over a long time, not just for a brief spell of distress. Where, in the 1940s, only 10 per cent of social beneficiaries had required means-tested supplements, it was now over 30 per cent, including no less than five million pensioners. Professor Jonathan Bradshaw calculated that, in 1992, a modest-but-adequate income was achieved by only 30 per cent of lone mothers and single pensioners, and that many social security dependants do not have sufficient incomes even for a 'low-cost' budget.

Welfare finance in the 1990s

In the year 1992–3, the Department of Social Security spent over £58 billion, and by a long chalk was Whitehall's leading spender. This is apart from another large sum – around £20 billion – expended by local authorities on, for instance, council tax benefits. Expenditure was estimated to rise significantly in the ensuing years. This bill of near £80 billion was eleven times the amount then spent on either education or transport, and represented a sevenfold real terms increase in social security since the inception of the scheme in the 1940s.

Unemployment benefit accounted for £7.4 billion of this great sum for 1992–3, and it was estimated to rise to close on £10 billion in the following year. Family benefits, including child benefits, cost almost as much, at £7.2 billion, while disability pensions, widows' pensions, war pensions and industrial injury benefits cost another £7.5 billion in total. Income support (£3.7 billion), housing benefits (£0.3 billion) and the social fund (£0.23 billion) make up another £4 billion plus, while it takes no less than £4 billion to administer the entire business. By far the biggest stake is the £27.5 billion for the contributory state pension, and it should not be forgotten that, outside of these figures, there is the £13 billion in tax relief for private pensions, almost a half of all that is paid out in state pensions.

The issue of privatism

That bargain over occupational pensions with the grand corporate pension funders is a neat example of what has been called 'privatism', in that it was not individualism. That is to say, it was not market forces freely operating, but a rigged market, with those who contributed to, and those who organized, private pension funds seeking advantage from friendly state assistance. The phenomenon of 'privatism' will reoccur when health, housing and education are under discussion.

Not that we need to wait that long, for 'privatism' very much influenced the expansion of private residential care during the 1980s, when the social security support of private fees rose from £18 million in 1980 to £2 billion in 1993, a startling jump. Along with the decrease in local authority spending in this field, and other factors, this was the main cause of a three-fold rise in residential care for elderly people in England over the decade. This was from about 30,000 to 90,000, whereas public sector residents fell from 120,000 to 100,000. Including some 25,000 voluntary places, this gave England a total of 223,000 residential placements. However, the proportion of older people in institutional care in the 18,000 residential care homes and nursing homes across the United Kingdom is still less than 4 per cent of those over 65, much the same figure as in 1895.

The Griffiths Report examined the provision of care in kind and was the fluent preface to, first, much argumentation, and then, second, government action by way of the Community Care Act of 1991. This introduced tighter controls of social care as from 1993, in the hope of halting the gallop towards institutional care, some of it not strictly required, and in the further hope of concentrating on care in the community through home helps and other forms of day and domiciliary assistance. Although this was castigated as a cost-cutting exercise – £565 million 'ringfenced' funding was made available in 1993–4, £250 million short of what was necessary, according to its critics – there was much to be said for a more coherent look at the provision of community care. Were local authorities able to draw statutory, private and voluntary services into the rational assessment, treatment and evaluation of individualized care 'packages' for those not able to live independently, then the reform would have not been in vain. There is little doubt that care in the community had grown a trifle stilted and rigid, yet also slipshod and fragmented, over the years.

The debates about care in the community illustrated graphically the dilemma facing the apolitical observer of the 1980s and 1990s scene. The New Right Conservatives, in their assault on the 'patronage' state, drew attention to inefficient, over-bureaucratized, wasteful and insensitive management, and aligned this with their bold belief in the durability of individuals to take their chances in an enterprise economy.

Even some of those who felt that their solution was likely to exacerbate the problem of social distress could see that their analysis had much to commend it; and social services were a case in point. Large public agencies had lost, if they ever enjoyed, the secret of efficacious and sympathetic relations with their users, the Post Office perhaps being an outstanding exception at this time. None the less, there were those who wondered whether the risks endemic in 'privatized' solutions could not be avoided by a third proposal, namely an insistence that the services in question be rendered more consumer-conscious and, in the phrase of the hour, 'user-friendly' by decentralized and community influence, even involving experiments in popular democracy.

In a summary sentence, the dilemma was that the public sector was good on needs and bad on wants, and the private sector was the reverse, good on wants and bad on needs.

Approach to ill-health

Ill-health, like poverty, refused to disappear; rather it extended its definition and changed its guise. And, as with social security, there were financial, administrative and policy issues with which to contend.

National Health Service – finance

The cost of the National Health Service for the year 1993–4 was £29 billion, and even that huge sum was £1.7 billion less than originally budgeted, owing to the nation's difficulty with public expenditure. It should be added that national insurance contributions had never paid for more than 20 per cent of the NHS costs, any more than they had paid for all the insurance and pension benefits – general taxation was still the main contributor.

The NHS employed a million people, including over 30,000 general practitioners and 17,000 dentists, but with only half of the staff strictly medical in vocation, leaving a vast swarm of technical, clerical and ancillary employees. That said, the NHS, by international standards, was efficiently run, less than 4 per cent of its 1988 budget, for instance, being devoted to administration.

By the late 1980s the NHS was providing over 30 million treatments annually, compared with eight million in 1949. Ten million eye tests, subject to charge from 1991, were made yearly, and the astronomic total of over 320 million prescriptions were made available each year. By 1993 the cost of these alone was £2 billion. Limitations were introduced into what drugs could be used, and although many retained the right to free prescriptions (children, old people etc.) charges for the remainder were such that, sometimes, it was cheaper to buy the proprietary equivalent.

National Health Service – administration

The health services were subject, like all parts of the welfare state, to the New Right critique, and there were suggestions that the NHS should be privatized. This did not occur, but the service underwent revision in the triple sense alluded to above: charges were raised or imposed, as we have already noted; 'internal markets' were introduced to increase competitive tendencies; central direction was confirmed and emphasized.

The 1983 Griffiths Report had led to a tightening of budgetary procedures and central management, all in an endeavour to render the service more business-like in style, and then, in 1989, the White Paper *Working for Patients* paved the way to an even more resolute essay in such practice. The chief measures were the adoption of general practice budgets, which doctors had to use as efficiently as possible and for which the other services had to compete as briskly as possible, and the establishment of trust status for hospitals and other agencies within the system. This was a form of opting-out, with the hospital managed by a self-governing trust. By 1993 there were about 450 of these striking examples of the quango approach, for all members of these boards were appointed by the Secretary of State for Health. New 'waves' of such trusts were promised.

At about this time, the notion of the Citizens' Charter enjoyed some vogue, with its message of consumer-orientated standards. It was devolved throughout the public services, and included a Patients' Charter, which was very hot, for instance, on waiting lists, which became something of a *cause célèbre* of hospital efficiency. Curiously, the waiting lists for hospital treatment had tended to cling to about 10 per cent of the annual total of hospitalizations since the onset of the NHS.

After 1983 the central administration of the NHS was split between the Health Services Supervisory Board and the NHS Management Board, and from 1988 the Department of Health was separated from its union with Social Security. Chief executives had been appointed to each of the regional authorities to provide managerial acumen. These moves were intended both to improve productivity and to ensure central oversight. Productivity actually doubled: bed utilization dropped from 19 days in the 1960s to eight in the 1980s; the same number of beds as in the 1940s – 400,000 – but with twice the staff, annually handled seven million inpatients, 40 million outpatients and 15 million emergency patients. It was quite a thriving concern.

National Health Service – policy

There was something of a contest between medical and managerial control of the service, while others bemoaned the fact that the NHS embraced too much of either side of that controversy. There were those who would have liked to have seen more environmental or preventive medicine practised, and there were those who would have preferred more democratic controls. The NHS had been deliberately steered clear of direct local government control, but there had been some indirect links, through, for example, the appointment of local councillors to management committees, or the continued use of municipal ambulance and allied services. These links, such as they were, were weakened still further by the revisions of the 1980s, with the 'trust' device an additional blow.

The opted-out hospital, like the opted-out school (which will be briefly discussed below), paradoxically tends not to develop close linkages automatically with its community, tends to be in-bred in terms of influences and tends to be over-reliant on its direct lines of command to the central bodies. Power, especially the authoritative power of the budget, seemed both to slip away from the districts and regions and to swell at the centre – the classic syndrome.

Finally, there was the continuation of private or commercial medicine. Unlike housing, where the majority had always been housed privately, health had for many years been the prime responsibility of the public and voluntary sectors. Even before the NHS, the poor law, the national insurance 'panel' and various charitable efforts had offered some non-commercial succour to the sick. Conversely, the NHS, despite the wishes of very radical thinkers, had not sought to abolish the private sector, and in the 1980s it continued to flourish. It did so more under the device of private insurance than the straightforward remission of fees to doctors which had characterized the pre-1947 situation. There had been precedents then – the British Hospitals Contributory Schemes Association had had no less than 10.5 million members, each of them putting aside a little for themselves and their families against the rainy day of a visit to hospital.

In the early 1990s approaching 4.5 million people, around 8 per cent of the population, enjoyed membership of private health care schemes, with BUPA being the notable front-marker. About 150 private hospitals provided 300,000 annual treatments, with the help of some 7,000 beds, and at a cost of £1 billion, while a further £500 million was spent on off-the-shelf private medicine. It remains an expensive alternative, and its bedrock is the investment of employers in membership for their staffs, hopeful of quick service and a fast return to the workplace. It has been estimated that a quarter of the professional and managerial classes are covered in this fashion. Tax incentives, such as rebates for those who insure elderly relatives, have been offered, and the Labour government's 1976 decision to phase out 'pay-beds' (NHS beds and relevant services used for consultants' private patients) was reversed in 1980. There are currently about 3,000 such pay-beds available. These elements amount to a mild dose of 'privatism'.

Left-wing critics chorus that this array of measures – free market business practices; heavy charging, especially for dental and optical treatments; encouragement of the private sector; over-centralized organization with insufficient local or democratic control – has led and continues to lead to a 'two-tier system'. It was well-known that the kind of geographical and social equalities touched on in Chapter 7 had not been addressed, and fears were loudly expressed that the divisiveness was worsening.

Housing – privatism and the 1980 Housing Act

Of all the Conservative government's actions in respect of welfarism none was more dramatic than the determination to revise and expand owner-occupation of housing. This it did by two complementary processes: the encouragement, notably by taxation and other financial incentives, of the private market; and the encouragement of the sale into private hands of council houses and flats.

During the 1980s annual tax relief on mortgages was worth an average of over £700 per owner-occupier, costing the nation £6.5 billion a year in lost revenue, a negative hand-out of surprising abundance. Needless to say, it was an advantage enjoyed by the better-off in society, with the south-east of England benefiting especially. By the mid-1980s, fuelled by advantageous credit terms, advances for mortgages were running at nearly £17 billion, with repayments reaching about 40–45 per cent of mortgagees' average salaries. The overall mortgage debt was eight times what it had been in 1968.

As for the municipal sector, the 1980 Housing Act required local authorities to sell council properties, with prices reduced by length of tenancy. This act also included a Tenants' Charter, but it was the effect of its main clause which was sweeping. During the 1980s and up to 1993, 1.4 million council houses and flats were conveyed into private hands, by far the most telling process of 'privatism' committed by the Conservatives under Mrs Thatcher. Sales had not been unknown or illegal, but this bargain transaction was equal to all the sales that had taken place between 1945 and 1979. The previous Labour government had reduced the expenditure on public housing by a quarter in the 1970s. The Conservatives now reduced it by another half in the 1980s, although, as a corollary to rents doubling to economic levels at a time of recession, rent rebates grew considerably during the late 1980s.

Housing – the position in the early 1990s

The 1988 Housing Act gave council estates the choice of opting for a landlord other than the local authority, and the government hoped to see the establishment of housing action trusts to take over the worst estates, on some of which half the flats might be empty. There was also legislation to end the control of private rentals, although security of tenure remained. These enactments had relatively little effect, compared with the sale of council housing.

The upshot was that, by 1988, 66 per cent of British homes (only 43 per cent in Scotland, however, where traditionally council housing was especially strong) were owner-occupied, compared with 55 per cent in 1979 and only 10 per cent in 1914. Some 90 per cent of personal savings and a third of personal sector wealth was tied up in owner-occupied properties. This left 24 per cent of homes as council tenancies and 10 per cent privately rented or run by housing associations. Something like a fifth of council accommodation had been transferred into private hands.

There was now precious little public building – there were only 20,000 starts in 1980, compared with over 100,000 in 1976 – while the 200,000 a year building of private properties in the 1980s also dwindled significantly as boom gave way to slump in the late 1980s and early 1990s. Moreover, the high-rise edifices of the 1960s were now condemned out of hand, and many were demolished, at an estimated replacement value of £10 billion.

All in all, housing standards, like health standards, had risen since 1945. Almost all housing units now enjoyed sole use of basic amenities, and no less than 70 per cent were centrally heated. None the less, it was rapidly ageing stock, with 2.4 million of the total 21.3 million housing units of Britain in poor repair.

More problematic than the houses were the householders. One million (a fifth) of council house tenants were in arrears, while in the private sector the 1990s recession brought soaring levels of repossessions of houses and record mortgage repayment arrears. Yet it was claimed that there were a million empty houses across the two sectors, and a million people were on the council waiting lists, whereas half the owner-occupiers had thankfully discharged their mortgage debt and 200,000 people had second homes. It was estimated that, in the early 1990s, there were 300,000 people who, from a variety of causes, were homeless. The 1977 and 1985 Housing (Homeless Persons) Acts had transferred the responsibility for this social ill from the social services to the housing departments, placing on them an obligation to find some shelter for those made homeless.

It was a hapless compound, reflecting the truism that housing, as a set of assets, is not flexibly amenable to national needs as they change; reflecting, too, the inadequacy over many years of British housing policy. Unlike in health, education and social security, there had scarcely been any attempt to construct a national blueprint. In practice, both main political parties accepted owner-occupation as the norm, and believed in its endorsement of political stability, rooting families, as it did, in the safety of their own property.

By contrast, the political establishment saw in the remnants of public sector housing little more than accommodation for the residual populace, those who could just not make the grade as house-owners. Any aspiration to construct less divisive and more integrated communities, through a national policy of land-use, planning and building development, was far from the thoughts of most politicians.

The grand sale of council houses, in the circumstances a most popular and successful measure, was an edict from on high, commanding the local authorities to retail their housing assets to sitting tenants. Of all the instances of the deployment of autocratic central power, directed at the extension of 'privatism', this was probably the most meaningful.

Approach to ignorance

It was in the education system that many of the traits of the reforming zeal of 1980s Conservatism were most lucidly exhibited.

The Thatcherite critique of education

As with other services, state spending on education has remained virtually static over the fifteen years from about 1977. For 1992–3, the budget was some £9.5 billion, of which over half, about £5.5 billion, was for higher education. About nine million pupils were being educated in United Kingdom schools in the early 1990s, at an average annual cost of roughly £1,000, while well over 250,000 students were engaged in full-time higher education. This was about 10 per cent of the age-group, and this percentage had remained the same since the late 1960s. The ratio of teachers to pupils had improved – for primary children from 1:27 in 1971 to 1:22 in 1986, for secondary children from 1:18 to 1:15 over the same period of time – while public examination results were showing a small but significant betterment.

The Thatcherite criticism of the schools was ideological in two senses. There was, first, an expressed fear that schools and colleges were wasteful of resources and not efficiently run. There was, second, an anxiety that educational standards were low, in part because of left-wing tinkering and soft-centred experiment. Thus there were twin siren calls, the one redolent of new Conservatism, in terms of value for money, the other a more traditional Conservative view about a concentration on the old-fashioned basics of reading, writing and arithmetic.

There was a flurry of Education Acts during the Thatcher years, in some way aiming to provide parents with more freedom of choice of schools, and enabling parents to be better represented on governing bodies, all in an attempt to make the education service more susceptible to the wishes of its consumers. Happily, and stemming chiefly from continental European leads, corporal punishment was abolished in the 1980 Act. However, the seminal statute was the 1988 Education Act, which laid down several major revisions of the public system.

The 1988 Education Act

Parents remained the focus. Information, about examination results, for instance, had to be made available to parents, and a school henceforth had to admit children desirous of entry up to its capacity, regardless of any plan or restriction imposed by the local education authority. Local government, with education its main component, suffered further. The Inner London Education Authority had already been abolished, with the responsibility transferring to the boroughs which had comprised that agency, but other edicts cut across the powers of all LEAs.

At the post-school level, restraints were placed on spending for further and continuing education. City technology colleges were planned, with the help of local business, to bring centrally controlled educational units to urban areas, although these were never established in the numbers to which the government had aspired. The polytechnics were taken from local authority supervision, and by 1992 were independent universities. Later, the LEAs lost control of the 550 further education and sixth form colleges. From 1993 they were no longer allowed to nominate members for the governing bodies of these places, which catered for something like a million students. Instead business executives had to fill half the membership of the boards, and all funding was henceforward distributed by another quango, the Further Education Funding Council.

At the school level, the 1988 Act gave schools virtual autonomy, primarily through the appointment and election of school-based governing bodies, and by the operation, under the acronym LMS (local management of schools), of delegated budgets. In the patois of the day, schools became cost centres. Furthermore, on a simple ballot of current parents (without, that is, any reflection of the feelings of the community at large) and with the temptation of initially favourable funding, schools were encouraged to 'opt out' and seek independence of the local authority. Although this was also a process that moved more ponderously than ministers had hoped – there were ambitions to render all secondary schools thus autonomous by 1997 – about 800 schools had taken advantage of this offer by 1993.

The 1988 Act also introduced the National Curriculum, with three core subjects, of English, maths and science, and seven 'foundation' subjects. This was done in a bid to improve the overall standards of education, and, perhaps strangely, received support across a wide body of opinion. It was underpinned by a series of age-related testing procedures, which caused much controversy. Then there was an insistence on the use of a privatized inspectorate, under the national regulation of the quango, Ofsted, labelled very much after the consumerist style of the period for national regulators: it was ranged alongside Ofgas, Ofwat, Oftel and so on. The old-style public inspectorate was disbanded in 1993.

Centralism and privatism in education

A national curriculum was not quite as novel as some imagined. The payment by results scheme, inaugurated during the late Victorian era and in use until 1898, had lain down the necessary syllabus, which was subject to inspectoral scrutiny pending the award of grants. A broad 'elementary code' existed until 1944, and even thereafter, and whatever the changes of methods in some schools, the teaching ethos itself, together with the intense pressure of public examination, had guaranteed a certain modicum of uniformity.

None the less, this reversion to a full-scale national curriculum, with ministers pronouncing on what history should be taught and when it should end, what religious knowledge should be presented and what literature was suitable for pupils to read, was a long step into an old-fashioned past. It represented a censorious approach to schooling long absent from much of British educational circles, almost as if the government wished to clone children for social and vocational ends. It was also out-moded in its failure to acknowledge the weight of home and neighbourhood influence on educational out-turns, placing a reliance on the school as a change-agent out of all reasonable aspiration.

The orthodox independent sector still enjoyed the kind of qualitative character associated with private health care, in spite of the sort of financial pressures that had hit the medical model. The proportion of children involved had remained very similar over time. About 5 per cent of children, including 8.5 per cent of secondary age children, were in fee-paying schools in the early 1990s, that is, about half a million youngsters in all. The Conservative government introduced an assisted places scheme to support indigent parents, at a yearly cost of some £50 million, and, with tax relief and other payments, the state did make available considerable sums to the commercial sector. The products of private education performed conventionally well: in 1985 half the Oxbridge studentship had been educated independently. However, one should recall that much of this might have reflected social background being expressed through the schools rather than the actual schooling itself – private education is probably 'a catalyst rather than a crucial determinant in its own right'.

Education was, then, a critical test-bed for the questioning of the welfare state. There were efforts to introduce 'privatism' and market-style consumerism into the system. There were attempts to halt the flow of public money, which left many schools, like many hospitals, a little too dependent on domestic fund-raising exercises. There were moves to reduce radically the power of the local authority, for so long, in varied guises, the bulwark of the system. There were, conversely, moves to gather enormous power into the bosom of the central authority. These were the features of an all-encompassing review of the old system of public education in Britain.

Approach to crime

Organizationally speaking, there was probably less movement in this social field than in the other three during the 1980s and early 1990s, but that is not to suggest that the problem of crime was any less demanding than sickness, poverty and ignorance. Indeed, crime continued to exercise many minds during this period.

Crime – its causes and incidence

The Conservative Party, traditionally the advocate of strong law enforcement, was faced with an unstoppable cascade of crime. Just as the Conservatives blamed what they deemed poor educational results on permissiveness, left-wing fanaticism and dysfunctional family life, they were inclined to find ill-disciplined home and communal life-styles culpable for the increasing crime wave.

Their opponents were quick to point to social ills as the continuing cause, and even Sir Peter Imbert, retiring Commissioner of the Metropolitan Police in 1993, was inclined to the belief that unemployment and poverty were chiefly to blame. There were also suggestions that a society in which enter-prising individualism was encouraged was bound to fall foul, among rich and poor, of those ready to overstep the legal mark. There were also noises about the xenophobia of a right-wing government, and the notion that some misbehaviour – racial harassment and football hooliganism in the world arena – was not unconnected.

It might be argued that the two aspects – unstable family life with loss of social values, and material deprivation – were not incompatible as explana-tions. Certainly, there was evidence, based, for instance, on a study of chil-dren and youth in the north-east in 1992, that deviance was more the consequence of uncommitted or ineffective parenting than of socio-economic impoverishment, yet the cultural context of life on run-down urban estates could well have helped to cause the social breakdown initially.

What no one could escape was the tidal wave of criminal statistics. The British Crime Survey 1992 indicated that three times as many crimes were committed as were reported, and for 1991 a gross total of 15 million crimes was estimated for England and Wales, embracing 5.5 million notified offences, but excluding drugs, fraud, shoplifting and commercial burglary. There had been 11 million offences in 1981, showing an increase of 36 per cent. However, 'acquisitive' crime, such as theft and burglary, had almost doubled in the decade, while attempted thefts, such as trying to break into cars, had risen by four times. It became obvious that, as the recession deepened in the early 1990s, burglary increased dramatically, at an annual cost to the victims of £1 billion, and at a rate of three burglaries every minute.

Although violent and sexual offences continued to give proper cause for disquiet, the huge burden of crime was against property, and this was un-equally spread, with the poorest municipal estates being three times more vulnerable than the average district. A 1992 estimate suggested that pro-fessional crime had a turnover of £14 billion, which, if true and if combined, would have made it the fourth wealthiest company in Britain. The 1980s also witnessed some civil disorder, some of it in connection with politics – anti-poll tax demonstrations, coal mining and printing disputes, for instance – and some in connection with inner-city difficulties – in Liverpool, Bristol and Newcastle upon Tyne, for example.

Crime – the public response

The state machinery for grappling with this dreadful problem had grown immense. In 1992 there were 130,000 police officers, 50,000 civilian staff in ancillary positions, 34,000 prison officers, 20,000 court and probation staff, a proportion of over 70,000 lawyers engaged in criminal practice and 175,000 security personnel. The barristers and solicitors excluded, this still left over 400,000 men and women in the battle against crime.

The Home Office spent about £5 billion a year on the police and about £1.5 billion on the prison service. There were moves to privatize parts of the prison service and, initially, a small number of prisons and some conveyance of prisoners to and from court were handed over to private firms. In a backward glance to a by-gone age of 'know-everyone' policing, there were endeavours to enlist communal volunteers. In the early 1990s there were some 60,000 Neighbourhood Watch schemes of variable energies, and there were some 350 victim support units, with 8,000 volunteers, advising 250,000 people each year.

On the other hand, there were moves to shave expenditure on legal aid, with the suspicion that more people would avoid the courts simply on grounds of cost. The courts, both civil and criminal, were faced with huge log-jams of work, despite the fact that over 90 per cent of cases were dealt with in local magistrates' courts. A Royal Commission, the first for many years, scrutinized the judicial process in the hope of making the procedure less hidebound and wasteful, and also in the hope of recommending how miscarriages of justice, of which several had come to light during the early 1990s, might be avoided. The resultant Runciman Report was published in 1993.

Nationally, there were moves toward centralization. This was largely an operational imperative, most overtly seen at the time of the mining strike in the mid-1980s, when the police were organized on a nationwide scale to oversee that sometimes fiery disputation. Other matters, such as the sharing of computerized intelligence and cooperation over major crime, like the drugs traffic, contributed to the trend.

In 1993 the Sheehy Report recommended changes in the operational and salary structure of the police, and at about the same time a Police Bill was published, which proposed further inroads into local accountability. It was intended that the local police authorities would, in future, be 16-member bodies, with fewer local government and more business representatives. An advisory body, with no direct elective representation, was suggested for the Metropolitan Police. As with other services, such as health and education, 'league tables' were proposed as a check on the efficiency of the police forces, and the process by which police forces merged was shortened. Reliable reports suggested that the Home Office was determined to reduce the number of police forces even further, from the then existing 43 to as few as 20, and to exercise the heavy hand of autocratic control over them.

The link with local government, as in health and education, was threatened and, indeed, the operational freedom of chief constables had, in effect, already been extended over the preceding years. The Benthamite tenet, so loved by the Victorians, of identifying as closely as possible the governed and the governors of services was fast losing favour. Local democratic accountability was being replaced, in the police as elsewhere, with financial accountability, aligned with forceful central autocracy.

Modern policing does pose a difficult question about its provenance and style. Unlike the settled location of schools and hospitals, the incidence of crime is restless and never static, and it ranges from international fraud of baffling complexity to vandalism in the local park. The police have never quite mastered the pyramidal trick of peak-to-base interface with the public – unlike the Post Office, where worldwide communication is somehow harmoniously matched by the cycling postman visiting the loneliest cottage.

The gradual diminution in the number of forces; the gradual encroachment of the central authority; the gradual reduction in the role of the elected local authority; the gradual assumption of power by the chief constables; and the gradual undermining of the popularity of and esteem for the police – these became the leading characteristics of police management before and into the 1990s.

Comparative features

Put briefly, all Britain's friends and rivals in the developed world underwent the same economic trauma to some degree after the mid-1970s. Inflation, unemployment and deficit budgets were everywhere to be found, not least in the Eastern European countries which had shed the yoke of harsh so-called communist dominion during the late 1980s. Even in Sweden there was talk of 'consolidation versus dismantling', as unemployment, hitherto almost unknown, grew, and tighter rules were introduced in respect of benefits.

The United States was faced in the early 1990s with a huge federal budget deficit of £230 billion annually and 7 per cent unemployment, twice as much as the norm. Austria was a little more successful in preserving employment, although a main object of that policy was an avoidance of rising security benefits, while Germany, now inclusive of what proved to be an expensive ex-East German Republic, was feeling the pinch. Japan, after something of a welfare bonanza, was also prepared to call a halt and seek for consolidation, and in Canada the limits of universality as a base for social welfare were, as elsewhere, being questioned. Both Australia and New Zealand introduced income-related rules for some of what had previously been universal benefits, and France initiated a freeze on pensions. Everywhere, there was, in a word, retrenchment.

An analysis of crime among industrialized nations, coordinated by the Netherlands Justice Ministry and published in 1993, demonstrated all too vividly that social ills know few frontiers. Crime has risen wholesale, and seems to be related to the degree of industrial and urban development. Measured as a percentage of the population criminally victimized, New Zealand emerged as the worst nation for criminality, with the Netherlands, Canada, Australia, the United States and Poland all above Britain. Switzerland, Japan and, excluding crimes associated with political activity there, Northern Ireland had fared better. As that short list makes apparent, differing political systems and differing police and sentencing policies had no marked effect either way. These facts offer a useful reminder of the international range of very similar social problems.

As in Britain, there were some attempts to depoliticize the economy and to liberate business people to promote trade as freely as possible, the aspiration being that all-round growth and profitability would eventually benefit all. The presidencies of Ronald Reagan and George Bush in the United States witnessed a similar anti-tax, pro-market approach to that of Britain, with similar cuts and curbs on the public services. Across the world, the crucial difference was between those politicians who felt exultant at the apparent failure of the welfare bureaucracies and those who felt uncomfortable about that seeming lack of success. The difference was, to put it another way, between those who took an atomized or individualist view of life, with the priority to be accorded economic 'spontaneity', and those with more collective of social democratic leanings. Both were challenged by the trauma of an unstable declining global economy.

It is true that there remained a high support across the developed world for state-provided services, and even President Clinton, during his successful election campaign in the USA in 1992, gained in strength from his avowal to right the wrong of American health care, dragged down, as it was, by heavy insurance premiums and the like. It is equally true to remark that what was on the political rack was the 'state', as the respondent to the requirements of 'welfare'. The post-1973 scene was one in which the problem was increasingly influenced by international factors, such as the activities of worldwide financial dealings and multinational companies. The nation-state had long been buffeted by the waves of the global market, but in the last quarter of the twentieth century those waves were very much stronger.

This led, in turn, to thoughts that possibly the solutions would have to be extra-state in response to this. A mild illustration of this was the inclusion in the European Community's Maastricht Treaty, ratified in 1993, and intended to assist the EC in its trading and allied ventures, of a Social Chapter. This offered workers across the European Community certain rights in regard of social conditions, such as pay and hours of work. It was not, however, accepted by the British government.

Specific features

Ethnic minorities

The 1980s were an ambivalent period for the so-called minorities. Assuming that the male Anglo-Saxon, employed or employable, is par for the national course, then the rest – the children, the disabled people, retired and elderly people, women and members of ethnic minorities – won most of the arguments but did not regularly gain advantages in consequence. Their rights to equal citizenship were vociferously and refreshingly heard but, in most part because of economic and social decline, there was little by way of material prizes to be found.

In an era of violent crime and economic dislocation, racism showed no signs of abating, and, for instance, there was much questioning of the attitudes of the police and the judiciary to Afro-Caribbean involvement in crime, or the protection made available to harassed Asian households and premises. The newly united Germany, occasionally France and the United States were other nations finding this problem almost endemic, while, in tragic particular, the warfare which attended the dismemberment of the former Yugoslavia in the early 1990s was a grievous illustration.

More optimistically, there were many in Britain who recognized the contribution made by incomers and the generations of their settled families: a third of NHS hospital staff and a fifth of Britain's general practitioners, for example, were from overseas.

Disabled people

In 1988 it was reported that over six million people in the United Kingdom suffered from some form of physical or mental handicap, one and a half million of whom were severely handicapped, and many of whom were reliant entirely on the state for their main income. At the same time, with several worthy pressure groups in the van, the struggle to secure, for instance, rational access to public buildings, transport and the like continued, so that by the 1990s there was a general acknowledgement that this was a just demand.

Of course, it was pressed by many of those in authority that the necessary resources were not readily available to put everything to rights. Still, there was great pressure to make adequate provision when new starts were made in buildings or in other facilities.

Retired people

There was also some growing recognition of retired people, now more positively described under the generic label of the Third Age, following the First Age of childhood and the Second Age of paid work and parenting. Many believed they should be regarded as active rather than passive members of society, as the inventors of their destiny rather than the recipients of patronizing hand-outs. 'Ageism' began to enjoy something of a meaning parallel with 'racism' and 'sexism', although, strictly speaking, age discrimination may affect, in varying ways, all age groups and not just older people.

There were at this time some 11.4 millions over 55 years of age and finished with paid work and/or parenting, an unprecedented fraction, although, again, one to be found in greater or lesser degree across the industrialized world. Many were healthy and wealthy, many were not: all deserved to be shown that citizenship and work were not identical, and that socially productive roles could be found for them. Once more, lack of funds was often the plea of the decision-makers.

Children

Children in need had their own legislation with the Children's Act of 1988, which produced what was felt to be a more unified legal code, principally for the operations in this regard of the local authority social services departments. The period was one in which the possibly long-submerged horrors of child abuse, sexual as well as physical, surfaced, and there were several pertinent cases, many domestic but others institutional.

The whole mood of social work was to move away from the institutional frame. In the early 1990s there were about 100,000 children in care at any given time, but only a quarter were now in large-scale homes, with the majority fostered or otherwise provided with more homely accommodation.

This switch from the austerity and aridity of the kind of institutional existence which had been a gloomy feature of British social practice since early Victorian times was also to be found in the 'care in the community' stance, whereby it was hoped that older and infirm people might, with help, stay in their own houses, and, not without many misgivings, that mentally ill patients might be re-established in the ordinary surrounds of home-life.

Women

There were, by this stage, over 160,000 divorces a year in Britain, which meant that, over time, one marriage in three and one child in five was affected. One-parent families were on the increase, some by choice but many – a point often forgotten by moralizing critics – through marital breakdown. One in nine of these were men, while, of the women, 19 per cent were widows and 63 per cent were divorced or separated. Eighteen per cent had never married, although the majority of these had cohabited for some time. There were roughly a million single-parent households, catering for a million and a half children, and about half of those parents were on income support. The 1984 Matrimonial and Family Proceedings Act made divorce simpler, by virtue of a year's separation, and it also tried to mend the fences of the maintenance field. In the late 1980s, 25 per cent of maintenance orders were unpaid and 55 per cent were in arrears.

The 1992 Household Survey demonstrated that although unemployment was having some marginal effects, the working mother was still in the as-cendant. Fifty-nine per cent of women with dependent children had jobs, and over the past ten years the number of mothers of under-fives with jobs, many of them part-time, had risen from 25 to 43 per cent. Almost 71 per cent of mothers of under-fives had their children cared for by others, made up of 21 per cent in nursery schools, 23 per cent with voluntary and private schemes or child-minders, 20 per cent with unpaid family or friends, only 6 per cent in local authority schemes and just 1 per cent in workplace creches. The desire and the need of mothers to find care for their young children, especially with a view to holding down jobs, had definitely grown, and was emerging as one of the critical social causes of the 1990s.

One gloss on this was the wish of women to harmonize domestic and vocational life, in a way that might have been familiar to their predecessors (albeit without the option, for the most part) in medieval society or most agricultural communities, or even some special-case industrial activities, such as textiles. Although there were other factors – the slaughter of putative male partners in two world wars, for instance – bearing on this statistic, there was a declining number of single women, many of whom had probably been faced in the past with the stark choice of career or marriage.

It must be concluded that, for all the advances on the feminist front, women still bore an unfair brunt of the domestic duties, in particular of caring for older or disabled relatives, while, the headline-grabbing exceptions apart, many of the professions, beginning with parliament itself, showed few signs of a dash for equity.

Conclusion

The 'privatized' re-casting of the welfare state from 1979 onwards, against a canvas of economic greyness, is too close to call in terms of its likely permanence. Strident as it was, it may well be that, assessed over the lengthier perspective, it will seem less dramatic and durable than first sight suggests.

Much will depend, as ever, on the circumstance of the economy, and whether the post-1973 turndown, with its succession of slumps, is a temporary or long-term condition. If, as some opine, it is the latter, then welfarism may have to face corresponding hardships. Conversely, public welfare policies do continue to go hand in hand with urbanized, industrialized economies, to the point where it is hardly thinkable that a country like Britain could have anything less than a tolerable system of social provision.

Some had believed that one of the hopes for the next cycle of welfare delivery was decentralization and a closer correspondence of users and facilities. Community schools, community policing, community health centres, centres for community care, each with a fair degree of popular democracy and communal accountability – these were the innocent thoughts of some reformers.

The nearest to that has been the practice of what some commentators, such as Vernon Bognandor, began to call 'fragmentation'. This arose in public services, where outright 'privatization' was impractical for one reason or another, and where forms of 'privatism' or other attempts to include market habits were introduced. These often led to a splitting up of an existing coordinated scheme or pattern, on the grounds that it was monopolistic and inefficient. The privatization of British Rail, with its plethora of service franchises, Railtrack zones and other divisions, is the most vivid example. However, with the NHS trusts, the opted-out schools, the privatized prisons and other instances, there were signs of this lack of a coherent pattern in parts of the social services.

None the less, it may be that, in time, the chief outcome of the Conservative revisions of the 1980s will be judged to be, ironically, not the practice of market forces and enterprise but the authoritative impact of strict centralism. That, of course, would be the antithesis of those communitarian aspirations, such as community schools or community hospitals, not least because the funding and the appointments to board or allied membership remains closely in the hands of the central, national authority. What might be called the quangoesque tendency is far removed from any hopes of popular democracy and empowerment.

Were this to be the case, then one of the major themes of this study would be justified; namely, the switchback of central and local authority, with first one and then the other finding itself in the ascendant. And, at the finale, the chief motif of this text – the relation of social provision to social stability and wherewithal – is also justified. Even in economic turmoil, even with governments keen to change from welfare spending, not only in Britain but across the world, that rule applies. Governments, however rigorous their rhetoric, are forced to stop short of risking the overall solidity of the realm. However reluctantly, social welfare, in all its forms, must be used to hold that balance.

The British government, faced with the possibility of a social security bill of almost £100 billion by the year 2000, and with the economy persisting in dragging its feet, is no more free from that central political question than was the nomadic Hebrew, with his public hygiene problem, that we met in Chapter 1, or the medieval peasant, scourged by famine, that we encountered in Chapter 2.

Advice on further reading

This concluding chapter has tried both to describe the situation of Britain's social provision in the early 1990s and to place that description in the context of an ongoing, and worldwide, critique of welfarism. For a final round-up of reading, therefore, we have, first, two references in respect of the social position of Britain in modern times.

Abercrombie, N. *et al.* (1988) *Contemporary British Society*, Polity Press, Cambridge (updated annually).
Central Office of Information (1992) *Britain 1992: an Official Handbook*, HMSO, London (an annual publication).

Second, three books address the questioning of the welfare state, both in Britain and overseas.

Ball, M., Gray, F. and McDowell, L. (1989) *The Transformation of Britain: Contemporary Social and Economic Change*, Fontana. London.
Mishra, R. (1984) *The Welfare State in Crisis: Social Thought and Social Change*, Harvester Wheatsheaf, Hemel Hempstead.
Paradakis, E. and Taylor-Goodby, P. (1987) *The Private Provision of Public Welfare*, Harvester Wheatsheaf, Hemel Hempstead.

The following select bibliography is largely devoted to very recent literature which deals in great detail with the contemporary situation.

General advice on further reading

There follows a select bibliography of literature which should enable students to continue their reading, beyond the introductory passages of the foregoing chapters, the better to equip them for the planning of essays, tutorials and so on. Each chapter has included some preliminary reading, usually chosen for its vintage character as well-tested source and ideas material, and some of those books suggested for such solid value may have to be sought in college libraries and elsewhere.

This final select bibliography is almost invariably composed of new, recent or revised publications, many of them necessarily concerned with the contemporary and near-contemporary scene. Care has been taken to provide an up-to-date list, and all the books recommended are in print and readily available. For ease of reference, the literature is divided into the same sections as each of the chapters.

Social and economic background

Briggs, A. (1983) *A Social History of England*, Penguin, Harmondsworth (2nd edn 1987).

Brown, R. (1991) *Society and Economy and Modern Britain 1700–1850*, Routledge, London.

Deakin, N. (1987) *The Politics of Welfare*, Routledge, London.

Dunleavy, P. (1991) *Democracy, Bureaucracy and Public Choice*, Longman, Harlow.

Elcock, H. (1991) *Change and Decay? Public Administration in the 1990s*, Longman, Harlow.

Halsey, A. H. (ed.) (1972) *British Social Trends since 1900*, Macmillan, London (revised edn 1988).

Kingdom, J. (1991) *Local Government and Politics in Britain*, Harvester Wheatsheaf, Hemel Hempstead.

Marwick, A. (1982) *British Society since 1945*, Penguin, Harmondsworth (5th edn 1990).

Peden, G. C. (1991) *British Economic and Social Policy, Lloyd George to Margaret Thatcher*, Philip Allan, Hemel Hempstead.

Wilson, T. D. (ed.) (1991) *The State and Social Welfare*, Longman, Harlow.

Common factors in social provision

Ascher, K. (1987) *The Politics of Privatisation: Contracting out of Public Services*, Macmillan, London.

Atkinson, A. B. (1983) *Social Justice and Public Policy*, Harvester Wheatsheaf, Hemel Hempstead.

Brown, P. and Sparks, R. (eds) (1989) *Beyond Thatcherism*, Open University Press, Milton Keynes (2nd edn 1990).

Challis, L. (1990) *Organising Public Social Services*, Longman, Harlow.

Culpitt, I. (1992) *Welfare and Citizenship; Beyond the Crisis of the Welfare State?*, Sage, London.

DiNitto, D. (1992) *Social Welfare: Politics and Public Policy*, Harvester Wheatsheaf, Hemel Hempstead.

Fraser, D. (1973) *The Evolution of the British Welfare State*, Macmillan, London (2nd edn 1984).

Gamble, A. (1981) *An Introduction to Modern Social and Political Thought*, Macmillan, London.

Glennester, H. (1992) *Paying for Welfare: the 1990s*, Harvester Wheatsheaf, Hemel Hempstead.

Ham, C. (1992) *The Policy Process in the Modern Capitalist State*, Harvester Wheatsheaf, Hemel Hempstead.

Hewitt, M. (1992) *Welfare, Ideology and Need: Developing Perspectives on the Welfare State*, Harvester Wheatsheaf, Hemel Hempstead.

Hill, M. (ed.) (1993) *The Policy Process: a Reader*, Harvester Wheatsheaf, Hemel Hempstead.

Johnson, N. (1987) *The Welfare State in Transition: the Theory and Practice of Welfare Pluralism*, Harvester Wheatsheaf, Hemel Hempstead.

Johnson, N. (1990) *Reconstructing the Welfare State: a Decade of Change, 1980–1990*, Harvester Wheatsheaf, Hemel Hempstead.

Loney, M., Boswell, D. and Clarke, J. (1983) *Social Policy and Social Welfare*, Open University Press, Milton Keynes (4th edn 1990).

Lowe, R. (1993) *The Welfare State in Britain since 1945*, Macmillan, London.

Manning, N. (ed.) (1985) *Social Problems and the Welfare Ideal*, Gower, London (3rd edn 1993).

Mishra, R. (1981) *Society and Social Policy: Theories and Practice of Welfare*, Macmillan, London.

Pierson, C. (1991) *Beyond the Welfare State? The New Political Economy of Welfare*, Polity Press, Cambridge.

Taylor-Gooby, P. (1991) *Social Change, Social Welfare and Social Science*, Harvester Wheatsheaf, Hemel Hempstead.

Approach to poverty

Alcock, P. (1987) *Poverty and State Support*, Longman, Harlow.

Alcock, P. (1993) *Understanding Poverty*, Macmillan, London.

Atkinson, A. B. (1989) *Poverty and Social Security*, Harvester Wheatsheaf, Hemel Hempstead.

Baugh, W. E. (1992) *Introduction to Social and Community Services*, 6th edn, Macmillan, London.

Bryson, L. (1992) *Welfare and the State: Who Benefits?*, Macmillan, London.

Spicker, P. (1992) *Poverty and Social Security*, Routledge, London.

Webb, A. and Wistow, G. (1987) *Social Work, Social Care and Social Planning*, Longman, Harlow.

Approach to ill-health

Health

Allsop, J. (1984) *Health Policy and the National Health Service*, Longman, Harlow.
Baggott, R. (1993) *Health and Health Care in Britain*, Macmillan, London.
Dingwall, R., Rafferty, A. M. and Webster, C. (1988) *An Introduction to the Social History of Nursing*, Routledge, London.
Ham, C. (1982) *Health Policy in Britain: the Politics and Organisation of the National Health Service*, Macmillan, London (3rd edn 1992).
Klein, R. (1989) *The Politics of the National Health Service*, 2nd edn, Longman, Harlow.
Walmsley, J., Reynolds, J. and Shakespeare, P. (1992) *Health, Welfare and Practice*, Sage, London.
Webster, C. (ed.) (1993) *Caring for Health: History and Diversity*, Open University Press, Buckingham.

Housing

Balchin, P. N. (1985) *Housing Policy: an Introduction*, Routledge, London (2nd edn 1989).
Birchall, J. (1992) *Housing Policy in the 1990s*, Routledge, London.
Clapham, D., Kemp, P. and Smith, S. (1990) *Social Policy and Housing*, Macmillan, London.
Malpass, P. and Murie, A. (1982) *Housing Policy and Practice*, Macmillan, London (3rd edn 1990).

Approach to ignorance

Ballantine, J. H. (1993) *The Sociology of Education: a Systematic Analysis*, Prentice Hall, Hemel Hempstead.
Gordon, P., Aldrich, R. and Dean, D. (1991) *Education and Policy in England in the Twentieth Century*, Woburn, London.
Lowe, R. (1991) *Education in the Post-war Years*, Routledge, London.
Meigham, R. (1981) *A Sociology of Education*, Cassell, London.
Simon, B. (1988) *Education and the Social Order*, Lawrence and Wishart, London.
Wexler, P. (1991) *Social Analysis of Education*, Routledge, London.

Approach to crime

Fitzgerald, M., McLennan, G. and Pawson, J. (1993) *Crime and Society; Readings in History and Theory*, 7th edn, Routledge, London.
Johnston, L. (1992) *The Re-birth of Private Policing*, Routledge, London.
Morris, T. (1989) *Crime and Criminal Justice since 1945*, Blackwell, Oxford.
Reiner, R. (1992) *The Politics of the Police*, Harvester Wheatsheaf, Hemel Hempstead.

Whitfield, R. (ed.) (1991) *The State of the Prisons – 200 Years on*, Routledge, London.

Comparative features

Bailey, J. (ed.) (1992) *Social Europe*, Longman, Harlow.
Cochrane, A. and Clarke, J. (eds) (1993) *Comparing Welfare States: Britain in International Context*, Sage, London.
Curran, D. J. and Renzetti, C. M. (1993) *Social Problems: Society in Crisis*, Allyn and Bacon, Hemel Hempstead.
Green, A. (1990) *Education and State Formation: the Rise of Educational Systems in England, France and the USA*, Macmillan, London.
Heidensohn, F. and Farrell, M. (1993) *Crime in Europe*, Routledge, London.
Mawby, R. I. (1990) *Comparative Policing Issues*, Unwin Hyman, London.
Mayo, M. (1993) *The Mixed Economy of Welfare*, Macmillan, London.
Mishra, R. (1990) *The Welfare State in Capitalist Society*, Harvester Wheatsheaf, Hemel Hempstead.
Power, A. (1993) *Hovels to Highrise: State Housing in Europe since 1850*, Routledge, London.
Room, G. (ed.) (1991) *Toward a European Welfare State?*, School for Advanced Urban Studies, Bristol.
Sullivan, M. (1992) *The Politics of Social Policy*, Harvester Wheatsheaf, Hemel Hempstead.
Thane, P. and Bock, G. (eds) (1991) *Maternity and Gender Policies: Women and the Rise of European Welfare States 1850s to 1950s*, Routledge, London.

Specific features

Race

Cashmore, E. and McLauglin, E. (1991) *Out of Order? Policing Black People*, Routledge, London.
Cross, M. and Keith, M. (eds) (1992) *Racism, the City and the State*, Routledge, London.
Hiro, D. (1971) *Black British; White British: a History of Race Relations in Britain*, Paladin, London (3rd edn 1991).
Skellington, R. with Morris, P. (1992) *Race in Britain Today*, Sage, London.

Disabled and elderly people

Coleridge, P. (1993) *Disability, Liberation and Development*, Oxfam, Oxford.
Jefferys, M. (ed.) (1989) *Growing Old in the Twentieth Century*, Routledge, London.
Johnson, P. and Falkingham, J. (1992) *Ageing and Economic Welfare,* Sage, London.
Oliver, M. (1990) *The Politics of Disablement*, Macmillan, London.
Swain, J., Finkelstein, V., French, S. and Oliver M. (1992) *Disabling Barriers – Enabling Environments*, Sage, London.
Tinker, A. (1981) *Elderly People in Modern Society*, Longman, Harlow (3rd revision 1992).

Family and gender issues

Allen, N. (1990) *Making Sense of the Children's Act*, Longman, London (2nd edn 1992).

Bradshaw, J. (1990) *Child Poverty and Deprivation in the United Kingdom*, National Children's Bureau, London.

Bulmer, M. (1987) *The Social Basis of Community Care*, Unwin Hyman, London.

Dale, J. and Foster, P. (1986) *Feminists and Social Welfare*, Routledge, London.

Glendinning, C. (1992) *Women and Poverty in Britain*, Harvester Wheatsheaf, Hemel Hempstead.

Ungerson, C. (1985) *Women and Social Policy*, Macmillan, London.

Glossary of terms

In a textbook of this kind, one invariably finds new, strange terms and concepts, often used as a sort of short-hand of 'isms' to facilitate the flow of the writing. The 'summary' preface to each chapter has ended with a note of the main terms mentioned in that chapter, and it is hoped that their meanings have been made reasonably clear from the text. It may be helpful to have these gathered together, with brief definitions and under relevant headings. In many cases, these concepts or ideas are twinned, e.g. centralism and localism, and it makes sense to refer to such pairs together. The terms in this Glossary have been numbered sequentially, and are accordingly referred to in the Index.

Basic concepts of social casualty

This study of social provision deals systematically with a four-fold division of social problems, sometimes referred to as 'social casualty' in the round, with the victims of such problems referred to as 'social casualties'. In terms of this book, these four kinds of problem have been defined as:

1 *Poverty*. The condition of people being insufficiently resourced to live adequate lives, relative to the norms of their community.
2 *Ill-health*. The condition of people reduced, by illness, from reasonable participation in normal communal life.
3 *Ignorance*. The condition of people unversed in the skills and information required for involvement in community life.
4 *Crime*. The condition of people deviating from the legal standards imposed by their community.

Basic socio-economic concepts

These refer to the type of social and economic structure in a given area, usually a nation-state (see 14 below)

5 *Natural-economy*. Where the economic means of production and distribution are predominantly based on the use of one's own produce and its exchange

in kind, rather than through the medium of money. *Naturalwirtschaft* is the German term.

6 *Money-economy*. The opposite, where the economic means of production and distribution are based on exchange through the use of money. *Geldwirtschaft* is the German term.

These are the two fundamental types of economic practice, but there are other concepts appertaining to one or both of them.

7 *Feudalism*. This may be used strictly to denote a particular form of land-tenure. It is used here more loosely to describe the 'feudal' tendency whereby, in much of medieval Europe, a landed warrior class and a tied peasantry were bound together in a balance of protection and service.

8 *Self-sufficiency (also self-help)*. Normally associated with the natural-economy (see 5 above). It refers to a family or small group existing largely by their own, usually agricultural, devices, without outside help or services.

9 *Subsistence*. Often 'subsistence level'. Existence at the lowest level consistent with social survival, although, like most of these concepts, this is often relative to the prevailing social norms.

10 *Mercantilism (bullionism)*. The policy whereby a nation seeks to improve its trading position through the use of customs and other regulations. In early modern times, this was assessed on whether the nation had acquired more gold bullion than it had dispersed; hence 'bullionism'.

11 *Protectionism*. A more modern term for the same policy of regulating trade in and out of the nation to seek favourable commercial outcomes. When Britain used such a policy in respect of trade to and from the British Empire, it was known as 'imperial preference'.

12 *Free trade*. The opposite of protectionism; in short, the policy of avoiding or abolishing customs, tariffs and other trade barriers, in the belief that freedom of commercial activity will reap the best trading rewards. See also *laissez-faire* (36 below) and individualism (37 below).

13 *Keynesianism*. A financial policy, based on the ideas of John Maynard Keynes, English economist, influential from the late 1930s and thereafter. A government of Keynesian orientation would use budget deficits to stimulate demand in recession, and budget surpluses to quieten demand in boom. In general, it might be said to fall part way between outright protectionism and free trade, being a more pragmatic attempt to 'manage' an economy by financial levers, such as interest and exchange rates, taxation etc.

Basic political concepts

These relate to the character of political control exerted over a given area, usually a nation-state. They obviously have affinities with the socio-economic references.

14 *Nation-state*. The basic political format of post-medieval times. The nation-state is a bloc of land and people, often identical with a uniform ethnic base, language and culture, where authority is vested centrally and without qualification. See omnicompetence (19 below) and sovereignty (20 below).

15 *Atomism*. To some extent, the opposite of the nation-state. The 'atomistic' society is one where small groups of people live self-sufficiently (see 8 above), without major reference to a more distant authority, such as the state.

16 *Communalism*. The widest possible spread of political control into local or community hands.

17 *Anocracy*. Literally, government upwards from the grass roots. Not anarchy, which is without government, but more government by local communities, instead of by the state.

18 *Particularism*. Used, especially in medieval studies, to denote a 'particular' region or district, relatively small but discrete and self-contained, within the wider ambit of political control: e.g. today Scotland might be regarded as a 'particularist' component of the United Kingdom.

19 *Omnicompetence*. Refers to the absolute and unqualified power and authority of the centralized nation-state, especially in relation to its officialdom.

20 *Sovereignty*. Refers to the source of absolute law and authority in a state. In Britain, this was once held by the king or queen (the 'sovereign') but is now vested in the Houses of Parliament as the sole and final maker and arbiter of law and power.

21 *Europeanization*. The tendency for almost all the world to have been occupied and colonized by or, if not, very heavily influenced by modern European civilization.

22 *Giantism*. The term used to describe the tendency of modern socio-economic institutions, in either the private or public sectors, to be large in scale and shape: e.g. a vast supermarket chain or the National Health Service. The implicit criticism of the term suggests that the 'giantist' institution has grown beyond human grasp and comprehension.

23 *Statism*. The tendency of the modern state to draw control of activities within its own direct authority. In critics' minds, the closeness of 'statist' and 'static' is not entirely coincidental.

Basic social or ideological concepts

These refer to ideas and theories which have helped to frame the thinking and practice of social provision.

24 *Utilitarianism (Benthamism)*. The theory, developed chiefly by the political scientist, Jeremy Bentham, and strongly held in nineteenth-century Britain, that 'utility' – 'what is the use of it?' – was the key to legislative and other action; and that 'the greatest happiness for the greatest number' was the best yardstick of the success of such action. Utilitarianism could lead to either more or less state intervention, depending on such judgements.

25 *Marxism*. The system of ideas, developed initially by the nineteenth-century political philosopher Karl Marx, which prophesied that, through the economically determined and revolutionary dictates of history, humankind would automatically proceed to a classless society, free of state authority and governmental control. The end product of this 'scientific socialism' would be the condition of 'communism'.

26 *State capitalism*. The so-called 'communism' of Eastern Europe and elsewhere, in Russia after 1917 and in other areas after 1945, became, in practice, a matter of heavy state domination or 'statism' (see 23 above). As the state controlled all the investment, funding etc. of the economy, this phenomenon was often described as 'state capitalism'.

27 *Socialism*. In general and popular terms, this is a less triumphalist and revolutionary doctrine than Marxism, hopeful that, through radical reforms, including the widespread state control of the economy, a fairer and more equal society might emerge.

28 *Christian socialism*. A nineteenth-century, mainly British, belief that socialist and Christian doctrines were capable of intertwining.

29 *Fabianism*. A late nineteenth and early twentieth century gloss (still with some influence today) on Socialism, urging the 'inevitabilty of gradualness' and the case for efficient, painstaking progress towards reform.

30 *Social democracy*. A late nineteenth and twentieth century variant of socialism, chiefly continental European in base, and predicated on achieving social reforms through parliamentary action.

31 *Idealism*. After the German philospher, Hegel, but in Victorian England and for social purposes associated with T. H. Green. The view that the moral 'ideal' should be embodied in the rights and duties connected with the state and its activities.

32 *Tory philanthropy*. Developed in the Victorian era, the notion within the Conservative or Tory Party that the well-to-do and more fortunate owed a duty to provide succour to the less well off.

33 *Fascism (Nazism)*. Twentieth-century political attitude aimed at making the state or race all-powerful, and, to this end, rather akin to the so-called Marxist communist (see 25 above) governments, subjecting people to a totalitarian and military regime of the strictest control.

34 *Collectivism*. Overall, a system of political control, usually democratically arrived at, whereby the state protects the individual from social ills and provides the social environment wherein he or she may reasonably prosper. In British practice, this has often been identical with 'nationalization', that is, the taking into central state ownership of some major service or utility, such as the health services.

35 *Mercantile collectivism*. A gloss on collectivism, relating to the mercantilist (see 10 above) view that the state must guarantee its own security. Hence the view that the modern industrialized state must develop schemes of collectivist welfare to ensure its stability.

36 *Laissez-faire*. Often used as a synonym for free trade (see 12 above) but applicable to 'free trade', that is, an absence of regulation, in other fields such as health or social welfare.

37 *Individualism*. Used here as an all-round term (see 12 and 36 above) describing the attitude that as many activities as possible, such as health care, education, pensions etc., should be left to the discretion of the 'individual' and his or her family, and that the state should interfere minimally. Thus individualism may be seen as the opposite of 'collectivism' (see 34 above).

38 *Privatization*. A late twentieth-century gloss on individualism, and associated with Margaret Thatcher, the Conservative premier, whereby 'collectivized' or 'nationalized' (see 34 above) services and utilities were sold in whole or contracted in part to the 'private' or commercial sector.

39 *Privatism*. A late twentieth-century 'individualist' (see 37 above) practice, whereby individuals are encouraged, for instance, by tax concessions, to choose private rather than public solutions to social questions, such as in health care, housing, schooling and the like.

The foregoing terms refer mainly to policies or attitudes. The remainder of this section refers to the application of such approaches to actual types of society.

40 *Functional society*. R. H. Tawney's descriptor for a society which tends to make the discharge of social duties and obligations its prime purpose.

41 *Acquisitive society*. The opposite of the functional society: Tawney's descriptor of a society where the right to acquire wealth, without any appropriate social purpose, is paramount.

42 *Welfare state*. A most important concept for this study. The welfare state aims to protect its members from social ill by public action and from cradle to grave, not least that they might be sufficiently resourced to make a reasonable contribution to civic and economic life. Its reverse – 'state welfare' – reminds us that it is the political ambit, the state, which is as meaningful as the social benefits and services – the welfare.

43 *Power state*. The opposite of the welfare state is now often deemed to be the individualist or free enterprise state, but initially it was envisaged as challenging the 'power state' of totalitarian method, in that this seemed to be providing for its citizenry materially, albeit with gross loss of liberty and civil rights.

44 *Social wage state*. A mainly Scandinavian gloss on the welfare state, whereby an emphasis on monetary benefits has amounted to a 'social wage', adequate enough to enable the recipient to live a life similar to that of those in work.

45 *Integrated welfare state*. One in which the management of the economy – the 'supply side' – is closely related or integrated with the management of social provision – the 'demand side'.

46 *Differentiated welfare state*. The opposite. Here the economy is largely left to find its own levels, without direct linkage with calls on the public treasury for social welfare and other services.

47 *Tutelary state*. The Victorian predecessor to the collectivist and then the welfare state. It demonstrates the 'artificial' wing of utilitarianism (see 24 above), whereby the state interfered to 'tutor' people towards a recognition of their own self-interest.

48 *Corporate state*. Describes the modern state, whereby 'corporations', that is, power blocs and vested interests of all kinds (e.g. industries, financial institutions, political parties, trades unions), parley, tilt and negotiate for compromise decisions about the political and allied condition of the nation. But also note corporate practices, 52 below.

Basic concepts of social provision

There are a number of ideas or interpretations which refer in general terms to all branches of social provision, and the way in which these are organized.

49 *Intolerability*. Coined to interpret Victorian responses, but widely applicable, this simply means that a mainspring of social reform and action is the reaction of people to a problem which they can stand no longer, and for which they are driven to find some solution.

50 *Expediency*. Much the same as 49. The notion that much social reform is forced on people by necessity, rather than, say, by moral or philosophic deliberation.

51 *Congregation*. Herman Finer's expression for the social condition of industrialism, whereby large populations are crushed into urban confines and cabinned workplaces.

52 *Corporate/contractual practices*. The medieval and early modern style of close-knit group or corporate existence (e.g. monks, a trade guild etc.) bound by strict group regulation, and based on a 'contractual' balance of give and take, duties and rights. See 48 above for something of a modern equivalent.

53 *Centralism/centralization*. The gathering of political power to the centre of the nation-state, into the hands of the national government.

54 *Localism/decentralization.* The opposite. The dispersal of political power to the localities, and away from the national to the local government.

55 *Bipartism.* Used in this study to describe the general tenor of centralism and localism (53 and 54 above) to be in shifting balance in Britain, rather than either being exclusively powerful. But note that the term 'bipartite' is sometimes used to describe the pre-comprehensive schools situation in Britain, when secondary education tended to offer two options, the grammar and secondary modern schools.

56 *Charitable/voluntary activity; the Church.* As well as the public and private sectors, there has always been in Britain a third sector of charitable and voluntary activity, neither paid for by the public purse nor pursued in search of private profit. Initially, it was almost wholly concerned with the Church, which still continues to play a role in that sector today.

57 *Institutionalism.* Used to describe the solution to social problems where social casualties are placed in 'institutions', such as hospitals, rather than treated in some other way, such as at home.

58 *The factory formula.* A previous coinage of the author, suggesting that the rash of 'institutions' (see 57 above) developed by the Victorians was influenced, consciously and unconsciously, by the success of the factory system.

59 *Felicific calculus.* Jeremy Bentham (see 24 above) believed that it was possible to measure – hence 'calculus' – the balance of pain and pleasure suffered by humans, further to the determination of their 'greatest happiness' – hence 'felicific'.

60 *Preventive (preventative) principle.* The precept, associated with Edwin Chadwick and others, that social reforms should aim at preventing the predisposing causes of social ills, and that legislation should be planned accordingly.

61 *Curative principle.* Coined in this study as the opposite; namely, social reforms which are instituted to treat the effects of social ills once occurred.

62 *Professionalism.* Describes the gradual move, especially from the middle of the nineteenth century, to introduce specialist expertise and separate professional groups into the field of social welfare. These replaced more general, amateur and domestic provisions.

63 *Prescribed qualification.* The phrase, coined by the social scientists Sidney and Beatrice Webb, to describe how, gradually, each separate profession developed standards, usually by examination, for entry and for career progress.

64 *Administrative procreation/momentum.* The phrase, coined by the historian Oliver McDonagh, to describe how 'professional' groups (see 62 and 63 above), such as civil servants, tend to expand in numbers and authority.

65 *Bureaucracy.* In its purer sense, and as defined by the sociologist Max Weber, it refers to the construct of a professional, rational and official efficiency in public affairs.

66 *Dilettantism.* The opposite, i.e. public affairs conducted in an amateurish, slovenly, even corrupt, manner.

67 *Universalism.* The offer of services, benefits etc. to everyone, that is, on a 'universal' basis, and as opposed to means testing or, in the current jargon, 'targeting' special groups for specific treatment.

68 *Embourgoisement.* Refers to the post-1945 phenomenon of working-class people (the proletariat) adopting middle-class (the bourgeoisie) habits and aspirations.

69 *Butskellism.* Refers to the political consensus, 1951–79, to preserve the welfare state and its attributes. It portmanteaus the names of Conservative and Labour politicians R. A. Butler and Hugh Gaitskell.

70 *Quango.* Acronym for 'quasi-autonomous non-governmental organizations' or, officially, 'non-department public bodies'. These are established and funded by government for a particular purpose and are not directly accountable to any electorate.

Specialist concepts of social provision and welfare

These are methods, ideas, approaches etc. which are usually an aspect of just one of the four areas of social reform under review.

Poverty

71 *Old poor law.* The system of relief of poverty in England and Wales from the end of the sixteenth century to 1834.
72 *New poor law.* The system of poor relief established in 1834, which continued, with variations, until 1929.
73 *Parish.* The major unit of British local government, especially for poor relief purposes, throughout the early modern period, and then in 'unions' of parishes for poor relief for much of the modern period.
74 *Justices of the peace.* These locally based and unpaid magistrates, drawn from the gentry of the shires, undertook much of the work of local government, poor relief as well as law and order, throughout the early modern period.
75 *Almshouses.* Established in medieval times, by the Church, for the institutional relief of poverty and sickness. Important as creating the precedent for 'institutional' care (see 57 above), they constituted, in fact, the first residential care and hospital provision in Britain.
76 *Workhouse.* Important as the emblem of strict, dour 'institutional' care (see 57 above), the workhouse was originally conceived as, literally, a place where poor people lived and worked, but after 1834 and the new poor law (see 72 above) it became the premier institution for all forms of social casualty during the nineteenth and early twentieth centuries.
77 *Less eligibility.* In poor relief circles also known as 'the workhouse test', but used more widely, and associated with the 'preventive principle' (see 60 above). The approach was to make the treatment so much more severe than the problem (e.g. the workhouse regime was intended to be harsher than life on the lowest working wage) that people would only choose it as a last resort, when nothing else was more 'eligible'.
78 *Contributory principle.* The ruling whereby people make contributions, usually from their salaries or wages over their working lives, to finance benefits, either for themselves directly or for collective provision. National insurance or pensions contributions are examples, and, obviously, 'non-contributory' benefits are the opposite of this.
79 *Dependency.* The condition of being 'dependent' on state aid and services. Over the past decade or so, it has been suggested by critics of welfare schemes that it is welfare itself which creates the dependency – hence 'dependency culture'.

Ill-health

80 *Sanitary idea.* This Victorian notion, well-founded in practice if not in theory, urged the introduction of clean water supplies, for domestic use and for the

proper drainage of sewage, as the solution to the grievous public health problems of the age.

81 *Miasmatic (pythogenic) theory of disease.* This nineteenth-century opinion believed that disease and death were caused by the 'poisonous exhalations' which arose from filth and sewage – hence the 'sanitary idea' (80 above).

82 *Germ theory of disease.* Introduced by chemists, such as Pasteur and Koch, towards the end of the nineteenth century, this argued that diseases were caused and spread by micro-organisms. It is simple to see how the clearance of filth, even when associated with 'miasmatic' attitudes (see 80 and 81 above), had good effects.

83 *Allopathic medicine.* The practice of treating illness by inducing an opposite condition, usually through drugs or surgery. This 'medicalized' approach may lead to iatrogenic or 'doctor-induced' illnesses.

84 *Naturopathic medicine.* The opposite. The 'alternative medicine' practice of treating illness naturally, working holistically with the body.

Ignorance

85 *Socialization.* The general preparation of children for their social role in society, undertaken by the family, but, to some extent and in modern times, also by the school. It reminds us that 'ignorance' and 'education' have been used in this study in a wider social sense, rather than just in terms of literacy or academic achievement.

86 *Monitorial system.* The system used in the middle decades of the nineteenth century to deal with large numbers of children in schools. With variations, older children were taught lessons which they then passed on, as 'monitors', to groups of younger children. Via such schemes as the 'pupil-teacher' system, it preceded the usual 'class' pattern in operation in schools today.

87 *Selective system.* The form of secondary education whereby children were tested and selected on academic grounds at the end of their primary schooling (normally at eleven years) for, usually, either the grammar or the less academic secondary modern school. See 55 above for a note on the bipartite system, as this came to be known.

88 *Comprehensive system.* The opposite, which largely replaced the selective system from the 1960s onwards, with often large comprehensive secondary schools. This amounted to a preference, on both social and educational grounds, for extending the 'common' school of the primary years right through to the end of schooling.

Crime

89 *Consensual policing.* A phrase coined by the sociologists J. Lea and J. Young to describe police-work reliant on the support and sympathy of the community.

90 *Military policing.* The opposite, where police-work is conducted in a community which is suspicious and unhelpful.

Final reminder: the Index includes a full list of these Glossary items, numbered accordingly.

Index

WORLD HEALTH AND DISEASE
Alastair Gray and Philip Payne

This book presents a global view of human health. It traces some of the major changes in the health and disease patterns affecting humankind, and sets these in the context of demographic change and economic development.

The book addresses a series of important questions: how and why have patterns of health and disease changed so dramatically in industrialized countries over the last century? And why, within a country such as the United Kingdom, is there so much variation in health between women and men, married and single, black people and white people, manual and non-manual workers? How different from these are the health problems confronting the populations of Third World countries, and what progress have they experienced? Does rapid population growth testify to health improvements, but does it also threaten them?

To examine these questions, the authors of this book have drawn together arguments and evidence from a wide range of disciplines, in particular demography, economics, nutrition, history, biology and epidemiology. The book also considers ways in which evidence, and in particular statistical data, can be used or abused. Over 120 tables and figures illustrate and augment the text.

Contents
Introduction – World patterns of mortality – Mortality and morbidity: causes and determinants – Livelihood and survival: a case study of Bangladesh – The world transformed: population and the rise of industrial society – The decline of infectious diseases: the case of England – Health in a world of wealth and poverty – Population and development prospects – Contemporary patterns of disease in the United Kingdom – Explaining inequalities in health in the United Kingdom – Food, health and disease: a case study – References and further reading – Answers to self-assessment questions – Acknowledgements – Index.

212pp   0 335 19078 2 (Paperback)

CARING FOR HEALTH
HISTORY AND DIVERSITY

Charles Webster (ed.)

This book considers the historical development of health care from 1500 to the present day. The authors adopt a broad interdisciplinary framework and draw on recent research in the fields of medical, social and economic history. While focusing primarily on Britain, they also trace the influence of European systems of health care in the former colonies, which continues in present relationships with the Third World. The central premise of the book is that the strengths and limitations of health systems around the world can only be understood in terms of their evolution from past practices and structures, many of which are inflexible to change.

Important themes explored in this book include: the growth of state involvement in health care, culminating with the welfare state model in the twentieth century; the shifting boundaries between formal and lay care, with particular attention to the role of women as health-care providers; the emergence of specialized health-care occupations and the phenomenon of professionalization; and the changing definitions of public health and community care. It offers a comparative analysis of current methods of delivering and financing health care in the developed and developing world, and asks if economic integration is leading towards a global health-care system.

Contents
History and diversity – Pre-industrial health care, 1500 to 1750 – The Industrial Revolution, 1750 to 1848 – The era of public health, 1848 to 1918 – The impact of war and depression, 1918 to 1948 –Mobilization for total welfare, 1948 to 1974 – The crisis of welfare, 1974 to the 1990s – Health care in the Third World, 1974 to the 1990s – International patterns of health care, 1960 to the 1990s – Conclusions – Appendix – References and further reading – Answers to self-assessment questions – Index.

Contributors
Virginia Berridge, Alastair Gray, Mark Harrison, Margaret Pelling, Gill Walt, Charles Webster, Paul Weindling.

224pp   0 335 19118 5 (Paperback)

DILEMMAS IN HEALTH CARE

Basiro Davey and Jennie Popay (eds)

This book considers the major dilemmas arising from the funding, organization and delivery of health care in the United Kingdom in the 1990s. 'Health care' is given the widest possible definition – stepping beyond the health service to include social, community, educational and government initiatives – in an analysis of the constraints on and opportunities for improving the nation's health.

The authors come from a wide range of academic and research backgrounds in health and social care. They examine the dilemmas inherent in providing care that is simultaneously effective in alleviating disease and in promoting health, cost-effective in its use of financial and human resources, delivered equitably to those who need it, and humane in its treatment of service-users and health workers. A number of contemporary themes are explored: the management of limited resources; the evaluation of inputs and outcomes; the relative power of 'consumers', doctors and managers, and the aspirations of the workforce; planning for the latest developments in medical technology; and balancing the provision of hospital, primary and community care, and the demand for curative and preventive services. The book concludes by examining the prospects for social and fiscal policies to make an impact on health.

Contents
Universalizing the best: an impossible dream? – *Managing health care: balancing interests and influence* – *Rationing and choice* – *The evaluation of health care* – *The consumer voice* – *Health work: divisions in health-care labour* – *Innovations in health care* – *Care in the community: rhetoric or reality?* – *Disease prevention and health promotion* – *Coronary heart disease: a cautionary tale* – *Poverty, economic inequality and health* – *Appendix* – *References and further reading* – *Answers to self-assessment questions* – *Index.*

Contributors
Basiro Davey, Alastair Gray, Stephen Harrison, Richard Holmes, David Hunter, Helen Lambert, Nicholas Mays, Klim McPherson, Gillian Pascall, Chris Pond, Jennie Popay, Kate Robinson, Clive Seale, Gerald Wistow.

224pp   0 335 19119 3 (Paperback)

A SOCIOLOGY OF MENTAL HEALTH AND ILLNESS

David Pilgrim and Anne Rogers

This new textbook provides a critical introduction to literature on mental health and illness of relevance and interest to undergraduate sociologists. The sociological analysis offered by this material will also be of particular relevance to mental health professionals from a wide variety of disciplines. Questions of race, age and gender are addressed, along with explorations of work on psychiatric treatment, the mental health professions, the organization of mental health work, legalism and service users. The book begins with an examination of the competing perspectives about mental health and illness, which have contributed to multiple understandings and terminologies, both inside and outside of sociology. A recognition of these diverse perspectives informs the way in which subsequent chapter topics are explored.

While there are several books which focus on sociological aspects of mental health, none of them has the same wide coverage of topics, and most of them have been available for some time.

(Dr Shulamit Ramon, London School of Economics)

Contents
Perspectives on mental health and illness – Gender –Race and ethnicity – Age – The mental health professions – Questions of treatment – The organization of psychiatry – Psychiatry and legal control – Users of mental health services – References – Index.

208pp   0 335 19013 8 (Paperback)   0 335 19014 6 (Hardback)